viii — 85

ELBOW ROOM

ELBOW ROOM

The
Varieties
of Free Will
Worth
Wanting

DANIEL C. DENNETT

CLARENDON PRESS · OXFORD
1984

Oxford University Press, Walton Street, Oxford OX2 6DP

London New York Toronto
Delhi Bombay Calcutta Madras Karachi
Kuala Lumpur Singapore Hong Kong Tokyo
Nairobi Dar es Salaam Cape Town
Melbourne Auckland
and associated companies in
Beirut Berlin Ibadan Mexico City Nicosia

Oxford is a trade mark of Oxford University Press

This book was printed and bound by Halliday Lithograph in the
United States of America

British Library Cataloguing in Publication Data
Dennett. Daniel C.
Elbow room : the varieties of free will
worth wanting.
1. Free will and determinism
I. Title
123   BJ1461
ISBN 0-19-824753-2
ISBN 0-19-824790-7 Pbk

Dedicated
to the memory of
Gilbert Ryle

Contents

Preface

Shortly after World War II, Gilbert Ryle was invited to write a book demonstrating how the new philosophical methods triumphed over old problems:

> . . . it was time, I thought, to exhibit a sustained piece of analytical hatchet-work being directed upon some notorious and large-sized Gordian Knot. . . . For a time I thought of the problem of the Freedom of the Will as the most suitable Gordian Knot; but in the end I opted for the Concept of Mind—though the book's actual title did not occur to me until the printers were hankering to begin printing the first proofs (Ryle 1970, p. 12)

Elbow Room is not, of course, the book on Free Will that Ryle would have written had he not found a more enticing project, but it does show his influence—to a degree that has often startled me. Combine that fact with my undying admiration and affection for the man, and my joy at being invited to return to Oxford to present these ideas on free will as the John Locke Lectures in 1983, and one can see that my decision to dedicate this book to the memory of my thesis supervisor was, while free, rational, and responsible, also predictable and even (in one sense) inevitable. I couldn't do otherwise.

In my own attempt to hew out a unified set of answers to the difficult questions about free will, I have been helped by many people, including many of the philosophers whose works I criticize. I owe a special debt to Bo Dahlbom and Douglas Hofstadter who in their very different ways led me away from many false trails and pitfalls, as they have often done in the past. I also want to thank Michael Berry, Gordon

Brittan, Carl Castro, Pat Churchland, Tony Coady, Richard Dawkins, Richard Gregory, Laurie Kahn-Leavitt, Christopher Peacocke, Michael Ruse, Teddy Seidenfeld, Michael Slote, Sue Stafford, and Andrew Woodfield, Hugo Bedau, John Mazzone, and my other colleagues and students at Tufts also helped with constructive criticism and suggestions. Finally, my thanks to the Sub-Faculty of Philosophy at Oxford for their kind invitation, and to all of Oxford for its gracious hospitality to me and my family.

Daniel C. Dennett
Tufts University
January 1984

ELBOW ROOM

Please Don't Feed the Bugbears

The philosopher is the one who
will contribute a paper on the
hangman paradox to a symposium
on capital punishment
—James D. McCawley

1. The Perennial Gripping Problem

The idea of Fate is older than philosophy itself, and since the dawn of the
discipline philosophers have been trying to show what is wrong with the
idea that our fates are sealed before we are born. It has seemed very
important to demonstrate that we are not just acting out our destinies
but somehow choosing our own courses, *making* decisions—not just
having "decisions" occur in us.

Ideas about causation were at the focus of attention in the early days
of Greek philosophy, and it occurred to some to wonder whether all
physical events are caused or determined by the sum total of all prior
events. If they are—if, as we say, *determinism* is true—then our actions,
as physical events, must themselves be determined. If determinism is
true, then our every deed and decision is the inexorable outcome, it
seems, of the sum of physical forces acting at the moment, which in turn
is the inexorable outcome of the forces acting an instant before, and so
on, to the beginning of time.

How then could we be free? The Epicureans, who were surprisingly
modern *materialists* (they believed that minds were composed of material
atoms, just like everything else), tried to extricate themselves from this
nightmare of predestined choice by breaking the fabric of universal causation here and there. They postulated that atoms occasionally exhibit
"random swerves."

> Again, if all movement is always interconnected, the new arising
> from the old in a determinate order—if the atoms never swerve so
> as to originate some new movement that will snap the bonds of fate,

the everlasting sequence of cause and effect—what is the source of
the free will possessed by living things throughout the earth? (Lucretius, *The Nature of the Universe,* II, lines 250–255, Latham translation 1951)

The oft-recounted difficulty with this proposed solution (and its more
modern variants) is that even if such random swerves happen, they don't
seem able to give us the sort of free will we want. If an atom in my brain
suddenly veers off with a random swerve, it must do so "for no reason at
all," and if this causes me to choose or decide something important, I am
completely at the mercy of these random swerves. Random choice, as
blind and arbitrary as the throw of dice or the spin of a wheel of fortune,
does not seem to be any more desirable than determined choice. Indeed
many have thought that it was *less* desirable, and have gone on to propose
alternative reconciliations of free will with determinism (different varieties of *reconciliationism* or, as it is more frequently called, *compatibilism*).
Some of these attempted reconciliations are hardly more appealing than
the dire prospect they are supposed to keep at bay.

The Stoics, for instance, urged that a certain sort of freedom could
be found in not struggling against the inevitable but rather adjusting
one's desires downward to meet one's circumstances. They encouraged
adopting an attitude of wise resignation which they called *apatheia.* And
while one should recognize that the concept got simplified and
cheapened as it took the etymological journey to our present-day *apathy,*
the fact remains that the Stoics liked to explain their doctrine with the
help of some particularly depressing metaphors. Each of us is assigned a
role to play in the tragedy of life, they suggested, and there is nothing for
us to do but say our prescribed lines as best we can; there is no room to
ad-lib. Or consider a dog on a leash being pulled behind a wagon; it can
trot along peacefully, or it can resist. Either way it will end up at the same
destination, but if it resigns itself to the destination and makes the most
of the journey, it will enjoy a certain kind of freedom. Being led through
life with a rope around one's neck—some freedom!

For more than two millennia philosophers have been trying to discover a doctrine about free will that is both more attractive and more
rationally defensible than these dire and unappealing beginnings. It is
often said (plausibly, but I wonder how accurately) that more has been
written on free will than on any other philosophical topic. Any philosopher ought to feel at least a little embarrassed that with so much work so
little progress has been made.

The trouble with philosophy, some say, is that it isn't Science; if it
were more like Science it would solve its soluble problems and dissolve
or discard the rest. The trouble with philosophy, others say, is that it has

tried to be "scientific" about matters that can only be dealt with through Art. If it would give up its love affair with the Scientific Method, it would no longer have to cast its projects in terms that guaranteed failure. The trouble with philosophy, I think, is that it is much harder than it looks to either Scientists or Artists, for it shares—and must share—the aspirations and methods of both.

There are undismissable philosophical questions—"Do we have free will?" is one of them—that require clear, well-supported, soundly reasoned answers. We should not be bought off with allusive, impressionistic answers, however appealing or moving they may be. But most attempts to deal truly rigorously with philosophical questions—and questions about free will are no exception—run afoul of the problems of premature formalization. There is an abundance of self-consciously technical work by philosophers on the problem of free will that is, ironically, of only aesthetic interest (to connoisseurs of formula architecture or "logic chopping") because it simply fails to make contact with the real issues. Finding a method appropriate to the task is philosophy's perennial first problem, and there has never been much of a consensus about the right or best method. Any book on free will makes a declaration, *ipso facto,* about method, about how one ought to approach the problem. This book will more self-consciously address the issue of method, beginning now. My method, to be exhibited presently in action, takes science very seriously but its tactics more closely resemble those of art.

In my student days I thought I was going to be a sculptor, and I addressed myself more energetically to blocks of wood and stone than to either philosophy or science. It occurred to me while working on this book that I have never abandoned the methods I developed in the studio, but simply changed media. Unlike the draftsman, who must get each line just right with the first stroke of the pen, the sculptor has the luxury of nibbling and grinding away until the lines and surfaces look just right. First you rough out the block, standing back and squinting now and then to make sure you are closing in on the dimly seen final product. Only after the piece is bulked out in the right proportions do you return to each crude, rough surface and invest great labor in getting the fine details just so.

Some philosophers are very unsympathetic to this method when they encounter it in philosophy. They have no patience with roughed-in solutions and want to see nothing but hard, clean edges from the outset. I aspire to the same finished product that they do, but question their strategy. It is just too hard getting off on the right foot in philosophy, and nowhere are the risks of their strategy more evident than in the philosophical literature on free will, which is littered with brilliant but useless fragments. One of the themes of this book is that little progress has been made on the free will issue because philosophers, rushing in to deal definitively with what they consider to be the important parts of the free will issue and lavishing somewhat myopic attention on these topics, have simply failed to see the shape of the main body of the topic. Out of the opaque marble block of the problem emerge an exquisitely rendered face and some highly polished hands and feet—but no room has been left for the elbows. In this book most of the work will be on roughing out the shape of the parts philosophers usually rush past with a lick and a promise.

It is often remarked that the problem of free will is a uniquely engaging or even gripping philosophical problem: people who otherwise have no taste at all for philosophy can be brought to care quite deeply about the problem, and can be genuinely troubled by the prospect that the answers to the questions may turn out "the wrong way."

Why do people find the free will problem gripping? In part, surely, because it touches deep and central questions about our situation in the universe, about "the human condition," as one portentously says. But also, I will argue, because philosophers have conjured up a host of truly frightening bugbears[1] and then subliminally suggested, quite illicitly, that the question of free will is whether any of these bugbears actually exist.

This has contributed to the lack of progress on the problem, because philosophers, partly taken in by their own fearmongery and partly using that contrived urgency to "motivate" the elaboration of metaphysical systems and theories, have set themselves a variety of unattainable goals: the creation of impossible philosophical talismans to ward off nonexistent evils.

I do not mean to suggest that philosophers have deliberately and knowingly fanned the coals of anxiety, or that they have disingenuously exploited that anxiety to provide the spurious motivation for their metaphysical exercises. We philosophers are more the victims than the perpetrators of the induced illusions. After all, we are the main and intended readership of the literature that innocently conspires to engender the misapprehensions. And our complicity in protracting the lives of the errors arises in part from the natural and virtually universal desire to be engaged in a project whose importance can be made clear to bystanders. If this leads us to overdramatize things here and there, to heighten a few contrasts and sharpen a few boundaries, we are only doing what everyone else does in their own line of work.

Notice for instance that one of my initial premises—that people

---

1. "A sort of hobgoblin . . . supposed to devour naughty children; hence, generally, any imaginary being invoked by nurses to frighten children." (*Oxford Shorter English Dictionary*)

care deeply about free will—has already undergone a familiar exaggeration in my hands. It is not as if *everybody* cares about having free will in the same way that everybody cares about avoiding pain or finding love, for instance. We might remind ourselves of the luxury of our own participation in this exploration. Most people—99 percent and more, no doubt—have always been too busy staying alive and fending for themselves in difficult circumstances to have any time or taste for the question of free will. Political freedom, for many of them, has been a major concern, but metaphysical freedom has just not been worth worrying about. As Dewey once said, "What men have esteemed and fought for in the name of liberty is varied and complex—but certainly it has never been a metaphysical freedom of will." (Dewey 1922, p. 303)

Most other people, then, have not been worried about free will. But it is comfortable for us (gentle reader) to believe that thanks to our leisure and intellectual inclinations we have seen deeper into their predicaments than they have. This may be true. But we should be cautious about accepting at face value our quite spontaneous and mutually accepted intuition that the problem of free will is one of the Great Issues. For we are a self-selected group. Note particularly that free will is an almost exclusively Western preoccupation. Could we be deluded? Could we only *think* that free will matters? Do we even think it matters? That is, outside the lecture hall, outside our professional activities or midnight bull sessions, does the question have much hold on us? As Ryle once noted, we all have our fatalistic moments: "Yet though we know what it is like to entertain this idea, still we are unimpassioned about it. We are not secret zealots for it or secret zealots against it." (Ryle 1954, p. 28) Fatalism, according to Ryle, "is not a burning issue," and the same can be said of the broader issue of free will. But it can certainly be made to seem a burning tissue.

If having free will matters, it must be because not having free will would be awful, and there must be some grounds for doubting that we have it. What are we afraid of? We are afraid of not having free will. But what exactly are we afraid of? And why? Anyone who dreads the prospect of not having free will must have some inkling about *what that terrible condition would be like.* And in fact there are a host of analogies to be found in the literature: not having free will would be somewhat like being in prison, or being hypnotized, or being paralyzed, or being a puppet, or . . . (the list continues).

I do not think these analogies are merely useful illustrations, merely graphic expository devices. I think they are at the very foundation of the problem. Without them to anchor the philosophical discussions, the free will problem would float away, at best a curious issue to bemuse metaphysicians and puzzlemongers. One aspect of this can be easily seen.

Suppose a philosopher claims to have solved the problem of free will; a layman might say, "Well, does your 'solution' allay my worries? Because if it doesn't, then whatever else it may be, it is no solution to what I have been taught to call the free will problem." So if we let tradition be our guide, the free will problem is essentially one we care about. Problems about the will that are of merely esoteric interest are just not *the* free will problem, however fascinating they might be to some specialists.

But there is more to it than that. The fears not only anchor the problem of free will; they also provide its content and shape the dynamics of argument and exploration. One of my themes will be that the "classic," "traditional" free will problem of philosophy is far more an artifact of traditional methods and preoccupations of philosophers than has been recognized.

I propose to explore the role of these fears, and in so doing expose, and thus dissolve, some—but not quite all—of the worries and confusions that conspire to create "the free will problem." That problem will turn out to be a misnamed and misbegotten amalgam of overhasty problem *posing* and self-induced panic, the false pretext for much otherwise unmotivated system building and metaphysical tinkering.

There are some undeniably dreadful things in our experience, and when we fear that we don't have free will, it is always because we fear that something importantly like one of these dreadful things is our fate. It is only because we know these predicaments quite well, and hence abhor them for good reasons and fear that something similar might be our lot, that we care about free will at all.

I will present a catalogue of these bugbears and briefly analyze them. Each one drives a part of the traditional free will discussion. None of them is easily dismissed in all its forms, but investigating the fears first may permit some of them to vanish. That is (as Mother used to say), if we look them straight in the eye (and don't avert our eyes ever so slightly and make ourselves ever so busy devising theories) we may see that some of them are only figments of our imaginations. Having reminded ourselves of the bugbears at the outset, we will be able to discern their shadows in the explorations of further issues in subsequent chapters.

In *The Concept of Mind,* Ryle tried to shock us or shame us out of a bad habit of thought by adopting the tactic of referring to the view he was attacking "with deliberate abusiveness as 'the dogma of the Ghost in the Machine'."[2] I am similarly speaking with deliberate disrespect (and a

2. (Ryle 1949, pp. 15–16). The tactic was not quite foolproof. The neurophysiologist, Sir John Eccles, in his Waynflete Lectures of 1952 at Magdalen College, Oxford, presented his modern-day version of Cartesian interactionism and closed his peroration with what he must have supposed was a graceful bow to the

smidgen of caricature in this first chapter) when I speak of these bug-bears. For it is my view that these metaphors have done most of the work behind the scenes in propelling the free will problem, and that they do not in the slightest deserve the respect and influence they typically en-joy. So my point is to heighten sensitivity to them, and to undercut their traditional eminence with my pejorative characterizations. Once im-mobilized, they will be addressed in a more surgical spirit in subsequent chapters.

2. The Bogeymen

The first of the bugbears are quite literally bogey*men*—bogeypersons if you insist—for they are all conceived as *agents* who vie with us for control of our bodies, who compete against us, who have interests anti-thetical to or at least independent of our own. These fearsome fellows are often used by philosophers as reverse cheerleaders (gloomleaders, you might call them) ushered onto the stage whenever anxiety flags, whenever the urgency of the topic under discussion becomes doubtful. As intricacy piles on intricacy, the reader begins to yawn and fidget, but is quickly regalvanized by a nudging analogy: "But that would be like finding yourself in the clutches of . . ."

   The Invisible Jailer: Prisons are dreadful. Prisons are to be shunned. Anyone who fails to understand this is not one of *us*. Well, if prison is bad, what does it contrast with? If one is not in prison, one is free (in one important sense), and each of us can reflect gratefully on how glad we are not to be in prison. "Aha!" says the fearmonger. "What makes you so sure you're not in prison?" Sometimes it's obvious when one is in prison, but sometimes it isn't. A sly jailer may conceal the steel bars in the window mullions, and install dummy doors in the walls (if you opened one, you would see a brick wall behind it). It might be some time before a prisoner realized he was in prison.

   Are you *sure* you're not in some sort of prison?[3] Here one is invited to consider a chain of transformations, taking us from obvious prisons to unobvious (but still dreadful) prisons, to utterly invisible and undetect-

---

Waynflete Professor of Philosophy: "If one uses the expressive terminology of Ryle, the 'ghost' operates a 'machine,' not of ropes and pulleys, valves and pipes, but of microscopic spatio-temporal patterns of activity in the neuronal net. . . . It would appear that it is the sort of machine a 'ghost' could operate. . . ." (Eccles 1953, p. 285)

3. Berlin (1954, p. 68) says that determinism, "for all that its chains are decked out with flowers, and despite its parade of noble stoicism and the splendour and vastness of its cosmic design, nevertheless represents the universe as a prison."

able (but still dreadful?) prisons. Consider a deer in Magdalen College park. Is it imprisoned? Yes, but not much. The enclosure is quite large. Suppose we moved the deer to a larger enclosure—the New Forest with a fence around it. Would the deer still be imprisoned? In the State of Maine, I am told, deer almost never travel more than five miles from their birthplace during their lives. If an enclosure were located outside the normal unimpeded limits of a deer's lifetime wanderings would the deer enclosed be imprisoned? Perhaps, but note that it makes a difference to our intuitions whether some*one* installs the enclosure. Do you feel imprisoned on Planet Earth—the way Napoleon was stuck on Elba? It is one thing to be born and live on Elba, and another to be put and kept on Elba *by someone*. A jail without a jailer is not a jail. Whether or not it is an undesirable abode depends on other features; it depends on just how (if at all) it cramps the style of its inhabitants.

The Nefarious Neurosurgeon: How would you like to have someone strap you down and insert electrodes in your brain, and then control your every thought and deed by pushing buttons on the "master" console? Consider, for instance, the entirely typical invocation of this chap by Fischer (1982, p. 26): the ominous Dr. Black, who arranges things in poor Jones' brain so that Black can "control Jones' activities. Jones, meanwhile, knows nothing of this." First, we may ask—as we always should—why is this other, rival *agent* introduced? Why bring Dr. Black into it? Couldn't the example get off the ground just as well, for instance, if Jones had a brain tumor that produced odd results? What makes Fischer's version more dreadful is that Jones' control of his own activities has been usurped by another controller, Dr. Black. A tumor might cause this or that in someone's brain, and it would be terrible indeed to have a debilitating brain tumor, but it would take an awfully smart tumor to *control* someone's brain.

Variations on the Nefarious Neurosurgeon are the Hideous Hypnotist and the Peremptory Puppeteer. We all know about stage hypnotists (we think we do, in any case) and what is particularly chilling about them is that unlike the Nefarious Neurosurgeons, they may leave no physical trace of their influence. Recall that Jones was stipulated to know nothing of Dr. Black's intervention—an important point to which we will return in later chapters. But more insidious still, stage hypnotists display their victims before an audience: they hold you up to ridicule before people who are in more desirable circumstances. It "helps" if you imagine their laughter as your plight is demonstrated to them. The Peremptory Puppeteer is a bit different, for he can be imagined to control your coarse-grained *motions* in spite of your *efforts* and *desires*. In the clutches of the Peremptory Puppeteer you may struggle vainly, like the Stoic's dog, and may at least hope to reveal your conscientious objection to your audience by sneaking in a frown or a whimper, a consolation apparently unavailable to the Hypnotist's victims.

We have never seen an actual human puppet, but we know all about slavery, and know it is an abhorrent condition if anything imaginable is. Which would you rather be: the Zombie of Dr. Svengali, or the Pitiful Human Puppet? Would you rather be a slave or a prisoner? These are all somewhat different fates, each horrible in its own ways, but there are other villains to fear as well.

The Cosmic Child Whose Dolls We Are: Nozick writes "Without free will, we seem diminished, merely the playthings of external forces." (Nozick 1981, p. 291) How undignified to be a mere plaything, a toy! But how could one be the plaything of a mere impersonal force? There can be no playthings without players. And players aren't just agents; they are playful, childish agents. (It's nowhere near as demeaning to think of yourself as God's *tool*—as many an evangelist will tell you.)

Stanislaw Lem explores, and explodes, the familiar philosophical supposition that we might be mere playthings in his short story, "The Seventh Sally *or* How Trurl's Own Perfection Led to No Good" (Lem 1974), and a delicious parody of this classic philosophical horror story is found in Tom Robbins' novel, *Even Cowgirls Get the Blues:*

> For Christmas that year, Julian gave Sissy a miniature Tyrolean village. The craftsmanship was remarkable.
> There was a tiny cathedral whose stained-glass windows made fruit salad of sunlight. There was a plaza and *ein Biergarten*. The *Biergarten* got quite noisy on Saturday nights. There was a bakery that smelled always of hot bread and strudel. There was a town hall and a police station, with cutaway sections that revealed standard amounts of red tape and corruption. There were little Tyroleans in leather britches, intricately stitched, and, beneath the britches, genitalia of equally fine workmanship. There were ski shops and many other interesting things, including an orphanage. The orphanage was designed to catch fire and burn down every Christmas Eve. Orphans would dash into the snow with their nightgowns blazing. Terrible. Around the second week of January, a fire inspector would come and poke through the ruins, muttering, "If they had only listened to me, those children would be alive today." (Robbins 1976, pp. 191–192)

The craftsmanship of this passage is itself remarkable. Notice how the repetition of the orphanage drama year after year (echoing Nietzsche's idea of eternal recurrence—that everything that has happened will happen again and again) seems to rob the little world of any real meaning. But why exactly should it be the repetition of the fire inspector's lament that makes it sound so hollow?

Perhaps if we looked closely at what that entails we would find the sleight of hand that makes the passage "work." Do the little Tyroleans rebuild the orphanage themselves or is there a 'RESET' button on this miniature village? Where do the new orphans come from? Or do the "dead" ones come back to "life"? As we shall see, a close inspection of such fantasies often reveals that the real work is being done by some tacit feature of the example that is strictly irrelevant to the philosophical thesis being presumably motivated by its invocation.

The Malevolent Mindreader: This agent is essentially an opponent, but he does not cause or control your moves; he just foresees them and stymies them. Playing "rock, paper, or scissors" against this fellow is hopeless, for since he knows exactly what rut you're in, what policy you're following, he can see in advance which move you intend to make and always counters successfully (Hofstadter 1982a). If only you could shield your mind from him! If only you could find a strategy of unpredictability that would be proof against his calculations! Then you wouldn't be so impotent, so vulnerable in the game of Life. Predictions matter in a special way when one has a stake in them, when they are not merely future tense statements but rather wagers which one might want to *make* come true and an opponent might want to make come false. In real life one often comes into competition with other people, and even with other organisms (outwitting the rat or mosquito, for instance), but in the cosmic game of Life against whom is one wagering?

I cannot prove that none of the bogeymen in this rogues' gallery really exist, any more than I can prove that the Devil, or Santa Claus, doesn't exist. But I am prepared to put on a sober face and assure anyone who needs assuring that there is absolutely no evidence to suggest that any of these horrible agents exists. But of course if any of them did, woe on us! A closet with a ghost in it is a terrible thing, but a closet that is just like a closet with a ghost in it (except for lacking the ghost) is nothing to fear, so we arrive at what may turn out to be a useful rule of thumb: whenever you spy a bogey*man* in a philosophical example, check to see if this scary agent, who is surely fictitious, is really doing all the work.

3. Sphexishness and Other Worries

There are other fears fueling the free will problem that do not have personified objects. It often seems to people that if determinism were true, there would have to be something "mechanical" about our processes of deliberation that we would regret. We could not be free agents, but only *automata,* insectlike in our behavior. Consider the digger wasp, *Sphex ichneumoneus:*

When the time comes for egg laying, the wasp *Sphex* builds a burrow for the purpose and seeks out a cricket which she stings in such a way as to paralyze but not kill it. She drags the cricket into the burrow, lays her eggs alongside, closes the burrow, then flies away, never to return. In due course, the eggs hatch and the wasp grubs feed off the paralyzed cricket, which has not decayed, having been kept in the wasp equivalent of deep freeze. To the human mind, such an elaborately organized and seemingly purposeful routine conveys a convincing flavor of logic and thoughtfulness—until more details are examined. For example, the Wasp's routine is to bring the paralyzed cricket to the burrow, leave it on the threshold, go inside to see that all is well, emerge, and then drag the cricket in. If the cricket is moved a few inches away while the wasp is inside making her preliminary inspection, the wasp, on emerging from the burrow, will bring the cricket back to the threshold, but not inside, and will then repeat the preparatory procedure of entering the burrow to see that everything is all right. If again the cricket is removed a few inches while the wasp is inside, once again she will move the cricket up to the threshold and re-enter the burrow for a final check. The wasp never thinks of pulling the cricket straight in. On one occasion this procedure was repeated forty times, always with the same result. (Wooldridge 1963, p. 82)[4]

The poor wasp is unmasked; she is not a free agent, but rather at the mercy of brute physical causation, driven inexorably into her states and activities by features of the environment outside her control. In "Can Creativity be Mechanized?" Hofstadter (1982b) has proposed that we call this unnerving property, so vividly manifested by the wasp, *sphexishness*. One of the most powerful undercurrents in the free will literature is fear of sphexishness.

We are a lot cleverer than *Sphex,* thank goodness, but just as we reflect gratefully on this, the fearmonger asks again: "What makes you so sure you're not sphexish—at least a little bit?" Wouldn't it simply follow from materialistic determinism that human beings, as physical organisms however fancy, must be just as much at the mercy of the environmental impingements raining down on them? The Godlike biologist reaches down and creates a slight dislocation in the wasp's world, revealing her essentially mindless mechanicity; could a superior intelligence, looking down on us, find a similar if more sophisticated trick that would unmask us? Even when we remind ourselves that so far as we know, there are no

4. The same passage also occurs in Wooldridge 1968. For an account of other philosophically interesting features of wasp behavior, see Dawkins 1980: "Good Strategy or Evolutionarily Stable Strategy?"

such superagents out there determined to thwart our lives, the mere possibility in principle that we are imperfect and vulnerable in this way is distinctly unsettling.

Notice the parallel between the fear of the Invisible Jailer and the fear of sphexishness. One starts with a simple, clear case of something awful (being literally imprisoned, or being *just* like the wasp), and then, letting that awfulness sink in, one grants that in one's own case, matters are much more complex—almost too complex to imagine—but still importantly similar. Presumably then, our own case inherits the awfulness thanks to the similarity chain. But is this really so?

Here I want to point to a dangerous philosophical practice that will receive considerable scrutiny in this book: the deliberate over-simplification of tasks to be performed by the philosopher's imagination. A popular strategy in philosophy is to construct a certain sort of thought experiment I call an *intuition pump* (Dennett 1980 and Hofstadter and Dennett 1981). Such thought experiments (unlike Galileo's or Einstein's, for instance) are *not* supposed to clothe strict arguments that prove conclusions from premises. Rather, their point is to entrain a family of imaginative reflections in the reader that ultimately yields not a formal conclusion but a dictate of "intuition." Intuition pumps are cunningly designed to focus the reader's attention on "the important" features, and to deflect the reader from bogging down in hard-to-follow details. There is nothing wrong with this in principle. Indeed one of philosophy's highest callings is finding ways of helping people see the forest and not just the trees. But intuition pumps are often abused, though seldom deliberately.

Perhaps the most frequent abuse is deriving a result—a heartfelt intuitive judgment—from the very simplicity of the imagined case, rather than from the actual content of the example portrayed so simply and clearly. Might it not be that what makes the wasp's fate so dreadful is not that her actions and "decisions" are *caused* but precisely that they are so *simply* caused? If so, then the acknowledged difference between the object of our intuition pump and ourselves—our complexity—may block our inheritance of the awfulness we see in the simple case. Perhaps we should laugh, not shudder; perhaps this intuition pump is like that nightmare snake who swallows his tail and keeps on going until he's completely eaten himself up.

But only a detailed examination will tell. Are we sphexish? Are we importantly sphexish? We certainly know some people who are: the radically insane, the retarded, the brain-damaged. (For instance, Whitaker (1976) describes a brain-damaged woman who could no longer comprehend any language at all, but who parrotted back everything that was spoken to her exactly—except for grammatical errors, which she always corrected!) Many unsettling experiments by psychologists seem to reveal something about the dimensions of our sphexishness: Milgram's classic horror story about the obedient torturers (Milgram 1974), experiments on human irrationality by Kahneman, Tversky and many others (Kahneman, Slovic, and Tversky 1982),[5] and of course the famous, if officially unsubstantiated, anecdotes about students using Skinner's operant conditioning techniques to get their psychology professors to scratch their ears while lecturing (Brewer 1974). The likely extent of our sphexishness will be a central topic in the second chapter.

The Disappearing Self: Another feature lurking in the tale of the wasp is that spooky sense one often gets when observing or learning about insects and other lower animals: all that bustling activity but *there's nobody home!* We are looking at a world that appears to have been cleverly designed but then deserted by its designer. The ants and bees, and even the fish and the birds, are just "going through the motions." *They* don't understand or appreciate what they are up to, and no other comprehending selves are to be found in the neighborhood. This is the fear of the incredible Disappearing Self.

Again, we seem to know of clearly intermediate cases between the insects, the fish, and ourselves. The insane and brain-damaged, for instance, often do seem to be quite appropriately described as having no selves, as being alive and animated, but having no *animae*. When we look "too closely" at our own mental activities, the same vanishing act often occurs. As Mozart once said of his musical ideas: "Whence and how do they come? I do not know and I *have nothing to do with it* [emphasis added]."[6] If determinism is true, it seems, there is no elbow room left for our selves, and no work for our selves to do. Can we find our selves, or is science on the verge of showing that they (*we?*) are illusions—like the illusion that the wasp is (or has) a self?

Science takes us inside things, and the inner, detailed view of our brains that science provides is not likely to reveal to us any recognizable version of what Descartes called the *res cogitans* or thinking thing we know so well "by introspection." But if we lose our view of our selves as

5. Milgram found that a sufficiently "institutional" setting can induce appallingly compliant behavior from many apparently normal people: subjects were enlisted as "research assistants" and asked to administer apparently severe electrical shocks to "subjects" (actors, in fact) as part of a training program. Kahneman and Tversky have demonstrated in a variety of experiments that even sophisticated researchers are often fooled by elementary fallacies of inductive reasoning, such as the Gambler's Fallacy (if heads has been coming up most often, tails is getting more and more likely on the next toss). For important philosophical discussion and review of the experimental literature, see Cohen 1981 and Kyburg 1983.

6. See my discussion of Mozart, Poincaré, and creativity in Dennett 1975.

we gain in scientific objectivity, what will happen to love and gratitude (and hate and resentment)?

> But what can I do if I don't even feel resentment? . . . My anger, in consequence of the damned laws of consciousness, is subject to chemical decomposition. As you look its object vanishes into thin air, its reasons evaporate, the offender is nowhere to be found, the affront ceases to be an offense and becomes destiny, something like toothache, for which nobody is to blame. (Dostoevsky, *Notes from Underground,* quoted by Bennett 1980)

The Dread Secret: Science often seems to be on the verge of telling us too much, of opening Pandora's Box and revealing some Dread Secret or other; as soon as we hear it, it will paralyze us. It will paralyze us by shattering some illusion that is absolutely necessary for the maintenance of our lives as agents. Our own rationality will undo us, because once we've seen the truth, we will be unable to deceive ourselves any longer.

It is easy enough to see how the paralysis is presumably accomplished by the Dread Secret, for it is by analogy, once again, with something that often happens, and can indeed be paralyzing and often pathetic. Suppose, for instance, we spend the day in Oxford debating the relative merits of the restaurants in London, trying to decide which to try in the evening. Then we learn the trains are not running, or all restaurants are closed for the day, or we are locked in the room in Oxford, or it is simply too late to get to London. We have just learned that that particular exercise of deliberation was utterly futile. There was no real opportunity for us to act; there were no real alternatives to decide among. Now if science were to show us that there really aren't ever any opportunities, wouldn't that—shouldn't that—lead us to cease deliberation altogether?

As Tolstoy says in the last line of *War and Peace,* "It is necessary to renounce a freedom that does not exist and to recognize a dependence of which we are not personally conscious." But this would be awful, it seems, for wouldn't it lead to a truly pernicious and self-destructive resignation and apathy? Think, for instance, of the obscene resignation of those who see nuclear war as utterly inevitable and hence not worth trying to prevent. Shouldn't we deplore the promulgation of any claim (even if it is true—perhaps especially if it is true) that encourages this sort of attitude?

What is the Dread Secret supposed to be? Perhaps it is the fact of determinism. (Or the fact of indeterminism!) In any event, it seems that we should bring it out into the open very gingerly, since its implication is that freedom is an illusion. Note that the fear here is not that a certain proposition is true, but that true or false it may come to be believed.

After all, if determinism is true now, it always has been true. While many people's lives in the past have been quite horrible, many others have led lives apparently well worth living—in spite of their living in a deterministic world. Modern science isn't *making* determinism true, even if it is discovering this fact, so things aren't going to get worse, unless it is believing in determinism rather than determinism itself that creates the catastrophe.[7]

Could the discovery of determinism not only ruin our own lives but reveal retrospectively that all those earlier good lives were not what they seemed to those who led them? Some of the most haunting images in the philosophical literature play on this worry. Anscombe (1957, p. 6) tells us of a lecture in which Wittgenstein invited his audience to consider autumn leaves floating down to the ground, saying to themselves "Now I'll go this way . . . now I'll go that way." Hobbes devised a similar fantasy:

> A wooden top that is lashed by the boys, and runs about sometimes to one wall, sometimes to another, sometimes spinning, sometimes hitting men on the shins, if it were sensible of its own motion, would think it proceeded from its own will, unless it felt what lashed it. And is a man any wiser, when he runs to one place for a benefice, to another for a bargain, and troubles the world with writing errors and requiring answers, because he thinks he doth it without other cause than his own will, and seeth not what are the lashings that cause his will? (Hobbes, Molesworth, ed., 1841, Vol V, p. 55)

Some illusions are almost irresistible. The golfer is watching his putt curving slowly toward the cup. He squirms and twists and leans, as if to get the ball to alter its course, as if his gyrations could actually make a difference. But it's too late, of course. There is a term for such antics: *body English.*[8] Body English is always futile, sometimes comical, sometimes pathetic, and often irresistible. What science threatens to show us is that all our striving is just so much body English. Wouldn't it be awful if all our mental gymnastics, our deliberations and strivings and resolutions and struggles were just so much body English? They would be, if they were (however irresistible) utterly incapable of making any real difference to the outcomes of the events that matter to us. This bugbear looms large in discussions of fatalism, but that is not its only hunting

---

7. See, for instance, Strawson 1962: "What effect would, or should, the acceptance of the truth of a general thesis of determinism have upon these reactive attitudes [our normal, interpersonal 'participant' attitudes, such as gratitude and resentment]?"

8. I discovered in Oxford that this term is an Americanism, largely unknown in England, as is its parent, "putting English" (spin) on a ball.

ground. For the moment it might be useful to contrast body English with something quite similar, for this might help save us from a fear.

Consider follow-through.[9] The golfer has been told by the golf pro to *keep his head down* until he has completed his swing. But how can this be good advice? The ball leaves the club head in midswing, and after it has begun its trajectory, nothing that happens on the tee can alter that trajectory. Isn't the attention to details of the swing that occur after the ball leaves the club head just so much body English? Not necessarily. For it may be that the only way to get the right thing to happen up to the moment of impact is to look ahead and fix a more distant goal, counting on one's efforts to satisfy that goal to produce bodily motions that traverse just the right space at just the right speed. One would be foolish indeed to disregard the pro's advice on the basis of the argument given above that it couldn't make any difference. It could make all the difference. Sometimes the only way to get what you really want is to try to do something else. (These suggestions will be amplified in the fifth and seventh chapters.)

So I am willing to fight fire with fire. The fearmonger calls up the everyday image of body English, and gets you to transport your shudder of embarrassment or anxiety into the metaphysical realm of free will. I counter with the everyday image of follow-through, and ask why you shouldn't just as well transport its more congenial moral to the high metaphysical ground. But there ought to be a better way of proceeding, and there is. The more or less traditional philosophical practice is to move briskly through the analogies to a conclusion which then becomes the starting point for exquisitely careful theory construction and argument. For instance, it is taken as "obvious" that the sort of free will we all want is such that one has free will only if one "could have done otherwise," and then great care and energy is taken to spell out the necessary and sufficient conditions for this sort of power or circumstance.

This then creates the curious desire in some people that it should turn out to be true of any of one's acts that if *exactly the same* physical state of affairs should obtain again, some other act could issue forth. Much ingenuity has been expended in trying to say what this thesis amounts to, and what its chances are of being true, but surprisingly little attention has been given to the question of why anyone should care about this metaphysical might-be—aside from "reminding" the reader that if it weren't true, why, that would be like being in prison, being paralyzed, hypnotized, a wasp, a puppet, a plaything. The allusions to the awful alternative are sometimes so swiftly traversed that quite obvious

9. Compare the brief discussion of follow-through in Nozick 1981, p. 311.

incoherence is overlooked—incoherence that would never survive the careful attention philosophers devote to their theorizing proper.

4. Overview

So far I have not tried to prove anything about free will. Instead, I have been circling the topic, roughing out our sense of the issues, drawing attention to a few curious features of the raw material—a tempting shape here, a vein in the marble there. I have been concerned to draw attention to ways in which the free will problem *may* be in large part an artifact of the methods typically used to study it, and this preliminary consciousness-raising will be useful in keeping us out of some perennial ruts as we traverse the traditional terrain. Before we are finished, we will cover virtually all of the traditional topics and arguments in the free will literature, but my method will be *to go slow where others go fast,* pausing over the familiar analogizing instead of rushing headlong into theory construction and refutation.

A fairly vigorous institution of professional repression has submerged for us the centrality and influence of intuition pumps in the development of philosophy. It is not just in the free will area that intuition pumps have been the dominant force. I suggest that reflection on the history of philosophy shows that the great intuition pumps have been the major movers all along. Think of Plato's Cave, Meno teaching geometry to the slave boy, Descartes' evil demon, and Hobbes' state of nature. Think, more recently, of Quine's (1960) linguists trying to translate "Gavagai," Goodman's (1965) grue-bleen puzzle, Rawls' (1971) Original Position, and Farrell's (1950) seductive question about what it would be like to be a bat,[10] to say nothing of Putnam's (1975) notorious Twin-Earth, and Searle's (1980) even more notorious Chinese Room.

One might say that these intuition pumps are the enduring melodies of philosophy, with the staying power that ensures that they will be remembered by our freshmen, quite vividly and accurately, years after they have forgotten the intricate contrapuntal surrounding argument and analysis. A good intuition pump is more robust than any one version of

10. Yes, it was Farrell, in 1950, who first asked (and answered) the philosophically enticing question made famous in Nagel's (1974) classic paper, "What is it Like to be a Bat?" (reprinted, with commentary, in Hofstadter and Dennett 1981). Farrell's discussion of the question appears in his evergreen paper, "Experience," first published in *Mind,* and reprinted in the very successful anthology edited by Chappell (1962). I draw attention to Farrell's priority not to embarrass Nagel—we all are liable to reinvent what we admire—but to underscore my point below about the robustness of a good intuition pump, which is like the robustness of a good, unforgettable melody.

it. (How many variations have been trotted out on the themes of Rawls' Original Position or Putnam's Twin-Earth?)

Intuition pumps are powerful pedagogical devices. Descartes' "cogito ergo sum" thought experiment is generally agreed to be logically suspect, if not downright defective. It has inspired literally dozens of reinterpretations and defenses; many philosophy professors would dismiss all these commentaries while never dreaming of removing Descartes' dramatic idea from the syllabus. Even great intuition pumps can mislead as much as they instruct. When we teach Descartes, for instance, we typically do not teach his thought experiment as revealing the truth— or even as leading to the truth—about knowledge. In fact, we typically blame Descartes and his seductive intuition pump for leading philosophers on a three-century wild goose chase. At best we are grateful to him in the same way we might be grateful to someone who gave us the wrong directions, but whose directions led us on a fascinating misadventure from which we happened to learn a great deal.

The central role of intuition pumps in philosophy shows that philosophy is not, and could not reasonably aspire to be, science. Philosophy without intuition pumps occasionally succeeds in purifying and regimenting a conceptual area sufficiently for science to take over, but these are not mainstream philosophical triumphs, by and large. Philosophy with intuition pumps is not science at all, but in its own informal way it is a valuable—even occasionally necessary–companion to science. It should not embarrass philosophers to acknowledge that intuition pumps do much of the enduring work of philosophy (for better and for worse). After all, an intuition pump should be the ideal tool in the philosopher's kit, if we take seriously one of the best-known visions of what philosophy is *for*. It is for enlarging our vision of the possible, for breaking bad habits of thought. As Wittgenstein said, "Philosophy is a battle against the bewitchment of our intelligence by means of language." (Wittgenstein 1953, sec. 109) For such tasks, the regimented marshalling of rigorous argument is seldom more than an insurance policy, a check on the freewheeling intuition mongering that has laid down the lines of some new vision.

In the following chapters, I maintain that the free will problem *is* the family of anxieties briefly sketched in this chapter. My method will be to examine them, and the analogies and intuition pumps that feed them, to see what actual threats to our self-esteem and aspirations might be in the offing, and what residual philosophical problems of genuine interest might remain to be solved.

In chapter two I turn to questions about our biological status as rational animals, and examine the grounds for our fear of sphexishness.

In chapter three I examine the concepts of *control* and *self-control*, two concepts that are utterly central to the questions of free will and determinism, but which, so far as I know, have never been carefully analyzed by philosophers. Central questions will be: how does one thing control another—or itself—and what sorts of things can be controllers? (Here is where the bogeymen keep interfering.)

In chapter four I turn to the concept of a *self* or *agent,* and see how it can be kept from disappearing under the onslaught of science.

In chapter five we see what can be made of Kant's claim that when we act, we must "act under the idea of freedom." In what ways do we need to think about the future and about our powers for some things to be seen by us as "up to us" while others are seen as not "up to us"? Does the elbow room we must take ourselves to have when we deliberate really exist? J. Alfred Prufrock asks

> Do I dare
> Disturb the universe?
> In a minute there is time
> For decisions and revisions which a minute will reverse.
> ("The Love Song of J. Alfred Prufrock," T. S. Eliot)

But how could anything *count as* disturbing the universe? Science seems to need the idea (See *Disturbing the Universe,* Dyson 1979) while it overthrows it at the same time. Can we have it both ways?

In chapter six I investigate the meaning of the word "can" and the pivotal phrase "could have done otherwise." As Austin famously said, "In philosophy it is *can* that we seem so often to uncover, just when we had thought some problem settled, grinning residually up at us like the frog at the bottom of the beer mug." (Austin 1961, p. 179) How true, but first we must drain all the beer. Then we will find a much more manageable frog to deal with.

In chapter seven I ask why we want free will in the first place, and show why we are wise to want it, given the implications of our necessary imperfection as agents. The questions here turn practical and personal. Are we deceiving ourselves—or being deceived by society—when we maintain our interest in being *held responsible?* When and why is our responsibility diminished? Are we ever truly guilty when we have done wrong?

My conclusions are neither revolutionary nor pessimistic. They are only moderately revisionary: the common wisdom about our place in the universe is roughly right. We do have free will. We can have free will and science too. The conclusions reached will not exhaust the topic of free will, of course, and further challenges to our composure can be expected. But my review of the results of the earlier chapters will yield some advice on how to respond to these future challenges.

2

Making Reason Practical

1. Where Do Reasons Come From?

A recurring but still controversial theme in the free will literature is the idea that true freedom of the will consists (or would consist) in a complete subjugation of the will to the *dictates of reason*. Kant is of course the philosopher who made this idea the centerpiece of his theory, but he was hardly the first to recognize the appeal of perfect rationality as the ideal against which to measure all imperfections, all regrettable bindings of will or agency. Thus Spinoza, in "On Human Bondage" claims to prove:

> To act absolutely in obedience to virtue is in us the same thing as to act, to live, or to preserve one's being (these three terms are identical in meaning) in accordance with the dictates of reason on the basis of seeking what is useful to one's self. (*Ethics,* IV, Prop. XXIV, Elwes translation 1891, p. 204)

Descartes expresses similar views in *Meditation IV*,[1] and Dr. Bramhall, Bishop of Derry, in his debate with Hobbes, delivers quite a hymn on the subject:

1. "For in order to be free, it is not necessary for me to be indifferent about the choice of one or the other of the two contraries, but rather, the more I lean to one, either because I see clearly that it contains the (preponderance of) both of goodness and truth or because God so guides my private thoughts, the more freely do I choose (and embrace) it. And certainly, divine grace and natural understanding, far from diminishing my liberty, rather augment and strengthen it. Moreover, that indifference which I feel when I am not moved more toward one side than the other by (the weight of) some reason is the lowest degree of liberty, and is rather a defect in the understanding than a perfection of the will. For if I always understand clearly what is true and what is good, I would never need to deliberate about what judgment and what choice I ought to make, and so I would be entirely free without ever being indifferent." See also his letter to Mersenne (*Oeuvres de Descartes,* 1897–1913, vol. III, pp. 381–382): "I move the more freely towards an object in proportion to the number of reasons which compel me; for it is certain that my will is set in motion with greater ease and spontaneity."

> Reason is the root, the fountain, the original of true liberty, which judgeth and representeth to the will, whether this or that be convenient, whether this or that be more convenient. (Hobbes, *Works*, Vol. V, p. 40)

Locke, whose views are not otherwise recognizably "Kantian," comes up with rhetorical support as effective as anything in Kant for this ideal of living by the dictates of reason:

> If to break loose from the conduct of reason, and to want that restraint of examination and judgment which keeps us from choosing or doing the worse, be liberty, true liberty, madmen and fools are the only freemen: but yet, I think, nobody would choose to be mad for the sake of such liberty, but he that is mad already. (*Essay Concerning Human Understanding*, II, XXI, sec. 51)

This idea of freedom as perfect rationality is expressed in the literature so often that there is probably something deeply right about it, but it is expressed so vehemently that there must also be some counterbalancing error in it, something counterintuitive and worrying about it, that creates the resistance against which these and other authors proclaim their insight. In chapter three, I will turn to an exploration of the sources of this skepticism about the ideal of rationality (or perhaps more accurately, the lack of fondness for it), but here I want to review the strengths of its appeal and show how we can realistically aspire to such rationality.

How could reason ever find a foothold in a material, mechanical universe? In the beginning, there were no reasons; there were only causes. Nothing had a purpose, nothing had so much as a function; there was no teleology in the world at all. The explanation for this is simple: there was nothing that had interests. But after millennia there happened to emerge simple replicators,[2] and while *they* had no inkling of their interests, and perhaps properly speaking had no interests, we, peering back from our Godlike vantage point at their early days, can nonarbitrarily assign them certain interests—generated by their defining "interest" in self-replication. That is, maybe it really made no difference, was a matter of no concern, didn't matter to anyone or anything whether or not they succeeded in replicating (though it does seem we can be grateful that they did), but at least we can assign them interests conditionally. *If* these simple replicators are to survive and replicate, thus persisting in the face of increasing entropy, their environment must meet certain conditions: conditions conducive to replication must be present or at least frequent.

2. See Dawkins 1976 for a lucid and elegant version of this history. For a different, supporting, perspective see Monod 1972, chapter 1, "Of Strange Objects," on the birth of what Monod calls "teleonomy."

Put more anthropomorphically, if these simple replicators want to continue to replicate, they should hope and strive for various things: they should avoid the "bad" things and seek the "good" things. Still more dramatically, were we to imagine ourselves as guardians of their interests, we could see quite clearly that there would be steps to be taken, assistance to be rendered, warnings to be issued.

This is not saying very much yet, for it is also true that if we imagine ourselves to take a fancy to some particularly beautiful rock formation spewed up millions of years ago by some volcanic eruption, we can readily imagine the steps we would have to take to preserve it—to protect it from erosion, from being buried in sediment, from being broken by subsequent volcanic eruptions, and so on.

What is the difference? In what way did the interests of replicators take on a life of their own? Just this: the replicators began to turn into crude guardians of their own interests. Indeed their power of self-replication depended on it. Unlike the volcanic sculpture, they were not utterly helpless and dependent on the solicitude of others; they could fend for themselves, a bit. The day that the universe contained entities that could take some rudimentary steps toward defending their own interests was the day that interests were born. The very tendencies of these organisms to preserve this and that (their varieties of *homeostasis*) helped sharpen the definition of their interests. Only certain sorts of homeostasis tended to be self-preserving in the long run; those kinds were replicated and hence persisted, and hence *gave further definition* to the crude, primordial "interest" in self-preservation and self-replication. Thus if body-temperature maintenance played an important role in the self-preservation of members of a species, body-temperature maintaining control systems that evolved would persist. And that species' catalog of interests would come to include the maintenance of a certain (range of) body temperature.

The basic themes of this story have been well presented many times. Food seeking, predator avoiding, mate locating, mating, and health maintaining (self-repairing, trauma avoiding, energy conserving, and so on) are the highest-level subgoals of replicators. In interaction with the particular species' circumstances, these subgoals breed other, instrumental subgoals: odor detecting, hole digging, locomoting, pattern recognizing, pain feeling, mate impressing, and so forth.

By the time we arrive at such a sophisticated creature as our *Sphex*, we can assign quite an elaborate catalog of interests to the creature. If it were not so, if we did not have a clear and detailed vision of where her interests lay, her performance in the strange experiment described in chapter one would not seem so pathetic. We measure her performance against her interests and see how poorly she does. Were we to act as her guardian, we could advise much better courses of action to her—if only she could take our advice![3] She is a very imperfect guardian of her own interests, it seems.[4] Moreover, we can say why she is so imperfect: she apparently has no inkling of her interests, or even that she has interests. One is even inclined to wonder if she has any inkling of her own existence!

Her supposed utter obliviousness to her own interests does not prevent her from "having" those interests—any more than a comatose person ceases to have interests once he or she becomes oblivious to them and unable to act in their defense. (When such an unfortunate person is assigned a guardian, there is something to guard, and it is not just the living body; a guardian is not just a curator. (I will resist the digression that would take us into a consideration of such issues as the persisting interests of the deceased.)

When an entity arrives on the scene capable of behavior that staves off, however primitively, its own dissolution and decomposition, it brings with it into the world its "good." That is to say it creates a point of view from which the world's events can be roughly partitioned into the favorable, the unfavorable, and the neutral. And its own innate proclivities to seek the first, shun the second, and ignore the third contribute essentially to the definition of the three classes. As the creature thus comes to have interests, the world and its events begin creating *reasons* for it—whether or not the creature can fully recognize them. Thus poor *Sphex* has as much reason to hide from the biologist as to provide nourishment for her progeny, but while she is designed to act (and not at all crudely) on the latter reason, she is apparently oblivious and helpless with regard to the former. This is to be expected of course. Evolution takes time, and it takes a nonnegligible amount of pressure on one's ancestors (more precisely, on one's ancestors' less fortunate contemporaries). It is easy enough to see why nothing in the wasp's heritage should have prepared her to recognize, and respond to, this novel reason she now has for action.

The reasons for action that came first in creation were rather like Platonic Forms, pure *abstracta* whose existence, while dependent on the existence of strivers and seekers, was independent of their being explicitly recognized or represented by anyone or anything. Consider, for instance, the set of reasons, composing what we may call a rationale, for

3. We may be underestimating her, of course. On the pitfalls of premature verdicts of stupidity in the wasp, see Dawkins 1982, pp. 48–50. See also Dennett 1983b.

4. But perhaps she is quite good enough. The costs of a larger brain, for instance, might well outweigh whatever benefits she could gain from it.

deceptive coloration among insects. The rationale can be quite elaborate: the precise color and location of deceptive markings such as the "eye-spots" on the wings of many moths is "dictated" by reasons of some subtlety, drawing on the visual acuity and color sensitivity of the relevant predators, the probably location and posture of the moth at the critical moment, and many other factors. Such rationales, which pre-Darwinian thinkers were constrained to place in the mind of God the Creator, can now be seen to be, and to have always been, "free-floating": a set of reasons that were appreciated by, thought out by, and rendered explicit by *no one*. The subtlety and deviousness of this thinking-without-a-thinker is often more than a match for the thinking we thinkers do.[5]

Lower animals, such as *Sphex,* are constitutionally oblivious to many of the reasons that concern them. They are like the stock character in spy fiction who plays out his role in a complex project without an inkling of the real import of the events he is involved with—until the denouement. The CIA and MI5 have their famous "Need to Know" principle: explain as little as possible and tell one's field operatives only what they absolutely need to know to perform their roles. Mother Nature is similarly stingy when she apportions comprehension, it appears. When larger "goals" can be achieved by cleverly organized armies of uncomprehending agents, such as ants, the "Need to Know" rule is ruthlessly invoked.

Consider, for instance, the strategy of "predator saturation," as followed by Ridley's sea turtles: the newly hatched young emerge in near unison from the safety of their nests under the sand and participate in a sort of reverse Anzio Landing, dashing by the thousands from their holes on the beach through a murderous gauntlet of massed predators that kill perhaps nine out of ten before they can reach the relative safety of the sea. Their strategy is clear: flood the predators with more opportunities than they can handle. But unlike the all-too-knowing participants at Anzio, they surely have no inkling of the point of their well-synchronized march.

Mother Nature abides by the "Need to Know" principle, but we appreciate a contrary principle: our ideal is to be completely savvy, to be

---

5. Francis Crick speaks of "Orgel's Second Rule: Evolution is cleverer than you are." "Free-floating rationales" are defined in Dennett 1983b. Interests, like reasons, are best conceived as abstractions; they are often definable even in cases where we believe, on theoretical grounds, that they *cannot* be systematically pursued. The most obvious case is that of the interests of species or groups as opposed to the interests of individuals (or their genes). If the "group selectionists" are wrong, the interests of a species, or a particular population of a species, are free-floating in a stronger sense: they are (let us grant) definable, so we can tell when they *happen* to be furthered, but it would be a mistake to invoke them in any explanatory role.

able to notice *all* the reasons that concern us, to be in the dark about nothing of relevance to us, to be the completely and perfectly informed guardians of our own interests. That is what it would be to be able to choose one's course of action always as reason dictated.[6]

We often say that "reason dictates" a certain course of action to an actor in a certain circumstance. We do not mean by this that there is some strange personified force, a Dictator called Reason who has issued an edict. Obviously we mean something abstract: we mean that a certain problem (abstractly considered—that is, whether or not any creature has explicitly expressed and addressed it) has a certain (optimal) solution. The problem is defined by the circumstances and interests of the actor in question. But the subliminal image of wise old Reason, *telling* what to do, has had quite a strong effect on the way the issue has been conceived by philosophers.[7]

Kant draws our attention to the distinction between merely doing what reason dictates and doing what reason dictates *because reason dictates it.* One might, in the first instance, just happen to do "the right thing," or be caused by extraneous and irrelevant factors to do the right thing. However fortunate one might be to fall into such a circumstance, this is to be distinguished from the good fortune enjoyed by one who has the marvelous further power to be *moved by reasons.*

Intermediate between the actor who purely coincidentally "does the right thing" and the actor who is moved by the right reasons to do the right thing is the actor who tends to do the right thing (because the actor was designed to tend to do the right thing), but nevertheless does the right thing (when it does) unwittingly. This intermediate actor, it seems, does not attend to the wise voice of Reason directly, cannot itself actually hear and comprehend Reason's dictates; however, it seems as though the process (or agent) that designed the actor was thus responsive to Reason's dictates. Our *Sphex* is an example. *Sphex,* in her normal surround-

6. Wolf (1980) discusses the case of someone whose thinking is determined, but determined in such a way that "what reasons he *has* for being generous depends on what reasons there *are.*" (p. 158) Williams (1981), in "Internal and External Reasons," discusses a similar but narrower notion.

7. One effect is to foster a certain vision of Reason as a "faculty" of the mind, competing with others, as portrayed in this passage from Hume:

> 'Tis impossible reason cou'd have the latter effect of preventing volition, but by giving an impulse in a contrary direction to our passion; and that impulse, had it operated alone, wou'd have been able to produce volition. Nothing can oppose or retard the impulse of passion, but a contrary impulse; and if this contrary impulse ever arises from reason, that latter faculty must have an original influence on the will, and must be able to cause, as well as hinder any act of volition. (*Treatise of Human Nature,* II, III)

ings (that is, when tricky biologists are not interfering), typically does what reason dictates, for surely reason does proclaim the wisdom of reconnoitering her pathways ("Look before you leap!"). But she doesn't do it because reason dictates it *to her;* it is rather that her designed behavior cunningly approximates in this one regard the responsiveness of what we might call, doing violence to Kant, Pure Practical Reason.

Consider another example. The Oxford zoologist John Krebs has investigated a remarkable case of what we might call *apparent reason* in birds (Krebs, Kacelnik, and Taylor 1978). He and his colleagues place great tits (*Parus major*), one at a time, in an experimental situation known as a two-armed bandit. There are two perches several meters apart that the birds may press in order to obtain food on random but differently weighted schedules. Since they can be assumed to have an interest in gathering food as efficiently as possible, their "task" is to determine, by exploratory pressing, which perch has the better average yield for their efforts (and hence should be exclusively pressed, once it is identified). They maximize their food intake during their fixed stay in the apparatus if they find the best possible balance between "exploration" and "exploitation." On the one hand they should avoid settling too early on the lower-yielding perch, while on the other hand they should avoid prolonging inefficient exploration. Optimal solutions to this set of problems can be calculated by an elaborate dynamic programming algorithm. In other words, reason dictates a certain course of action (on plausible assumptions about the birds' interests and circumstances). Wonderful to say, the birds approximate very closely to this optimal solution—they really do what reason dictates—but as Krebs hastens to insist, there is no reason to suppose the etiology of their action includes any sophisticated calculation, let alone any appreciation of the principles (for example, Pontryagin's Maximum Principle) which dictate the optimal solution.

A mathematician faced with a similar problem might actually be capable of working out the optimal solution, and *because of* her full appreciation of it (her grasp of the meaning of her own calculations), take it as the grounds for her action. That would be a case of being moved by reason, if anything was. But how can the gulf between the the birdbrain and the mathematician be bridged? How might more advanced creatures such as ourselves be capable of responding directly to reasons? How, to paraphrase a question of Kant's, is a truly rational will possible?

2. *Semantic Engines, Perpetual Motion Machines, and a Defective Intuition Pump*

It has seemed to many that there is no gradualist bridge to be built between the "blind," "mechanical," only seemingly clever behavior of the birds and bees, and the human capacity to contemplate and be moved by reasons, to "grasp" meanings, and to enjoy genuine "intentionality." If meaning is not a physical property of things in the world, how *could* there be physical or mechanical meaning-transducers, meaning-detectors, meaning-recognizers? The underground (seldom explicit) argument is straightforward: physical discriminator-mechanisms can only discriminate physical properties; they can sort oranges by weight, color, or shape—but not by whether or not they are beautiful, or once belonged to a widower. Events can be physically discriminated according to their duration or location—or, say, by the presence or absence of light of some particular wavelength, or tone of some particular pitch and volume. But events cannot be physically discriminated according to their meaningfulness or lack thereof. *We,* however, can discriminate meanings; we can respond directly to the import, sense, or relevance of things that we encounter. Therefore we are not (merely) physical discriminator-mechanisms.

Here is a somewhat different underground argument to the same conclusion. To do something because reason dictates it is to be caused by (the appreciation of) a reason so to act. But reasons are not physical conditions in the world. Therefore, if any act of mine is caused by physical conditions in the world, it is *ipso facto* not caused by (the appreciation of) a reason. Thus the only hope of having a rational will involves the exemption from physical causality of one's mind.

The distinction between reasons and causes has often been inflated into a complete segregation of reasons and causes, so that they are seen to be antagonistic. Consider, for instance, this observation of Wittgenstein's:

> The causes [*Ursachen*] of our belief in a proposition are indeed irrelevant to the question what we believe. Not so the grounds, which are grammatically related to the proposition, and tell us what proposition it is. (Wittgenstein 1967, i. 437)

This passage is precariously poised; it is easy to read as claiming that the grounds or reasons for holding a belief could not be the causes of holding that belief, and as implying that if a belief is caused (has causes) it cannot be believed *for reasons*—which is simply false. I doubt that Wittgenstein meant this claim to be read that way, but it certainly invites that reading, and many philosophers have accepted the invitation with pleasure.

Kant apparently fell for some version of this underground argument. He could not see how a human act could be *both* the effect of physical causes and also the execution of a decision of a rational will. As one Kant commentator puts it, Kant claims that "to have a will simply means to be capable of being moved by reason *rather than* [emphasis added] by natural causes." (Wolff 1973, p. 216) Thus his vision of the mind was forced, by his vision of the will as one of its parts, into a dualistic cul-de-sac.

Dualism, the idea that minds (unlike brains) are composed of stuff that is exempt from the laws of physical nature, is a desperate vision which richly deserves its current disfavor. But if we are quite confident today that one way or another we can account for the mind's powers in terms of the brain's purely physical powers, we must acknowledge that if we are to do this we must break the back of these underground arguments somehow. What are brains for? They are not, as Aristotle is reputed to have thought, just for cooling the blood; they are for controlling the bodies they are perched in by discriminating the meanings of the impingements or stimuli that those bodies encounter. In short, brains are meaning manipulators, information processors, or, as I shall say, *semantic engines* (Dennett 1981a).[8]

But at the same time brains are just very complicated physical organs; whatever they react to must be some physical change or difference in the stimuli they encounter. In short, as physical mechanisms they can only be *syntactic engines,* responding only to structural or formal properties.[9] According to the traditional distinction in linguistics, a sentence's form or syntax is one thing and its meaning or semantics is another. Now how does the brain manage to get semantics from syntax? It couldn't.

Syntax all by itself doesn't determine semantics. It is a relatively straightforward task to design and build machines that test for acidity, or for temperatures below forty degrees Fahrenheit, or for dot-dot-dot-dash-dash-dash-dot-dot-dot. But think of designing a machine that tests for the presence of hostility or love or danger or skepticism. *We* don't find it impossible to react to, recognize, or comprehend these properties. But it seems unlikely indeed that any combination of structural (and hence straightforwardly mechanically detectable) properties is equivalent to hostility, love, skepticism, or danger. Since meaning does not reside, like some rare ore, in physical features of stimuli, no alchemical extraction process could distill it and respond to it. But then the concept of a semantic engine is apparently like the concept of a perpetual motion machine: semantic engines are strictly speaking impossible machines!

But then what are brains for, if they are not semantic engines? The answer must be: brains only approximate the behavior of the (ideal, pure) semantic engine. The perfect semantic engine, the perfect Kantian

8. Haugeland develops the concept further in "Semantic Engines: an Introduction to Mind Design" (Haugeland 1981).

9. See also Fodor's discussion of what he calls the Formality Constraint (Fodor 1980 reprinted in Haugeland 1981 and Fodor 1981).

rational will, is indeed friction-free, infinitely alert to nuances of meaning, perfectly invulnerable to sphexishness—and physically impossible. Our brains, however, are very good substitutes. They are cunningly designed to be not infinitely but indefinitely sensitive to meaningful changes, not perfectly but practically invulnerable to sphexishness.[10]

How does a brain manage to approximate the competence of a perfect semantic engine? We have already seen, in *Sphex,* how a cleverly designed bit of mere physical reactivity can produce some of the right effects in normal environments, causing *Sphex* to behave *as if* responding directly to a present concern of hers, to a reason she has. What magnification of such powers can be achieved by combination and iteration of such basically sphexish mechanisms? The elaboration of ever more exquisite and sensitive pattern-recognition devices can be traced in phylogeny, and advances in Artificial Intelligence are beginning to reveal the strengths and limitations of such indirect, imperfect meaning-detectors. But as Hofstadter points out, the truly explosive advance in the escape from crude sphexishness comes when the capacity for pattern recognition is turned in upon itself. The creature who is not only sensitive to patterns in its environment, but also sensitive to patterns in its own reactions to patterns in its environment, has taken a major step.[11] Unlike *Sphex,* it can notice that it is caught in a futile loop or rut, and leap out of it.

One describes the patterns in a language—both syntactical and semantical—by making statements in a *meta-language.* More generally, one "goes meta-" when one represents one's representations, reflects on one's reflections, reacts to one's reactions. The power to iterate one's powers in this way, to apply whatever tricks one has to one's existing tricks, is a well-recognized breakthrough in many domains: a cascade of processes leading from stupid to sophisticated activity. (The most de-

10. Hofstadter (1982b) makes excellent observations about the manifestations of our inevitable, finite susceptibility to absurd ruts of the sort *Sphex* falls into. He claims persuasively that our ruts, unlike hers, are recognizable in such amiable quirks as artistic and cognitive styles—moderately disabling, on occasion, but a small price to pay for our ability to think fast under the pressure of real time.

11. As Hofstadter (1982b) also points out, this fact is clearly recognized by Lucas in his classic antimechanist argument: "Minds, Machines, and Gödel" (Lucas 1961). Having arrived at this insight, Lucas squanders it by committing a traditional philosophical error: holding out for absolutism. For no apparent reason Lucas insists that we human beings are perfectly antisphexish (and perfectly consistent—perfect semantic engines, in effect). As we shall see, this demand for absolute perfection and invulnerability frequently leads philosophical theory builders to ascribe magical (that is, impossible) properties to human agents.

tailed exploration of the power of this process of iteration is Hofstadter 1979.)

Thus (1) the blind trial and error of Darwinian selection creates (2) organisms whose blind trial and error behavior is subjected to selection by reinforcement, creating (3) "learned" behaviors that generate a profusion of (4) learning opportunities from which (5) the most telling can be "blindly" but reliably selected, creating (6) a better-focused capacity to generate (7) further candidates for not-so-blind "consideration," and (8) the eventual selection or choice or decision of a course of action "based on" those considerations. Eventually, the overpowering "illusion" is created that the system is actually responding directly to meanings. It becomes a more and more reliable mimic of the perfect semantic engine (the entity that hears Reason's voice directly), because it was designed to be capable of improving itself in this regard; it was designed to be indefinitely self-redesigning.

As the possibility of multiple iterations suggests, there are different varieties of reflexivity, with differing powers. At the simplest end of the spectrum there is simple reaction to some of one's own reactions. An automated door-opener that "counts how many times it works" and turns off after a certain number of cycles is about as simple as such a system can be. Something like those mechanisms, mere protectors against "excess" repetition, seem to be evidenced in nonhuman animals, but they sometimes produce unimpressive results. I once had a dog who loved to fetch tennis balls, but faced with two balls on the lawn and unable to hold them both in his mouth at once, he would switch rapidly back and forth, grabbing one and letting go of the other, mesmerized by his preference for getting over keeping—for perhaps several dozen cycles—until *something* clicked and turned off the behavior.

Much higher on the spectrum of modes of reflexivity is the *representation* of some of one's reactions, whether via expressions in a public language or other public system of representations, or via internal states that themselves have enough of the functional properties of vehicles of public representation to be worthy of the name.[12] (Just how a system with the power of explicit self-representation of some of its states might arise will be examined in the next section.)

---

12. Just how and why to draw the line between states or events that are and states or events that are not representations is an important topic I have discussed at length elsewhere (for example, Dennett 1978a, 1981a, 1981b, 1982a, 1983a). On this occasion I will attempt to skirt the controversies by appealing to representations only when their presence and implication in the matter is obvious to virtually everyone, myself included. Since I am myself one of the most extreme skeptics about mental representations, my use of this tactic ought to be quite safe.

A system that can reflect on its own activities in this way cannot reflect on all its activities at once. It may be able to reflect on its reflections on its reflections, but sooner or later it must run out of moves or room or time. Could there be a perfect self-watcher? Not a finite and nonmagical one. This is shown by the proof in computability theory that the "halting problem" has no solution: there is no program that can inspect any program and determine whether or not it contains infinite loops (Hofstadter 1982b, pp. 27–28). Now is anything short of perfection good enough for us? If we are not perfect, then we are, indeed, a little bit sphexish. That would mean that *in principle* we could be put in a ludicrous situation where we manifested our marginal, otherwise invisible irrationality (or better still, our *a*-rationality, or *syntactitude*—a term suggested to me by Hofstadter). But this should hardly come as a shock or disappointment. Which of us requires an argument from physical finitude and computability theory to convince us we are not perfect meaning-extractors?

So long as one concentrates in imagination on cases of imperfect rationality and incomprehension as dramatic as *Sphex*, it is easy enough to convince oneself that human beings are radically, qualitatively different sorts of beings. And of course the philosophers' perfectly reasonable penchant for simple, easy-to-follow examples leads them again and again to focusing on just such simple cases when contrasting *being caused to do something* with *doing something for a reason*. The entire "reasons and causes" literature in philosophy is infested with this species of spuriously contrasting examples.

Consider, for instance, the subtle effect wrought by MacIntyre: "If a man's behaviour is rational it cannot be determined by the state of his glands or any other antecedent causal factor." (MacIntyre 1957, p. 35)[13] Why his glands? No doubt the sort of causation that might arise from someone's glands would be a crude blast of some sort, a shove in one direction, a "blind" shift in the myriad switching patterns, not an almost indescribably subtle and delicate selection of a subsequent state. There is a commonly used term, I have discovered, for this species of crude causation in the brain; it is often called "psychological"! Consider the following remark drawn from an interview about free will with a university professor (not a philosopher):

> It's part of your responsibility to be aware of what you are doing, and why you are doing it. That's really your only chance to exercise some amount of free will, to be able to make a real choice *instead of*

13. This passage is discussed in more detail in Dennett 1973 (reprinted in Dennett 1978a). For another instance of the spurious contrast, see Anscombe 1957, p. 24 and my discussion of it in Dennett 1969, pp. 162–163.

being pushed by psychological determinants [emphasis added]. (Doan and Macnamara in preparation, ms. p. 7. 13)

To be led to a decision by an exhaustive consideration of the pros and cons is not to be "pushed" by "psychological" determinants, apparently. This use of "psychological" is apparently a cousin of the usage by American children of the word "mental"—as in "That kid's so stupid, he's mental!" This usage is obviously a truncation of "mentally retarded" or "mentally ill." The parallel use of "psychological" is probably due to the pride of place in popular imagination of *clinical* psychology; the word in this use apparently means *psychologically pathological.*[14]

Occasionally philosophers do make use of the fact that it does not follow from the fact that an action or decision is caused that it is not also done for (good) reasons. Thus Nagel notes that one can *hope* that even if one's actions are determined by causes, they are "not determined by causes in a way which implies that they are not justified by reasons." (Nagel 1981) This is not at all a logically forlorn hope, but it tends to be overlooked by philosophers. There is even a famous aphorism that strongly suggests that the hope is forlorn: *"Tout comprendre c'est tout pardonner."* Why would anyone think this was true?[15]

One reason might be that people reflect on it by imagining themselves to have complete understanding of the etiology of some act, and find themselves imagining something (sketchily) with a causal ancestry far too simple and direct to be a plausible candidate for a responsible act. Since the only causal processes we can completely understand at a glance (the sort of glance one gives to such matters in imaginary cases) are quite simple causal processes, we arrive at the intuition that causal understanding excludes rational evaluation and assignment of responsibility. This is a clear case of a misused intuition pump, where simplicity is doing all the work.

When we think of causation, we tend to think of nicely isolated laboratory cases of causation, where a single, repeatable, salient effect is achieved under controlled circumstances. Or we think of particularly clear cases of everyday causation: Hume's billiard balls, sparks causing

14. One also finds "biological" used this way—thus meaning something like *merely* or *crudely* biological. One sometimes sees the term "biological determinism," where one can tell from context that it means something like "genetic determinism." On the bogey of genetic determinism, see Dawkins 1982, pp. 9–29.

15. Not everyone does, of course. Strawson tells me that the claim once came up in the metaphilosophy discussion group in Oxford years ago, and Austin retorted: "That's quite wrong. Understanding might just add contempt to hatred."—Austin's sharp, shallow scalpel at its best.

explosions, one big salient thing bumping into another big salient thing. We know that on closer examination we would find every corner of our world teeming with complicated, indecipherable, tangled webs of causation, but we tend to ignore that fact. Thus when we think of someone *caused* to believe this or that, we tend to imagine them being *shoved* willy-nilly into that state. The person thus caused to believe is analogized to the billiard ball caused to roll north, or the liquid caused to boil in the test tube.

But in relying on these analogies we tend to ignore a major difference: test tubes and billiard balls are deaf and blind. You don't have to whisper in front of the test tube, or make sure the billiard ball doesn't see you watching it. People and higher animals, on the other hand, are designed to be highly sensitive to virtually everything that happens around them. It is, in fact, utterly impossible to get an awake, normal human being into exactly the same "cognitive state" (let alone the same microphysical state) on two different occasions, simply because time passes and unless one is comatose or in some other sort of Rip Van Winkle state, one *notices* and hence is constantly changing.[16]

But when one starts thinking about the implications of determinism—the thesis that everyone's beliefs are caused, for instance—one almost invariably shifts to a vision that ignores (or deliberately dismisses) the information-gathering apparatus that is our most impressive causal interface with our surroundings.[17]

Consider, for instance, the forces that tug at Ayer's imagination when he conjures up the following science-fictional intuition pump:

> Suppose that the requisite physiological or psycho-physiological theories were developed and that we could use them in everyday life to make mainly accurate predictions. Or if this be thought too fanciful, let us suppose that the theory of conditioning were developed to a point where it became possible to implant desires and beliefs and traits of character in human beings, to an extent that it could be deduced, at least in fairly general terms, how any person who had been treated in this way would most probably behave in a given situation, and that we lived under a regime in which these powers

16. This fact will be seen to have an important role to play in the correct analysis of "could have done otherwise" in chapter six. Lucas (1970, p. 79) notes the importance of this fact, but again cannot resist inflating his position into a demand for human "infinitude."

17. It was Norbert Wiener, in *Cybernetics: or Control and Communication in the Animal and the Machine* (Wiener 1948), who inaugurated the contemporary vision of human beings as "automata effectively coupled to the external world, not merely by their energy flow, their metabolism, but also by a flow of impressions, of incoming messages, and of the actions of outgoing messages." (p. 54)

were exercised upon us, let us say from early childhood. (Ayer 1980, p. 9)

A chilling vision, to be sure, and Ayer wants it to pump from us the intuition that "our interpersonal attitudes," our sense of ourselves and each other as responsible, blamable, lovable agents, would not withstand the knowledge we would then have of how agents would behave. Indeed it would not, I dare say, *under the imagined circumstances.* But those are circumstances in which, (to avoid being "too fanciful") the actual causation of the imagined beliefs and desires has been rendered drastically cruder, in which agents are zapped into their supposed "beliefs, desires, and traits of character" by a process of conditioning that presumably is powerful enough to override their delicate, information-gathering, information-assessing, normal ways of coming to have beliefs and desires.

What would it be like to live in such a world? "It would be as if we were spectators of a play in which we also participated, with no other option than to enact the roles allotted to us." (Ayer 1980, p. 10) But wait just a minute; suppose we began to giggle and whisper, and completely disrupted the play by pointing out to each other how pointless the plot was. Unfair to Ayer's example! We are not supposed to imagine ourselves being able to do that. But why not? Did Ayer stipulate that in this imaginary world people can no longer notice things, and react accordingly to them? The evil scientists who run this world can apparently peer through the armored glass at us without worrying that we will unexpectedly shake our fists at them and revolt. It must be because, without saying so, Ayer has turned us into much simpler creatures. (Compare the method of operation of Ayer's intuition pump with that of Robbins' tale of the tiny Tyrolean village discussed in chapter one.)

3. Reflection, Language, and Consciousness

If people's wills are determined, Hobbes is asked, "why do we represent reasons to them?" He answers: "because thereby we think to make them have the will they have not." (Hobbes, *Works* Vol V, p. 52) People, normal people in any case, have the good fortune of having wills that are determined (if they are determined) by a complicated causal process of perception and ratiocination that often includes, as Hobbes notes, causal volleys of communication. People often have reasons represented to them. And it often moves them, fortunately for them.

But is this way in which people are moved by reasons importantly different from "ordinary" causation is some way I have still overlooked or submerged? I have sketched a cascade of self-monitoring processes and claimed that it takes us from *Sphex* and her peers to creatures who, like us, are indefinitely sensitive to the import of the things that happen around them. Such creatures are reliable approximations of "genuine" semantic engines. But in the eyes of philosophical absolutists, such entities would be *mere* simulations, not the real thing at all.[18] What reason, aside from traditional dogma, does anyone have for insisting that *we* are the real thing? If we are very good approximations, any empirical litmus test would be confounded.[19]

What about an introspective litmus test? It is tempting to argue that our consciousness of reasons is what sets us apart. In sketching the sequence that crosses the gulf between *Sphex* and us, have I not also surreptitiously crossed another gulf: the chasm separating the unconscious from the conscious? When we speak of pattern *recognition* by *Sphex*, or *decision* in great tits, we seem to require scare quotes around our mentalistic terms; it is tempting to insist that these are mere mechanical analogues of genuine recognition, decision, and comprehension. The ever more sensitive "comprehension" capacities so far described are species of what we might call *merely behavioral* comprehension. This is to be contrasted, it may seem, with the genuine, conscious comprehension to be found in human beings.

It is far from clear, however, what this familiar but unanalyzed property of consciousness might add to the powers of "merely behavioral" comprehension systems. Could it be that this apparently sharp qualitative difference is another illusion, generated by paying too much attention to the extremes, and not enough attention to the intervening complications? It is certainly true that theorists dealing with these issues have typically settled firmly into one of two visions. Philosophers have traditionally adopted a purely introspective approach, where consciousness is presupposed, while biologists and computer scientists (and other scientific modelers of these processes) have tended to insist upon a pure "engineering" approach with a third-person perspective on the mechanisms they describe. The scientific modelers often draw explicit attention to the absence of consciousness or anything suspiciously like consciousness in their accounts.

Thus "ideas of reflexion" played a large role in Locke's theory of the mind, and all the elements in his theory, all the "ideas of sensation and

18. See Searle 1980 and Nagel 1974. On Searle's and Nagel's absolutism, see Richard Rorty's discussion of what he calls their essentialism (Rorty 1982) and my reply (Dennett 1982e).

19. Lucas thought he had found just such a litmus test in an application of Gödel's Incompleteness Theorem, coupled with the idea of a Turing Machine (Lucas 1961 and 1970). See my rebuttals (Dennett 1972 and 1978a, chapter 13) and Hofstadter 1979.

reflexion," were supposed to be present to the conscious awareness of a human agent. Locke had a keen sense of the value of meta-level activity, and in one fine passage was so bold as to define free will in terms of it:

> For, the mind having in most cases, as is evident in experience, a power to *suspend* the execution and satisfaction of any of its desires; and so all, one after another; is at liberty to consider the objects of them, examine them on all sides, and weigh them with others. In this lies the liberty man has; and from the not using of it right comes all that variety of mistakes, errors, and faults which we run into in the conduct of our lives, and our endeavours after happiness; whilst we precipitate the determination of our wills, and engage too soon, before due examination. To prevent this, we have a power to suspend the prosecution of this or that desire; as every one daily may experiment in himself. This seems to me the source of all liberty; in this seems to consist that which is (as I think improperly) called *free-will*. For, during this suspension of any desire . . . we have opportunity to examine, view, and judge of the good or evil of what we are going to do; and when, upon due examination, we have judged, we have done our duty, all that we can, or ought to do, in pursuit of our happiness; and it is not a fault, but a perfection of our nature, to desire, will, and act according to the last result of a fair examination. (*Essay*, II, XXI, 48)

As Locke sees, some of the most important thinking we do is not directly about the objects of our desires, but about our desiring those objects. This can set us to wondering whether they are worthy objects of desire, "all things considered." (As we shall see in the chapter four, it is important that *all* things cannot in fact ever be considered; not even all relevant things can always be considered.) We also have the important capacity to think about our beliefs, and wonder about whether they are as they should be.

Does this *thinking about beliefs and desires,* this reflexive, meta-thinking, have to be conscious thinking, or could it be merely behavioral "thinking"—the sort of reflexive "information processing" a computer can accomplish, for instance? A lot would seem to hang on the answer, for some of our strongest intuitions about freedom hinge on consciousness. When we become conscious of our reasons, we recognize them (unlike *Sphex* who merely behaves as if she recognizes her reasons). So the capacity for conscious recognition of motivation is apparently a necessary condition of real freedom. Strawson describes the case of a psychoanalyst who successfully treats a patient and notes that we "may and do naturally speak" of the psychoanalyst's "restoring the agent's freedom. But here the restoring of freedom means bringing it about that the agent's behaviour shall be intelligible in terms of conscious purposes rather than in terms only of unconscious purposes." (Strawson 1962 and 1968, pp. 90–91)

Even if we can make sense of some varieties of unconscious thinking, can we make sense of the idea of unconscious thinking about beliefs and desires? Could one be self-conscious, but only unconsciously self-conscious, or has the gulf between unconscious and conscious processes already been crossed once we have arrived at systems that are capable of treating some of their own internal "belief" and "desire" states as objects of "scrutiny," running their pattern "recognition" mechanisms over them, and so forth? Intuitions and feelings run high on this question. Some people just know in their hearts, they say, that no amount of merely behavioral quasi-comprehension could ever add up to conscious comprehension, or genuine intentionality.

Others (myself included) are just as sure that whatever "genuine consciousness" or "real intentionality" comes to, it must lie at the reachable top of that pyramid of natural, physical processes. I will try to make that view somewhat more appealing in intuition by developing some intuition pumps of my own. Although this requires a brief digression away from the topic of free will onto the battlefields of philosophy of mind, unless I say something to acknowledge and alleviate the skepticism on this score, I will be suspected of having pulled a fast one.

The creation and improvement of intelligence is one of evolution's most impressive products, but not all living things engage in the battle of wits, of course, or at any rate not with the same degree of commitment. Roughly speaking, the "choice points" in evolution are between the *Maginot Line* ("digging in" and opting for the immobile, armored, (relative) invulnerability of plants and clams and other living things of minimal behavioral virtuosity) and *guerrilla warfare* (hide-and-seek against the other players in the environment). Those species that "opt" for the latter are then entered in a cognitive arms race against the other creatures that have also "chosen" mobility and intelligence over armor. Note that the merely behavioral (or "information-processing") capacity to "wonder" about the evidential pedigrees of one's "beliefs" and the soundness and coherence of one's "desires" (the capacity Locke praises, minus the presumption of consciousness) is a major advance in that cognitive arms race. Even an imperfect capacity to "evaluate" some of one's own cognitive and conative states makes a big difference. Without it, one would be particularly gullible, and hence particularly vulnerable to manipulation by any (secret) agent who could discover ways of causing one to believe this or that.

Tacit appreciation of the power of reflexive monitoring can be seen in the tradition in the free will literature of thought experiments featuring sneaky manipulators. It is always essential in these thought experiments that the victim be kept in the dark about the very existence of the manipulator. For once a suitably adroit self-monitor becomes informed of abnormalities in the causation of its cognitive states (and particularly of the source and intent of the abnormalities), it can immediately undo the well-laid plans of its deceiver. The process of undoing a deception comes in two forms: the illusion persists but one learns to discount or discredit it (so-called "stable" illusions); or one's very loss of innocence renders one incapable of experiencing the illusion any more (or better still, one becomes more or less invulnerable to the illusion).

The evil trickster's job is difficult enough even with a gullible victim. Advanced sense organs have been superbly designed to be such high-fidelity causal links between the world and perceptual beliefs about the world that it is almost impossible to *sustain* an elaborate illusion in a victim who is permitted to engage in minimal exploration—who can just move his head and shift his gaze, or (more powerfully) shift his vantage point (Gibson 1966 and 1979). If the victim also just makes it a habit to reflect, periodically, on the evidential pedigrees and general coherence of his beliefs and desires, the evil trickster's job is rendered virtually impossible: only a justifying, veridical, proper causal ancestry can reliably sustain such beliefs and desires.

But how could this capacity of self-monitoring and self-criticism develop? We want to satisfy ourselves that such a development is possible. We can postpone the true details until science gets around to discovering them, so all we need at this point is a plausible "Just So Story."[20] Here is such a story.

Once upon a time there were creatures who had a full complement of working sense organs "informing" them of conditions in the world, but who were entirely unconscious. Their lives, however, were quite complex—so complex that when one applied the "Need to Know" principle to them, one found that they needed to "know" (in their merely behavioral way) quite a lot about the point of their activities. In particular, they had coordination problems with other members of their species, and the apparently optimal solutions to these problems required rudimentary forms of "communication"—rather like the bee dances and other forms of social insect message-passing, but differing in the fact that when one creature communicated to another, it "knew" what it was talking about and why. That is to say, it did not just communicate in a sphexish sort of way, whenever some environmental "trigger" presented

---

20. On the use and abuse of "Just So Stories," see Humphrey 1982, and the commentary and response in Dennett 1983b.

itself (like the bee "driven" to dance by the presence of sugar water in a certain location).

It (or its ancestors) had "noticed" that sometimes better results were obtainable when one "discriminated" between different audiences on different occasions, depending on what both parties "knew" and "believed" and "wanted" (in their merely behavioral way).

For instance, creature Alf wouldn't bother trying to get creature Bob to "believe" there was no food in the cave if Alf "believed" Bob already "knew" there was food in the cave. And if Bob "thought" Alf "wanted" to deceive him, Bob would be apt to "disbelieve" what Alf said.

There are Artificial Intelligence (AI) programs today that model in considerable depth the organizational structure of systems that must plan "communicative" interactions with other systems, based on their "knowledge" about what they themselves "know" and "don't know," what their interlocutor system "knows" and "doesn't know," and so forth. We may suppose that our imagined progenitors in the thought experiment were no more conscious than AI robots would be—whatever that comes to. (I have no idea what that comes to in the minds of those who insist upon it; my strategy is to concede whatever point it is to them at this stage.)

Now it sometimes happened that when one of these creatures was stymied on a project, it would "ask for help," and in particular, it would "ask for information." Sometimes the audience present would respond by "communicating" something that had just the right effects on the inquiring creature, breaking it out of its rut, or causing it to "see" a solution to its problem. Now for this practice to gain a foothold in a community, the askers would have to be able to reciprocate on occasion in the role of answerers. That is to say, they would have to have the behavioral capacity to be provoked into making occasionally "helpful" utterances when subjected to "request" utterances of others. For instance, if one system "knew" something and was "asked" about it, this might usefully have the normal (but by no means exceptionless) effect of provoking it to "tell what it knew."[21]

Then one fine day an "unintended" short-circuit effect of this new social institution was "noticed" by a creature. It "asked" for help in an inappropriate circumstance, where there was no helpful audience to hear the request and respond. Except itself! When the creature heard its own

---

21. The theoretical problems surrounding the evolution of communication are not trivial, but also not insoluble. One cannot assume that a cooperative spirit of mutual aid would have survival value, or would be a stable system if it emerged. See Dawkins 1982, pp. 55ff.

request, the stimulation provoked just the sort of other-helping utterance production that the request from another would have caused. And to the creature's "delight" it found that it had just provoked itself into answering its own question!

How could the activity of asking oneself questions be any less systematically futile than the activity of paying oneself a tip for making oneself a drink? So long as we adhere to "naive perfectionism" (Dawkins 1980) about the mind or self, and view it, as Descartes did, as an indivisible and perfectly self-communicating whole, the possibility that such reflexive activities could serve some purpose is hard to imagine.[22] But think of all the occasions on which we remind ourselves, commend ourselves, promise ourselves, scold ourselves, and warn ourselves. Surely all this self-administration has some effect that preserves it so securely in our repertoires.

Under what conditions would the activity of asking oneself questions be useful? All one needs to suppose is that there is some compartmentalization and imperfect *internal* communication between components of a creature's cognitive system, so that one component can need the output of another component but be unable to address that component directly. Suppose the only way of getting component A to do its job is to provoke it into action by a certain sort of stimulus that normally comes from the outside, from another creature. If one day one discovers that one can play the role of this other and achieve a good result by autostimulation, the practice will blaze a valuable new communicative trail between one's internal components, a trail that happens to wander out into the public space of airwaves and acoustics.[23] Crudely put, pushing some information through one's ears and auditory system may stimulate just the sorts of connections one is seeking, may trip just the right associative mechanisms, tease just the right mental morsel to the tip of one's tongue. One can then say it, hear oneself say it, and thus get the answer one was hoping for.

There is considerable evidence, drawn from experiments and from studies of aphasias and other disorders, showing that the processes of

22. Epistemologists and philosophers of mind have traditionally overlooked or underestimated the utility of such practices, which is surprising since, as Powers (1978) shows, it was a central but disguised theme in Plato's *Meno*.

23. Recent experiments with "split-brain" subjects (people whose corpus callosum has been severed, breaking the normal highway of interhemispheric communication) dramatically reveal the brain's virtuosity in finding and exploiting novel channels of communication. (Note that it is the brain or the cerebral hemisphere, not the whole person, who is to be credited with the clever discovery—the person is utterly unaware of the tricky communicative ploys the brain comes to exploit.) See Gazzaniga and Ledoux 1978.

speech production and speech comprehension are not mirror-images of one another; in hearing and understanding a sentence, one does not more or less just suck it in through the same brain machinery one otherwise uses for formulating and uttering a sentence, only running in reverse. So there is no reason to suppose that the process of formulating, uttering, hearing, and comprehending a sentence would simply leave one back where one started cognitively. In particular, the cognitive tasks "automatically" subcontracted in the course of sentence generation and comprehension would seem to be just the right sort of jobs to stir up otherwise dormant pockets of knowledge that might contain the missing piece of some current puzzle.

So in this Just So Story, the creatures got into the habit of talking (aloud) to themselves. And they found that it often had good results—often enough, in fact, to reinforce the practice. They got better and better at it. In particular, they discovered an efficient shortcut: *sotto voce* talking to oneself, which later led to entirely silent talking to oneself. The silent process maintained the loop of self-stimulation, but jettisoned the peripheral vocalization and audition portions of the process, which weren't contributing much. This innovation had the further benefit, opportunistically endorsed, of achieving a certain privacy for the practice of cognitive autostimulation. And privacy was especially useful when "comprehending" members of the same species were within earshot—for we must not suppose that the "helpful" commerce that was the seed for this process was an entirely altruistic and noncompetitive affair.

Thus a variety of silent, private, talking-to-oneself behaviors evolved in a social setting in which reciprocally useful communication occurred. It was not necessarily the best imaginable sort of cognitive process. It was relatively slow and laborious (compared to other unconscious cognitive processes) because it had to make use of large tracts of machinery "intended" for other purposes (for audible speech production and comprehension). It was as linear (limited to one topic at a time) as the social communication it evolved from. And it was dependent, at least at the outset, on the public words that composed the social practice.

Suppose such a phenomenon evolved on some planet. Would we call it consciousness? Would we be inclined to include creatures endowed with these "merely behavioral" activities among our conscious and self-conscious brethren? Or would their internal information-processing activity be just more merely behavioral, unconscious pseudo-thinking? To outward appearance they would be well nigh indistinguishable from us: cooperative but also devious, communicative but also secretive, and apt on occasion to sit mumbling and staring into space until some cognitive breakthrough occurred.

Would we find some temptation welling in us to deem their internal cognitive activity conscious? If my intuition pump has done its job, you should now be feeling some temptation to judge these creatures conscious.[24] That is all I ask: some temptation.

If you are still skeptical, note that we wouldn't have to restrict these internal activities to *talking* to oneself silently. Why do people draw pictures and diagrams for their own eyes to look at? Why do composers bother humming or playing their music to themselves for their own benefit? (Goodman 1982) We can suppose that the creatures in our Just So Story would also be able to engage (profitably) in internal diagramming and humming. And they would be just as capable as we are of benefitting from playing an "inner game of tennis." (Gallwey 1979)

The techniques of autostimulation are extremely various. Just as one can notice that stroking oneself in a certain way can produce certain only partially and indirectly controllable but definitely desirable effects (and one can then devote some time and ingenuity to developing and exploring the techniques for producing those desirable effects in oneself), so one can also come to recognize that talking to oneself, making pictures for oneself, singing to oneself, and so forth, are practices that often have desirable effects. Some people are better at these activities than others. Cognitive autostimulation is an acquired and intimately personal technique, with many different styles.[25]

But suppose your deepest intuition is that these imagined creatures would *still* not be conscious at all—not the way you are! So be it. Then I will change my tack. Recall that this digression about consciousness was inspired by Strawson's example of the psychoanalyst who "restored freedom" to a patient by rendering that agent's behavior intelligible "in terms of conscious purposes." The appeal to conscious (as opposed to unconscious, freedom-impairing) purposes suggested that before the treatment the patient had no freedom because she herself (the famous "conscious self") was *uninformed* about the wellsprings of her behavior. Once she was made capable of informing herself about these wellsprings, and

24. More intuition pumps, intended to enhance this effect still further, are to be found in Hofstadter and Dennett 1981.

25. Material in the preceding paragraphs is drawn from Dennett 1982c. Inspiration for such a Just So Story came from several sources, including especially Ryle's posthumous collection, *On Thinking* (Ryle 1979), Straight 1977, and Bennett 1976, which contains a wonderfully detailed Just So Story about the first language, Plain Talk, and the tribes—especially the Dullards and Condescenders—that spoke it. (chapters 5–7) If Bennett's speculations provide for the emergence of the rudiments of language, these rudiments in turn provide for the emergence of human consciousness, according to the equally inventive and ingenious (if less rigorous) Just So Story developed by Jaynes 1976. See also Humphrey 1982.

hence capable of bringing them into the arena of rational consideration and discussion, she was free. But our imagined creatures, once they have their linguistic and reflective information-handling capacities in good shape, would be equally susceptible to persuasion and equally able to engage in rational self-evaluation. They would be equipped to react appropriately when, as Hobbes says, we "represent reasons to them." Isn't that what freedom hinges upon, whether or not it amounts to consciousness?[26]

4. Community, Communication, and Transcendence

Rather do our ideas, our values,
our yeas and nays, our ifs and buts,
grow out of us with the necessity
with which a tree bears fruit.
—Nietzsche (On the Genealogy of
Morals)

The vast differences between *Sphex* and us are obvious enough. In fact, they are too obvious, and encourage the sort of absolutist exaggeration that leads philosophers to defend bizarre theses about our exemption from causation, our metaphysically unique and privileged status. The realistic reassertion of our fundamental kinship with *Sphex* then tends to create an unfocused anxiety about whether we have deluded ourselves about our powers as "rational agents." My sketchy review of the differences between *Sphex* and us, and the natural processes that created those differences, has taken us through several iterations of the basic Darwinian motif: in the beginning there was some relatively unstructured and unsophisticated raw material; mutations of one sort or another occurred; and out of this emerged something novel, bringing with it not only new sorts of concrete phenomena, but new *abstracta*. Out of an inorganic world came not only replicators (living things) but also the reasons their striving after replication created.

Out of tropistic and unlearning creatures, who only imperfectly "recognized" and "served" their own interests arose conditionable or learning creatures, who could redesign themselves in the direction of an ever closer sensitivity to their reasons, especially enhanced by their

---

26. It has been perhaps the central claim of my work during the last fifteen years that such creatures *are* conscious—we are these creatures—and I certainly do not mean to abandon that claim here. But my argument about freedom does not depend on it. Unconvinced readers are thus not importuned to subject themselves to all my other intuition pumps about consciousness before proceeding further with this analysis of freedom.

emerging ability to react to patterns in their own reactions to the patterns in nature. Out of the crude protolinguistic practices of some of these creatures emerged, by opportunistic mutation, an even more powerful reflexive activity: the representation of some of these activities, and the use of these representations in self-monitoring and self-evaluation. But there is still one more important step on this staircase from *Sphex* to the rational will Kant glorified for us.

The emergence of a population of communicators, with language, provides the raw material for yet one more Just So Story: the Origin of Morality. Several versions of it are celebrated in philosophy, but so far as I know, Hobbes was the first to see the need for, and theoretical beauty of, this tale. His version has the flaws, but also the virtues, of a pioneering effort; in particular, it is radical. At the beginning of this chapter I described how the birth of interests was in part a matter of interests being *constituted* by the sorts of steps creatures happened to take in the course of their "efforts" at self-preservation. A similar, radically constitutive process was described by Hobbes.

Once upon a time, he said, there was no right and wrong, and people lived in "the state of nature" and engaged willy-nilly in the war of all against all, and life was "solitary, poor, nasty, brutish and short." (*Leviathan,* 1651) Then it happened that some of them came together and formed a covenant, and thus began society, and with it *right and wrong came into existence.* Not just the ideas or concepts of right and wrong in the peoples' minds, but right and wrong themselves. Before the covenant nothing was morally right or wrong. It is not that when people did evil or good things they had no inkling of how evil or good they were. Nothing *was* evil or good—in a moral sense. For people lived then the way lions and tigers live now in the state of nature, and surely our intuitions do support the idea that there simply are no moral facts about the relationships between wild animals.[27] The covenant changed all that, by bringing into existence a different way of life, with *new* reasons for acting, just as the emergence of replicators brought into existence the first way of life, and with it the first sorts of reasons for acting.

Hobbes' Just So Story is certainly historically false; it is just as certainly a conceptual *over*simplification. It very misleadingly suggests that full-blown human consciousness and human language could flourish

27. Our intuitions are not univocal, however. If they were, they would not need regular reinforcement of the sort they receive, for instance, in almost every wildlife documentary, where the narrator must remind us, as we witness some horrific example of nature red in tooth and claw, that this is Nature's way; the lion has to eat, too.

in a presocial or asocial Hobbesian state of nature. The emergence of social order, language, consciousness, and morality was surely a tangle of interpenetrating and interacting developments for which Hobbes' account, considered as a "model," would be simplistic in the extreme. But Hobbes' story distills and isolates for thought one important strand: the social practices of verbal advocacy, mutual criticism and debate not only permitted the creation of a new relationship between creatures and their reasons (the relationship of *considering* those reasons); it also permitted the creation of new reasons to consider.

As Hobbes says, we represent reasons to other people "because thereby we think to make them have the will they have not." This practice of representing reasons to others is effective so long as the others are other people—don't waste your time representing reasons to trees or clams, or the mentally defective. In fact, the practice is so effective that it permits us, and only us among creatures on Earth, to "transcend our biology"—not in any mysterious, "contra-causal," vitalistic way but by permitting our cognitive control systems to acquire goals that *can not* be genetically controlled.[28] Dawkins, in the last paragraph of *The Selfish Gene* (which many of his critics have apparently never gotten around to reading), puts the point well:

> We have the power to defy the selfish genes of our birth. . . . We can even discuss ways of deliberately cultivating and nurturing pure, disinterested altruism—something that has no place in nature [that is, in a Hobbesian state of nature—DCD], something that has never existed before in the whole history of the world. . . . We, alone on earth, can rebel against the tyranny of the selfish replicators. (Dawkins 1976, p. 215)

So although we arrive on this planet with a built-in, biologically endorsed set of biases, although we innately prefer certain states of affairs to others, we can nevertheless build lives from this base that overthrow those innate preferences. We can tame and rescind and (if need be) repress those preferences in favor of "higher" preferences, which are no less real for not being directly biologically (that is, genetically) endorsed. (The "specter" of sociobiology looms only for those who fail to see this really quite obvious fact, and who think the only way biology could contribute to the understanding of the birth of morality would be by "reducing" all moral norms to some dimly imagined genetic imperatives. They fear "biological" explanations for the same reason they fear "psychological" explanations of their choices; they have an impover-

28. For an insightful analysis of the interaction between genetic and cultural evolution in ethics, see Campbell 1975.

ished sense of what a biological or psychological explanation of a phenomenon might be.)

It is our communal activity of mutual persuasion, reflection, and
evaluation that creates the values that then take precedence over the
cruder interests of our ancestors. How encompassing can this reflective
process be? We can not only try to talk people into doing or not doing
this or that; we can also systematize our persuasions into moral codes and
principles, and then reflect on these moralities in ethical theories, and
then engage in "meta-ethics," in which we reflect on the nature of ethical
theories, and then go on to consider the implications for the problem of
free will and freedom from sphexishness of our capacity to engage in
meta-ethics. And so on. Is all of this equally effective?

One would think at first that no one would ever want to call a halt in
this spiral, or to discover that we were constitutionally unable to continue. But in fact the claim to have exhausted our human powers of
consideration and meta-consideration is not all that unusual in philosophical discussions. Intellectual vertigo does set in on occasion, and
people begin to balk.

Nietzsche, for instance, has an unsurpassed capacity to make one
reel with his search for higher vantage points:

> This problem of the *value* of pity and of the morality of pity . . .
> seems at first sight to be merely something detached, an isolated
> question mark; but whoever sticks with it and *learns* how to ask
> questions here will experience what I experienced—a tremendous
> new prospect opens up for him, a new possibility comes over him
> . . . we need a *critique* of moral values, *the value of these values
> themselves must just be called in question.* (Preface, *On the Genealogy of
> Morals.*)

Foot (1973, p. 137) comments: "But how can one value values? The idea
of such a thing is enough to make one's head spin." One can certainly
evaluate some of one's values while clinging to others, but Foot is pro-
fessing dizziness when faced with Nietzsche's apparently more radical
project.

Is this the top of the pinnacle then? Or is it just the top of *our*
pinnacle, the point at which *we* reveal our sphexish streak and flounder
about foolishly in the face of higher thought? It is certainly difficult and
unpleasant to make oneself address this question and its kin, which
perhaps explains the paucity of careful discussions of this topic. One of
the few is Strawson's "Freedom and Resentment" (Strawson 1962),[29]

29. See also the excellent discussions of this piece by Ayer 1980 and Bennett
1980.

which presents and discusses a disagreement between an optimist and a pessimist about the implications of determinism for our vision of ourselves as agents and "participants." The pessimist urges that determinism has certain dire implications that "could, or should" lead us to abandon what Strawson calls the "participant attitude" towards others and ourselves. Strawson replies:

> It does not seem to be self-contradictory to suppose that this might happen. So I suppose we must say that it is not absolutely inconceivable that it should happen. But I am strongly inclined to think that it is, for us as we are, practically inconceivable. The human commitment to participation in ordinary inter-personal relationships is, I think, too thoroughgoing and deeply rooted for us to take seriously the thought that a general theoretical conviction might so change our world that, in it, there were no longer any such things as inter-personal relationships as we normally understand them. . . . (Strawson 1962, and 1968, p. 82)

For us/we are, abandoning the participant attitude is practically inconceivable. We are stuck with this conception, it seems, as surely as *Sphex* is stuck with her limited vantage point. *If* it is an illusion, it is a stable illusion—one that we find irresistible even though we can, with some attention, override it in a judgment. In chapter five we will examine this question of whether we are stuck and, if we are, what we should make of this.

In the meantime we should note that the conclusion that we had reached the top of *our* pinnacle should not necessarily be the occasion for self-deprecation and embarrassment, as if there were or even could be a "superior" observer who was to us as we are to *Sphex*. This prospect has been discussed illuminatingly but inconclusively by philosophers (Davidson 1973, Rorty 1979, and Fodor 1983, pp. 123–126). It is hard to see what should persuade us one way or the other here. Even if such a superior being is arguably inconceivable, one presumably is disbarred from arguing (in the usual way) that since it is inconceivable it is impossible, for we are presumably just as inconceivable to *Sphex*. The point of imagining this superior being, after all, is to challenge the traditional inference to impossibility from *our* incapacity to conceive.

At the same time, we want to protect ourselves from idle mystery-mongering, and can justly demand some reason for supposing there could be such a higher vantage point, inaccessible to us. It won't do to imagine a being who is merely a calculating prodigy or a walking encyclopedia, like Laplace's omniscient physicist, for it is dubious that such a being's conceptual scheme is superior to ours; it just knows more of the sort of facts we know. Fodor remarks, correctly, "One would presumably not be impressed by a priori arguments intended to prove, (e.g.) that the true science *must be* accessible to spiders." (Fodor 1983, p. 126) But this does not foreclose the possibility of an argument that the true science must be accessible to us, for it simply brandishes our kinship with spiders (and *Sphex*) without assessing the implication of the vast differences—another abuse of the intuition pump.

Even if there were higher vantage points of rationality, would they matter to us? Strawson thinks not. If the question is not what we would in fact do if we became convinced of determinism, but what we ought rationally to do, the standard of rationality to which we would and should appeal is not some dimly imagined extrahuman rationality, Strawson claims, but precisely the rationality that we have constituted by being the creatures we are, living the lives we lead:

> . . . if we could imagine what we cannot have, viz., a choice in this matter, then we could choose rationally only in the light of an assessment of the gains and losses to human life, its enrichment or impoverishment. . . . (Strawson 1968, p. 84)

The rationality we constitute is certainly not perfect. In this chapter I have assayed a Just So Story of considerable optimism; a story of higher historic fidelity would no doubt be somewhat darker. The possibility of cognitive and conative cancers must not be overlooked by tellers of Just So Stories. We may well be *designed* to be oblivious to certain truths, or to be obsessive inventors of comforting falsehoods, protecting ourselves from the irritating truth with pearly layers of persuasive myth. Do the scars of our genetic and cultural evolution show? We should not be surprised if they do. But do these scars cripple us? This question has a less obvious answer, and insofar as it is relevant to our concern with free will, it will be addressed in subsequent chapters.

The rationality Nature has endowed us with is practical; it makes a difference by moving us, for the most part, in appropriate directions. But we must not suppose that it is only practical, that it is an endowment tied directly and rigidly to serving the biological ends that gave birth to it. As we have seen, a particularly powerful part of that endowment derives from our capacity for language, which itself could only emerge under the pressure of no doubt very specific (if still dimly understood) environmental demands and constraints. Without having an important biological function to serve, something as complex as language could never evolve. But once it has arrived on the evolutionary scene, the endowment for language makes room for all manner of biologically trivial or irrelevant or baroque (nonfunctional) endeavors: gossip, riddles, poetry, philosophy. In seeing how evolution has made reason practical, we have also seen how evolution can give birth to impractical reason.

Let me summarize the results of this chapter. I have not offered a proof that rationality is possible for physical entities. What would be the point of such a proof? I take it that we already have an abundance of reasons for believing both that we are physical entities and that we are rational. So we need to understand *how* it might be so, and how it might have come about.[30] The biological speculations, by helping us imagine in more detail how our capacity to be moved by reasons is ensconced in the universe, removes at least some of the temptation to retreat into absolutist dogmas about our status as agents.

The perfect Kantian will, which would be able to respond with perfect fidelity to all good reasons, is a physical impossibility; neither determinism nor indeterminism could accommodate it. But that does not leave us in *Sphex*'s predicament. We are not infinitely but only extraordinarily sensitive and versatile considerers of reasons. If that is not enough, if free will and responsibility requires *absolute* freedom from sphexishness, if no modicum of responsibility can survive in anything but a perfectly sterile environment, then we must either overthrow the scientific vision of ourselves altogether or admit defeat. But these dire alternatives are not yet pressed upon us. We have hardly begun to see how much of what we want to be true about ourselves can be illuminated—not threatened—by an application of the scientific, naturalistic vision.

---

30. Nozick (1981) urges philosophers to consider abandoning formal proof in favor of a particular sort of philosophical explanation, in which we bring ourselves to see how something we want to believe in could be possible. This is excellent advice, in my opinion, and I take my project in this chapter (and indeed in the entire book) to be an exercise in Nozick's brand of explanation.

3

Control and Self-Control

No one has ever announced that
because determinism is true
thermostats do not control
temperature.
—Robert Nozick (1981, p. 315)

1. "Due to Circumstances Beyond Our Control"

One is often invited, in discussions of determinism, to cast one's mind back to a time before there were people, or even wasps, or even organic molecules, on this planet. If determinism is true, it is pointed out, the total state of affairs back then (at some arbitrarily chosen instant) has determined every subsequent event up to the present and into the future. As Laplace saw,

> Given for one instant an intelligence which could comprehend all the forces by which nature is animated and the respective situation of the beings who compose it—an intelligence sufficiently vast to submit these data to analysis—it would embrace in the same formula the movements of the greatest bodies of the universe and those of the lightest atom; for it, nothing would be uncertain and the future, as the past, would be present to its eyes. (Laplace 1820)

What is dreadful about this, apparently, is that if this is so, then all one's deeds are determined by events in the distant past over which one certainly has no control, so one never really controls any of one's deeds; one is controlled by the past or by current events caused by events in the past and beyond one's control.[1] At best one has the illusion of control. One is in fact entirely controlled by external factors, locked into a life story that was written at the dawn of creation, like a puppet that was destined to

---

1. "Every true proposition about the way things were before there ever had been any rational beings is such that no one has, or ever had, any choice about whether it is true." (van Inwagen 1983, p. 149)

play Punch and Judy even before its wooden face was carved and painted. One seldom sees this account of the dreadfulness spelled out in any detail, and small wonder, since it is so laden with confusions that it cannot survive the light of day.[2]

What we fear—or at any rate a very important part of what we fear—in determinism is the prospect that determinism would rule out control,[3] and we very definitely do not want to lose control or be out of control or be controlled by something or someone else—like a marionette or puppet.[4] We want to be *in control*, and to control both ourselves and our destinies. But what is control, and what is its relation to causation and determinism? Curiously, this obviously important question has scarcely been addressed by philosophers.[5]

What we must do, then, is perform a long overdue bit of "ordinary language philosophy," to see what we actually have in mind when we yearn for control and fear its loss.[6]

2. Suspicions about the familiar tactic of pointing to a prehistoric moment have been expressed by several writers. Nozick (1981) considers "how we naturally tend to express our worry about determinism":

> Why is that addendum made about causes before we were born, why is it so natural—rather, what function does it serve, what other possibility is it introduced to block or to cut off? Well, it is clear, isn't it, that if the causes go back to a time before we were born, then we don't control them and so, since they control our decision, we don't control our action. (p. 314)

And Slote's suspicions are raised by the fact that "with the sole exception of Wiggins, all the proponents of the new form of incompatibility argument single out past events occurring before the birth of an agent, in speaking of what that agent cannot do anything about." (Slote 1982, p. 19)

3. Fischer (1982) notes that "it is usually thought that determinism erodes control." Lucas (1970) says, without argument or other support, that "determinism deprives [people] of any real say" in their lives (p. 28).

4. "It will be pointed out that we are not extremely simple input-output devices, much internal processing takes place, involving feedback loops and other delightful 'software'; however, does that not make us merely more complicated puppets, but puppets nonetheless? True, much of these causes occur 'inside' us—is it better to be a hand puppet than a marionette?" (Nozick 1981, p. 310)

5. To my knowledge. Greenspan 1978 makes tangential remarks about the concept, as does Holmstrom 1977. Fischer 1982, Nozick 1981, and Slote 1982 all mention control; none refers to any earlier literature on the subject.

6. This exercise will be recognized as a close kin of earlier "ordinary language" defenses of free will against determinism, in particular, the appeal to a Paradigm Case argument of the sort best exemplified, perhaps, by Flew 1955 (See esp. pp. 149–163). (See van Inwagen 1975 and 1983 for critical discussions of Flew's argument.) Unlike Flew, I am not arguing that we have rock-solid ordinary

2. Simple Control and Simple Self-Control

What then is control? What is it—or would it be—to be in control of something? After we have answered that simple question, we can go on to look at controlling one's destiny, at varieties of self-control, and at other embroiderings on the basic concept. Dictionaries define "control" by piling up near synonyms—*command, direct, overpower, dominate, call to account*—a reliable sign that the concept is too basic to admit of straightforward definition.

The root idea of control, which has been elevated into a technically precise concept in cybernetics and automata theory, is (in ordinary terms) that *A controls B* if and only if the relation between *A* and *B* is such that *A* can *drive B* into whichever of *B*'s normal range of states *A* wants *B* to be in. (If *B* is capable of being in some state *s* and *A* wants *B* to be in *s*, but has no way of putting *B* in *s*, or making *B* go into *s*, then *A*'s desire is frustrated, and to that extent *A* does not control *B*.) This definition makes it clear from the outset that for something to be a *controllee* it just needs to have a variety of different states it can[7] be in, but for something to be a *controller* its states must include desires—or something "like" desires—about the states of something (else). (Recall the brain tumor of chapter one, which had to be "smart" enough to control poor Jones; it could not control Jones without having something like desires about Jones' states.)

It will be useful to remind ourselves of some features of this everyday concept of control by exploring an example. Suppose you buy a model airplane, a working model with a motor. You start it up and off it flies, crashing into a tree. "Needs to be controlled," you mutter, and fasten long wires to one wingtip. Now you can control it, making it go up and down—whichever you want, whenever you want—as it goes round

---

"criteria" for being in control that are proof against any discoveries science might make. I am, however, somewhat like Flew, drawing attention to an obvious empirical fact: we care about control (if we care at all), because *our ordinary concept* of control has a meaning according to which we distinguish certain circumstances we dislike as "our being out of control," "our being controlled by someone else," and so forth—and certain circumstances we like as "being in control," "controlling oneself," and so forth. If some concept of control fails to permit these distinctions, we will not know whether we ought to care about whether, in *that* sense, we are ever in control. Since the problem of free will is "essentially" one we care about, we should *begin* any investigation that relies on the concept of control with the tentative and defeasible assumption that whatever versions of the concept there might be, it is one of its "important" versions (if there are any) that is at stake.

7. Note that this "can" is Austin's frog at the bottom of the beer mug, to which we will return in chapter six.

and round in a circle "Not enough *degrees of freedom*," you mutter, so you replace the wires with a wireless radio "remote control" system. Now you can control the direction, height, speed, turning, diving, and banking of the plane. There are many more degrees of freedom, and they are all under your control, but not until you have discovered the parameters of the plane's degrees of freedom and the causal relationships between those parameters and your joystick-moving acts—an epistemic problem that is often not trivial and must always be solved before control can be effected.

If your model airplane happens to fly out of range of your radio remote control unit, it flies *out of control*, but of course it is still just as subject to the causal forces in its vicinity as ever (no more, no less). It might happen to wander back into the sphere of your control, and hence come again to be controlled by you. You can test this by seeing whether or not you can make it do what you want it to do. Of course you can't make it do anything you want it to do. You can't make if fly straight up, or hover motionless. Those are not capacities of airplanes. Helicopters have those capacities, but there are other things helicopters can't do: they can't fly as fast as airplanes, for instance, or do loop-the-loops and barrel rolls. One can control only those states or activities of a thing that fall within the range of its degrees of freedom, or in other words, within the range of what it can do. (We speak of what a model airplane *can do*, and of its *degrees of freedom*, but in doing this we are not attributing to it the sort of agency or freedom we attribute to a moral agent, of course. Still, the advanced sorts of agency and freedom certainly have the simple sorts as prerequisites. Before jumping to any metaphysical conclusions about the limitations of these simpler concepts, we should see a bit more about how they work.)

How do you know for certain when your model airplane is in your control? Suppose someone comes along while you are flying your plane, and he has a control box just like yours in his hands. Which of you, you wonder, is controlling the plane? Can you still make the plane do what you want, when you want? If not, you certainly are no longer in control. What if the other person mimics your hand motions as you make them, so you can't be sure whether or not he's controlling your plane? There is a possibility, after all, that your sense of control is illusory, but this is an empirically explorable possibility.[8] In fact, you are in a position to per-

---

8. In principle the illusion could be very hard to detect, as witnessed by poor Dennett, at the end of "Where Am I?" (Dennett 1978a, chapter 17) when his brain output was no longer causing his body to move, but only spilling ineffectually into the air, while a duplicate computer-brain was really in control. Another even more farfetched case is Descartes' example of the evil demon who could be deceiving him about everything.

form a classic "controlled" experiment. Using what is often called Mill's method of agreement and difference, you deliberately alter the circumstances in ways that will disrupt the relationship between your hand motions and the mimic's, and thereby isolated the factors that are actually implicated in the control of the plane.

Suppose the other person is actually in control of the plane. If you can control the other person's mimicry—if, that is, you can make him continue in his "mimicking state"—you can go right on controlling your plane through him! This is somewhat less reliable control, perhaps, than direct, "hands-on" control of your plane (and remote control is already less direct, causally, than contiguous hands-on control), but it is often quite reliable enough for us. Control that runs through another agent is quite enough control for sea captains, for instance, who seldom touch the helm themselves. (There are, as we shall soon see, importantly different ways in which an agent can control something via controlling an intermediary agent.)

A few other obvious facts about this case are worth mentioning before we turn to complications. When you control your plane perfectly, you don't do it by controlling all the causes that influence it. The weather, the density of the air, and the force of gravity, for instance, are all beyond your control, and they are the largest forces that act on your plane. The fact that your plane is constantly under the influence of gravity does not prevent you from controlling it—in fact in some regards gravity helps you, just so long as you *know* its effects on the plane. But a sudden and unanticipated gust of wind may upset your control, either temporarily or permanently.

What is important about the difference between the gust of wind and gravity is not the steadiness of the latter and the suddenness of the former, but the (relative) unexpectability of the former. If you are clever enough about gusts of wind to be able to predict them, they may be exploited by you in controlling your plane just as reliably as you exploit gravity. Sailors, for instance, use their foreknowledge of gusts, which can be readily seen approaching on the water, to help control the direction and speed of their boats. A bobsledder on a familiar course is much more in control, thanks to foreknowledge of conditions, than one who is on a maiden run.

Foreknowledge is what permits control. Circumstances that are clearly beyond our control may nevertheless not disrupt or prevent our control of the events we wish to control—if we know about those circumstances in time. For if we know about them in time, we can plan in the light of our expectations, and take steps to prevent, avoid, preempt, avert, harness, exploit, or accommodate ourselves to those circumstances. We are *at the mercy of* only those causal chains that either creep up on us without warning ("blind-siding" us, as one says in football) or that leave us no paths by which we can avoid their unwanted effects. (For a discussion of avoiding, see chapter five.) That Boston is more than 3,000 miles from Oxford is a circumstance quite beyond my control, but knowing it, I was able to take the appropriate steps to arrive in Oxford on time for my lectures. I could not change that circumstance, but I could accommodate myself to it. Foreseeing, moreover, that there would be a queue for transatlantic airplane reservations in April of 1983 (a circumstance equally out of *my* control—but not, perhaps, out of President Reagan's control), I reserved places early.

When you control something else, you must stay in contact with it. In the case of the model airplane, the size of the sphere of your control is fixed by the power of your radio equipment—up to a point. As the NASA engineers and scientists responsible for the Mars and Venus explorer vehicles will tell you, the speed of light becomes a non-negligible factor when distances get large. Detailed remote control of those vehicles became strictly impossible, since the time required for a round trip signal was greater than the time available for appropriate action. There was not enough time for the controllers to be caused to know the relevant conditions so that, armed with reliable expectations, they could wisely choose a command to issue. So these vehicles could no longer be *puppets*; they had to become *robots*. Since controllers on Earth could no longer reach out and control them, they had to *control themselves*. They had to be equipped with (rudimentary) desires—or something "like" desires—and enough "knowledge" about their circumstances so that they could reliably do the work the controllers would have done, had they been near enough to intervene.[9]

The people back on Earth maintained some secondary, partial control over the robots, for they could still send them general messages about what project to undertake next. Moreover, they had designed the robots to "deliberate" in particular ways on particular occasions.[10] So

9. A particularly fascinating case is that of "The Autonomous Viking," (Hutchings 1983) In this instance, the engineers figured out how to release the Viking spacecraft from their control, and make it "autonomous," after it was already circling Mars.

10. Dawkins (1976), discussing how genes "control the behavior of their survival machines, not directly with their fingers on puppet strings, but indirectly," uses the excellent science fiction story, *A for Andromeda* by Hoyle and Elliot, to illustrate the way an agent or quasi-agent can *delegate* fine control to other agents who are not practically within the sphere of the agent's direct influence (pp. 56–57). (Reprinted in Hofstadter and Dennett 1981.)

these robots were not only not "totally out of control"; they were to some degree still controlled by the people on Earth.[11]

As we have seen, it does not follow from the fact that x controls y that some other thing z doesn't also control y—by controlling x. There can be transitivity of control under some conditions.[12] This is true even when x and y are identical (when x controls itself); I can control something that is self-controlled—if I can control the states of the world that cause it, in controlling itself, to act. Suppose we replace the human controllers of an oil refinery with a computer control system. *It* controls the refinery just as much, it seems, as the people did. (Or stepping back a bit and looking at the whole refinery including its control system, we can say that the refinery is now *self*-controlled.) But we can drive the refinery into certain states by driving its computer into certain control states. If we switch the grade of crude oil coming in, it will have to respond by changing the refinery operations accordingly. And if it is sensitive to fluctuations in the price of aviation fuel on the open market, and we are able to artificially raise or depress that price, we can indirectly control the computer's control of the refinery.

It is tempting to insist at this point that the sort of control that we could thus impose on the computer-controller of the refinery is in some very important way unlike the sort of control we could impose by using the same tactics on human operators of the same refinery prior to automation. But it is far from clear that this is true. Human beings might have more ways of eluding control than the imagined computer, but since the ways the computer has were not specified, we have been given no reason to believe this. The computer might have a remarkably layered and versatile and tricky sort of self-monitoring system; so it might well be much harder in practice to control the computer than to control any human controller. Whatever tricks *we* have to play with (and I will shortly discuss a few of them), they do not seem yet to be of a different order from the sorts of tricks the computer system might rely on.

Moreover, even if it is true that for some reason and in some regards people would be importantly less subject to control in such circum-

---

11. It might be useful to reflect on the responsibility of the people on Earth, under various conditions, for "actions" performed by one of their robots. The jury would want to know if the robot had got out of control, was no longer even self-controlled, and so forth. Did it, perhaps, *seize* control of itself? Was it to some degree self-controlled? (Once again, the simple form of self-control already enjoyed by robots is not *our* form of self-control, the sort of self-control one learns, or is supposed to learn, as one approaches adulthood. That topic comes later, in chapter four.)

12. Nozick (1981, p. 314) asks "But is the notion of control transitive?" and does not stay to answer his question.

stances, there is still no denying that the imagined exercises in controlling the controllers are precisely the sort of activities we human beings dislike, resent, and seek to avoid. We don't like being controlled by others in this sort of way, so apparently we do feel that we are controlled (to some extent) by such activities. We don't feel immune to the sort of control the computer is vulnerable to; we don't exempt ourselves on grounds of our humanity, or even on grounds of our capacity to make free choices (compare Frankfurt 1973).

3. Agentless Control and Our Concept of Causation

When one agent attempts to control another agent (who may be trying to control the first) things get complicated. If we are to make any progress toward understanding that important phenomenon, we must first clear up some confusion at the foundations of our concept of control. As we just observed, an outside agent can control the refinery-controller by controlling features of the refinery's environment. I control the refinery-controller by artificially depressing the aviation fuel market, but if neither I nor anyone else engages in such manipulation, should we say that the market itself, or its fluctuation, controls the refinery-controller? Can we view the environment itself as a sort of minimal agent, and say that *it* does the controlling?

This view of matters is not unknown. It is a central theme in B. F. Skinner's vision of behaviorism. (See for instance Skinner 1953, especially "The Controlling Environment," (pp. 129–141) and "'Self-Control,'" (pp. 227–242).) We can see one reason (there are surely more) why it is chilling: it hints subliminally at the dark idea that the environment *wants* us to do this and that, and acting on the desire, *makes* us do what it wants. But that is not the way Skinner seems to see it. In Skinner's view there are no such phenomena as desires, even in people and other organisms, so certainly the whole environment can have no desires or intentions—good, evil or indifferent. Nevertheless he sees a distinction between mere environmental causation (for example, the effects of sun, wind, and rain on the condition of an organism's skin) and the control exercised by those features of the environment singled out as stimuli. And contrary to our chilling vision, he sees this control as benevolent—as just what we should want in fact (if there were such a thing as wanting!): "We may disagree as to the nature or extent of the control which it ["the world about us"] holds over us, but some control is obvious. Behavior must be appropriate to the occasion" (Skinner 1953, p. 129) Thus Skinner would say that the goal of the NASA engineers was to design the explorer vehicles so that they would come to be controlled appropriately by the Martian world about them.

Skinner constantly talks of behavior being "under the control" of various stimuli, but he does not emphasize the distinction between being controlled appropriately by the world about us, and being controlled inappropriately. If a robot explorer on Mars is caused by patterns in its environment to destroy itself, it is acting under the Skinnerian control of Martian stimuli, but not in a way it would "like"—if it could like. If being under the control of stimuli is a good thing, as Skinner suggests,[13] it must be only when one is under the control of stimuli in just the right way.[14]

What is the right way? What could it be except *just the way we would want, if we knew everything about our interests and the way the world really is?* For one thing, then, the right way is the truthful or veridical way. If the world will relentlessly cause us to know the truth about it we shall be quite happy so far as that aspect of the world's effect on us goes. As Wiggins puts it, "The libertarian ought . . . to be content to allow the world, if it will only do so, to dictate to the free man how the world *is*. Freedom does not consist in the exercise of the (colourable, but irrelevant) right to go mad without interference or distraction by fact." (Wiggins 1973, p. 34) It would be nice, that is, to have one's beliefs controlled by the way things actually were. (Compare Nozick's (1981, chapter 3) account of knowledge as "belief tracking truth.")

A truly benevolent world would keep us well informed about itself—but also, of course, the news it would tell us would be good news! If that bed of roses is too much to hope for, at least we might expect a benevolent world to "tell us what to do," while a malevolent world would "trick us" and "lure us into traps," and "go out of its way" to foil our plans. Is our actual world either of these, or does if often just appear to us in these different guises? The world as a whole, of course, is neither "for" us nor "against" us, although some of its parts may be tonic or toxic, our friends or our enemies.

The benign tendency that Skinner's words seem to impute, most

13. On the one hand it has always been shocking, and hence rhetorically self-defeating, for Skinner to quietly suppress the difference between *mere* brute control by the environment and its pleasanter proper part: *systematically helpful* brute control by the environment. But on the other hand Skinner has had his reason for this: he has seen, like the adaptationist, that this brute control will *tend* to be benign. (The sort of systematically murderous control imagined above, which leads the robot to destroy itself, is self-cancelling in even the short run; it wipes out its prey.) But he oversells his case, and quite deservedly fosters suspicion; of course not all "stimulus control" is a good thing simply in virtue of being a sort of control, and Skinner can't get away with pretending that it is.

14. Compare this to the reliance on "the right way" in causal theories of knowledge and reference, where the causal chain between object and thought must be of the "right" sort—the nature of rightness to be specified later, typically.

implausibly, to the immediate environment of "stimulation" is in fact a two-level affair: a benign tendency of the selecting environment, over the evolutionary long run, to design creatures that have *in themselves* a benign tendency to make the right discriminations—for themselves. The environment is not designed to *tell* us what to do; we are designed to *figure out* from the indifferent environment what to do. So it is unwise, even in the light of this indirect but systematically helpful tendency over the long run, to speak of the environment controlling us.[15]

Skinner's concept of control, as we have seen, is importantly different from our everyday notion in that no agent, no harborer of desires, is implicated. In the Skinnerian sense of "control" we say that A controls B if and only if changes in A are reliably reflected or registered in changes in B. This is not an eccentric concept of control, even if it is not just our ordinary concept. The grooves on the phonograph record control the vibrations of the loudspeaker, in this sense, and the amount of rainfall over a period of time controls the height of the river. The thing in the A slot need not be an agent, and the thing in the B slot need not be an organism—or something with interests. Thus there may be no question of whether the changes in B controlled by changes in A are appropriate for the organism which is B (or in which B resides). Skinner's concept might seem, then, to be just the familiar concept of physical causation under another name, but in fact it occupies intermediate ground, and helps propel the illusory slide from causation to control that feeds our fear of determinism.[16]

Part of the explanation for the confusion of causation with control arises from our common scientific practices, and more particularly from our imaginative understanding of them. In a typical good experiment, the experimenter is careful to *control* for various conditions, with an eye to establishing, in the manner of our model airplane remote controller, that a particular variable, the dependent variable, is *under the experimenter's control* (in the familiar sense) by being reliably linked to ("controlled by" *in Skinner's sense*) some independent variable or stimulus that the experimenter controls. The rationale for this practice is familiar. A pat-

15. Monod, in fact, sees reason to insist on the contrary: the environment does not and cannot control a living being. "[A living being] is thus a structure giving proof of an autonomous determinism: precise, rigorous, implying a virtually total 'freedom' with respect to outside agents or conditions—which are capable, to be sure, of impeding this development, but not of governing or guiding it, not of prescribing its organizational scheme to the living object." (Monod 1971, pp. 10–11)

16. Skinner's concept of stimulus control is in fact at least a close kin of the concept in information theory of a reliable (non-noisy) signal; the variation in B carries information about the variation in A. See Dretske 1981.

tern is observed in some phenomenon, and the question is: what causes it? If the experimenter's deliberate acts can drive the pattern this way and that "at will," the causes are uncovered—implicated in the chain of control leading from the experimenter to the observed phenomenon. In order to achieve these effects, we must render circumstances epistemically tractable; that is, we must isolate the phenomenon from unpredictable "outside" influences and render the immediate environment as uniform and simple as possible, so that we can keep track of the plausibly relevant features and thereby obtain effects that are reliably repeatable at will. Our successes under these "controlled conditions" flavor our imagination when we think about causation in general.

We know perfectly well that causation can be entirely inscrutable—utterly lost in a tangled web of coincidence—and still be causation. What caused *this* grain of sand to be right where it is on the beach? Something did—or rather some billions of things over billions of years did. We ignore cases like this. But if the grain of sand is part of a footprint on the beach, we focus in on one cause—the cause of its being *depressed* from the position it otherwise would presumably be in. When we think of cases of causation we almost invariably think of cases where the relationships are laid bare, where the actuality or at least the practicality of *control by an agent* is manifest. After all, we speak of "the" cause of an event or phenomenon, knowing that causation is always an indefinitely multifarious matter from which we can sometimes extract, by an intellectual act, a certain salient feature—that is, an epistemically tractable and hence controllable feature—and usefully call it "the" cause. These are "good, clear cases" of causation. We tend to forget the equally good cases of causation that are virtually indescribable and utterly uncontrollable by us.

In fact, some such cases of causation are called "randomizing" processes (shuffling cards, throwing dice, flipping coins)—precisely because of their uncontrollability. In reflective moments we think of the helter-skelter bouncing of the ball in the roulette wheel as entirely caused—indeed determined—by the state of the wheel and its immediate surroundings and the initial impetus given to the wheel and the ball. But since this behavior epitomizes (and was of course designed to epitomize) an uncontrollable ("random") process, it is easy to forget that it is no more exempt from causality than the billiard ball which rolls inexorably and with delicious predictability across the table under the expert control of a fine player (who relies on the uniformity of the table in planning the shot). An expert roulette ball thrower, or card shuffler, who could control the outcome in the way the expert billiards player can control the outcome, would defeat the element of "chance" in those games and be disallowed. For in such a game the outcome is intended to be independent of the beliefs and desires of all the participants regarding the outcome.

Laplace's superior intelligence would presumably fail to see the difference, and if offered a job in a casino, would be just as capable of controlling a game of roulette as any billiards expert would be capable of controlling a game of billiards.[17] Such a superhuman intelligence could also, no doubt, control one of us as easily as we control *Sphex*, but this superhuman, after all, is just another one of those imaginary agents we needn't worry about. Perhaps there could be such agents, for all we know, inhabiting other planets. It would be as reasonable for us to dread them as it is unreasonable for us to conjure them into existence on the premise of determinism.

4. Agents in Competition

The environment, not being an agent, does not control us. And yet the environment, over evolutionary time, has done a brilliant job of designing us. It may well seem that I am urging an inconsistent policy of "imagination management" here. On the one hand, I am warning against spurious personification of the environment as an evil opponent, while on the other I have defended as a usefully graphic vision the personification of evolution and its trends as wise, benign old Mother Nature whose "invisible hand" designed us all. Is this just the advice of Pollyanna to try to look on the bright side? I think not.

The standard antidote recommended for abuse of the Mother Nature vision is to remind oneself constantly that evolutionary processes operate *with no foresight and no goals*. If we are careful to remind ourselves of this we can go on to use the agency metaphor—what I call description "from the intentional stance" (Dennett 1971, 1978a)—to describe and explain the pattern of development that accounts for all the well-designedness we see in nature. Now it is open for some genius of pessimism to discover for us some sort of contra-Darwinian patterns of motiveless malignity which would permit us to reconceptualize our view of nature as a sort of Manichaean struggle between Mother Nature and

17. This need not assume that the superior intelligence has a total knowledge of its own microstates and transitions (which is logically impossible), for it might gate its interferences in the world (its "acts" in the casino) through some filters whose properties it knew intimately—an application of the same principle a normal human being could rely on if we let him use a precision-built dice-throwing machine at the craps table. On the impossibility of complete self-knowledge, and its implications for free will, see the classic papers by Popper (1951) and MacKay (1960).

the Evil One, but so far as I know, no such patterns have been seriously entertained.[18]

Sometimes things do happen to be against us. The environment may be indifferent to us, but we much prefer some ways the world might be to others—and for good reason: some arrangements of the world's objects better suit the pursuit of our interests than others. Nature does occasionally "conspire" to thwart us, constricting our choices, compelling—if not coercing—our actions.[19] But if we remember to apply the evolutionists' antidote to the appealing metaphors of "vicious" storms and "forbidding" cliffs, we will perhaps be able to keep our imaginations in proper check. Just remember: there are no bogeymen out there, except in philosophers' examples.

If an airline pilot is informed that there is a dangerous thunderstorm ahead, a storm so severe that were he to enter it, he would risk *losing control* of his plane, he can divert the plane to another course in order to preserve or enlarge the margin of control he maintains. (This fundamental tactic of minimizing uncertainty is a deeply explanatory concept in evolutionary theory. See Wimsatt 1980.) In the middle of a storm, only split-second, highly accurate reactions to circumstances will preserve the plane's safe course; in clear air, there is a wider margin for error. The smaller the margin for error, the less freedom of choice the pilot has, the more constrained and limited he will be in pursuing his course to his destination. Recognizing this, the pilot not only strives to control the plane at all times; he also engages in meta-level control planning and activity—taking steps to improve his position for controlling the plane

18. Humor is another matter. I recommend to all the classic expression of this vision by Paul Jennings, who in his "Report on Resistentialism," describes the Left Bank philosophy of Pierre-Marie Ventre, the author of *Resistentialisme* and the play *Puits Clos*. *"Les choses sont contre nous"*—that is the aphoristic heart of Resistentialism. "Except for his German precursors, Freidegg and Heidansiecker, all previous thinkers from the Eleatics to Marx have allowed at least some legitimacy to human thought and effort. . . . In the Resistentialist cosmology that is now the intellectual rage of Paris, Ventre offers us a grand vision of the Universe as One Thing—the Ultimate Thing (*Derniere Chose*). And it is against us." According to Jennings, Resistentialism has a scientific base: it all began when Clark-Trimble, a psychologist at Cambridge "who was not primarily a physicist" accidentally made his great discovery of the Graduated Hostility of Things. "Ventre's work brings us a great deal nearer to the realization of the Resistentialist goal summed up in the words, 'Every Thing out of Control.'" A version of the "Report on Resistentialism" originally appeared in the *Spectator;* a revised version appeared in America in *Town and Country* and is reprinted in Jennings 1963.

19. Greenspan (1978, p. 235n) says that compulsion seems to be a broader notion than coercion: "only the latter requires the direct intervention of another agent, as author of the threat."

by avoiding circumstances where, he can foresee, he will be forced (given his goals) to thread the needle between some Scylla and Charybdis.

This is just a particularly clear case of what we all always want: lots of elbow room. We want a margin for error; we want to keep our options open, so that our chances of maintaining control over our operations, come what may, are enhanced.[20] When we look ahead to see what obstacles we are apt to encounter, we should of course include any obstacles we carry with us—such as a craving for sweets, for instance, which might inspire us to adopt the higher-order strategy of not having sweets around the house, where the temptation would be too great. Higher-order strategies designed to maximize elbow room can in this way depend critically on the self-knowledge of the strategist.

When calculating the likely future constraints on our options, the presence or absence of a competitive agent makes all the difference, just because when there is an information-gathering, feedback-loop-closing agent out there, one's activities may be predicted by this agent, and hence foreseen and systematically thwarted.[21] It is important that the airline pilot, in evading the thunderstorm, doesn't have to worry about hiding his true intentions from the storm, which might, if it knew, switch its own course and come after him!

If agent A is to control object B, A must solve the epistemic prob-

---

20. Fischer says, "When we associate responsibility with control, we normally mean that a person is responsible for a particular event only if there is some alternate sequence open to the agent in which he performs a different act (or brings about a different event by performing some act that issues in the event)." (Fischer 1982, p. 34) We will have to see in chapter five what "open to the agent" means. Fischer goes on to speak of "control (freedom to do otherwise)" (p. 37)— but this is a fatal slide, as we shall see in chapter six.

21. This is, in slightly different guise, one of the founding insights of game theory. As von Neumann and Morgenstern note in the first chapter of *Theory of Games and Economic Behavior* (1947), while a lone "Robinson Crusoe" agent can view all problems as seeking maxima, as soon as other (maxima-seeking) agents are included in the environment, strikingly different methods of analysis are required, for

> A guiding principle cannot be formulated by the requirement of maximizing two (or more) functions at once. . . . One would be mistaken to believe that it can be obviated . . . by a mere recourse to the devices of the theory of probability. Every participant can determine the variables which describe his own actions but not those of the others. Nevertheless those 'alien' variables cannot, from his point of view, be described by statistical assumptions. This is because the others are guided, just as he himself, by rational principles— whatever that may mean—and no *modus procedendi* can be correct which does not attempt to understand those principles and the interactions of the conflicting interests of all participants. (p. 11)

lem of identifying the parameters of *B*'s operation. When two agents compete, each trying to control the other, there is thus competition for information, with each trying to conceal as much as possible about its own plans, its knowledge of the other's plans, and so forth, while obtaining as much "intelligence" as possible about the other.[22] This delicate and scary circumstance might well lead an agent to reflect: "If my opponent gets the edge, it may be able to find some way of treating me the way the biologist treated poor *Sphex*, some way of controlling my activity *in the wrong sort of way*, a way that is contrary to my interests."

This fear is just below the surface in a host of philosophical intuition pumps.

> Consider the frequently discussed case of the demonic neurologist who directly manipulates a person's brain to induce all his desires, beliefs, and decisions. (Fischer 1982, p. 37)

Indeed this case is frequently discussed, but this time let us consider the effects of certain traditionally favorite words in it. Why a neurologist, and not, say, an orator, or teacher, or philosopher? What difference does it make that the neurologist "directly manipulates" the victim's brain? With thought experiments, just as with actual experiments, one should not neglect to run the control experiments. For thought experiments that are intuition pumps, this is done by "turning the knobs"—trying out different settings of the various values and seeing what happens (Hofstadter 1981). Suppose then we revise the case:

> Consider the *in*frequently discussed case of the eloquent philosopher who indirectly manipulates a person's brain by bombarding his ears with words of ravishing clarity and a host of persuasively presented reasons, thereby inducing all his desires, beliefs, and decisions.

We may still feel that this agent is a bit more overbearing than we'd like. As Nozick notes (1981, "Introduction"), philosophers have an ulti-

---

22. There is considerable anxiety among the general public about the power that psychologists may come to have—may already have—over ordinary people in virtue of their (proclaimed) greater knowledge of the workings of the human mind. This widespread fear is firmly and wisely put in perspective by Neisser 1976, pp. 182–188. In particular, ". . . the psychologist cannot predict and control anyone who knows more . . . about the situation than he does, or who picks up information that he has left out of his reckoning." (p. 183) So *practical* freedom from prediction and manipulation by others (psychologists or dictators or whomever) is best achieved by the acquisition of knowledge in general. The more you know, the harder you are to control; as the Bible says, the truth shall make you free—or at least protect you from one kind of bondage.

mately unpleasant and unfriendly penchant for "coercive" argumentation, but we can soften the picture in a variety of ways. For instance:

> Consider the delightful case of the well-informed, truthful oracle who indirectly manipulates a person's brain by bombarding his ears with lucid and accurate warnings, made all the more irresistible by the citation of all the evidence in their favor and a frank account of the entire evidence-gathering operation.

By the time we've reset the dials on our intuition pump and tuned it to the image of a wise and friendly advisor, who uses only *epistemically warranted* communicative interactions to achieve only cognitive effects ("the truth and nothing but the truth"), will it still bother us that our beliefs, desires, and decisions are being thus "induced"? First note that the very fact that we might know (or have very good reasons to believe) that this—and only this—was what was going on would be vastly reassuring. We would know we were being influenced by this agent, but not "unwittingly influenced" (Greenspan 1978, p. 237); we were being, quite literally, wittingly influenced—influenced by influences that depended on, relied on, and exploited our wits and nothing but our wits. No "dirty tricks." Such influences yield decisions that are "in equilibrium." "An act in equilibrium withstands knowledge of its own causes." (Nozick 1981, p. 348) It withstands this knowledge because the knowledge reveals the act to have been caused just as we would have wanted—by a clear view of reality and the best of intentions.[23]

Of course we might want to eliminate the middleman altogether; we might prefer "first-hand" acquaintance with the world to even the best "hearsay." Why? Because it gives us an opportunity to learn things, to notice things, unfiltered by the epistemic interests and biases of another agent. It also diminishes the opportunity for betrayal: we really don't like to have to trust other agents. Our caution is surely reasonable. Bogeymen, if there were any, would be worthy objects of dread.

Suppose I am in the supermarket, trying to decide which can of soup to buy. I have heard disturbing rumors about the tricks advertisers use to

---

23. Ayer (1954) raises, and roundly dismisses, the curious, indeed apparently ridiculous, view that defines freedom "as the consciousness of necessity." Perhaps the insight lurking behind this dark doctrine is this: we especially fear *unrecognized,* hidden, unacknowledged influences on our wills—for the reasons just reviewed. And what would a perfect absence of this dreaded condition be? Perfect knowledge of the springs of our desires and beliefs. Thus if freedom is what we should aspire to, then freedom is perfect consciousness of the causation (necessity, in one sense) of our beliefs and desires. Freedom would be having one's acts in equilibrium (in Nozick's sense) and knowing it.

"control" my buying habits, and I certainly don't like that idea. But do I then hope that when I get to the soup shelves *nothing* will control my purchase decision? Do I want the sort of "radical freedom" that would make me impervious to important and relevant features of the candidates? I don't want my purchase decision controlled by the color of the can, or its location on the shelf, or whether or not it has a picture of someone I admire on it. But shouldn't I be content to let my choice be "controlled" by quality, price and availability—if only I can arrange it? What else would I rather have influencing my decision?

Well, maybe I do have a reason for a modicum of "radical freedom," if it will protect me from the wily advertisers out there who are always trying to "read my mind." Just as the pilot's meta-level control planning leads him away from situations in which he *risks* a diminution of control, so our meta-level control thinking may lead us to want to eschew tactics or control strategies that run the risk of being too fully understood, and hence anticipated, by a competitor (if ever one should appear).[24]

5. The Uses of Disorder

Consider the simple two-person game of "rock, paper and scissors." Sometimes when you play this game, you get the feeling you have locked onto the mind-set of your opponent. You home in on the pattern of your opponent's play, and just clean up. Imagine a case in which you have done just that; you have just won twenty consecutive throws of rock, paper and scissors against your friend, Mary. Thereupon she invites you to open the sealed envelope she had casually placed on the table at the outset of the game. Inside is a slip of paper with the message "I will now attempt to *lose* twenty consecutive throws of rock, paper and scissors to my friend. [signed] Mary" Now who was controlling whom?[25] Where did the power really lie? Why would it be so threatening to learn such a thing—and even from a friend? Well, if she can do it, someone else who wasn't so friendly could probably do it, too.[26] So I have a reason, a meta-

---

24. This meta-level control rationale in favor of the tactic of "poker face" unpredictability need not be *our* (conscious, explicit) rationale; it may be a free-floating rationale honored in our biological design. See Dawkins 1976, pp. 82–83, on the conditions under which a poker face is an evolutionarily stable strategy.

25. The answer is obvious if we mean Skinnerian control: your moves were controlling Mary's. This case brings out clearly what it is in the ordinary concept of control that is missing from Skinner's concept.

26. "Undercut, Flaunt, Hruska, behavioral evolution and other games of strategy" (Hofstadter 1982a) is an enlightening discussion of the powers and dangers of adopting detectable policies in such circumstances.

level reason, for wanting my mind to be unreadable, and this might well require that I avoid putting patterns into certain of my activities.[27] The only way of assuring that there is no readable pattern in those activities is to make them random.

The one way to guarantee that no opponent can anticipate one's moves is to make them directly dependent on some genuine quantum-mechanical indeterminacy—the sort of freedom that consists in the absence of causality. Since *in principle* these quantum effects are unpredictable, even Laplace's superior intelligence is stumped by them. But that sort of randomness is not necessary in our world.

There are many macroscopic (not quantum-level indeterministic) processes—such as coin flipping—that yield results that are random in a mathematically powerful sense that has nothing directly to do with causality. A series is said to be random in this mathematical or information-theoretical sense if it is informationally incompressible, that is, if the shortest, most efficient way of "sending" the series from A to B is to send it *verbatim*; no recipe or algorithm for the series (and no blueprint of a device that will generate the series) can be specified in less bits of information than it takes simply to transmit the series (Chaitin 1976). (See also Berry 1983 and Ford 1983.)

Then there are the pseudo-random series, of the sort generated by the "random number generators" in most computers. These are not only not causally indeterministic; they are also not informationally incompressible. Simple, briefly statable algorithms or functions generate such series, but "from the outside" such a series is virtually impossible to distinguish from a real random series. This sort of utter pattternless-ness—or perhaps we should say: utter *inscrutability* of pattern—has more bearing on free will and the nature of *possibility* than one might at first think, as we shall see in chapter six. In the meantime, I want to exhibit some of the roles it plays in our techniques of control and self-control.

----

27. The erratic flight of insects is an example of this strategy in a free-floating rationale; it makes it much harder for insectivorous birds to plot their trajectories and hence "lead their targets." Birds found a countermeasure; by greatly increasing the flicker-fusion rate of their vision, they could sample the insects' trajectories more often, and hence more accurately. (If our flicker-fusion rate were as high as a swallow's, we would see a motion picture as a rather rapid slide show. Perhaps a more useful way of thinking of it: the bird perceives its world "in slow motion.") See Wimsatt 1980.

The tactical problem thus solved by birds was the necessity that mothered the invention of the field of cybernetics. Wiener (1948) tells how a consideration of the problem of directing antiaircraft fire against planes taking evasive measures led to the fundamental insights of control theory and cybernetics.

We have already seen the strategic value of deliberately relinquishing pattern in some game-playing situations: this ensures that your opponent will not pick up your pattern and exploit it to seize control of you. In addition to games against (real) opponents, however, there are "games against nature."[28] Suppose you wish to learn about a large domain and haven't the time (or money, or inclination) to check every item in the domain. You settle on a "spot check" method, a small sample—say, five percent—from which you intend to extrapolate about the rest. How, though, should you choose your sample? Should you take the "nearest" or "first" five percent? Should you divide the domain into a grid of equal squares, numbered in order, and then systematically sample one out of twenty squares: squares 1, 21, 41, 61, and so forth? No. The traditional wisdom of statisticians says that you should draw your five percent sample randomly from the domain. Why? To minimize the danger of using a pattern of sampling that coincides with the very pattern in the world you are looking for.[29]

Suppose Martians send a space probe to Earth to learn about our climate. It can sample only 365 times before its batteries run out. It lands in northern Maine in January. If it samples once every ten minutes till its power runs out, it will never see February, let alone August. If it samples once a day for a year at exactly the same time (midnight, as it happens), it will uniformly blanket the annual domain with samples, but miss the existence of daylight altogether. There are thousands of patterns that might be relevant to the data-gathering mission; if any of them that are in phase—that is, if their *absence* is in phase—with the pattern of sampling, they will be invisible. The way to give oneself the best chance of seeing what is out there to be seen is to disorder one's search. An ordered, systematic, patterned search will necessarily be blind to any and all patterns in phenomena that are in phase with the search.[30]

---

28. See also Hintikka's work on game-theoretical semantics and a game-theoretical approach to induction in Hintikka 1976 and Saarinen 1979.

29. As this book was going to press, Teddy Seidenfeld drew my attention to the controversy among statisticians and probability theorists about the presumed rationale for relying on randomization in experiments. (This is lucidly set out and analyzed in Seidenfeld 1981.) While his arguments against the usual epistemological defenses of the practice strike me as devastating, I think that the reflections I offer here, which stress the practical desideratum of minimizing the risk of periodicities in phase, are independent of those arguments. But I have not had time to get anywhere near the bottom of this important issue. Here is just one of the areas where my hunk of marble is only crudely roughed out.

30. Of course any pattern in the phenomena that happens to be in phase with

The wisdom behind the practice of shuffling a deck of cards before playing with it has many applications in the world of designed systems (biological or artifactual), but so does the wisdom of another familiar technique of evoking "chance": flipping a coin. We flip a coin to settle things that could often presumably be settled in a more rational, if laborious, process of consideration. Instead of trying to decide which team "should" kick off, or which of two excellent restaurants it would *make sense* to try first (we could probably dream up some quite compelling reasons, if we really put our minds to it), we get on with life by letting an arbitrary coin flip "decide" for us.

It is surely rational of us to do so. That is, it is (higher-order) rational of us to cede a bit of our (lower-order) rationality in the interests of efficient, speedy decision making.[31] The "cost" is a slight risk of overlooking truly compelling and important reasons for one course of action over another. The "benefit" is avoiding the otherwise large risk of deliberating too long and missing the deadlines for meaningful action. Once again, it is important that the coin be (supposed to be) *decoupled* from whatever its behavior is being used to decide—now not so much in order to avoid pattern-matching as to obviate any time-squandering activity of checking to make sure the coupling was "right." (Compare Dretske 1981, chapter 5) (If you want to choose a restaurant, you can use a pair of dice, or an elaborate *gourmetoscope*, updated daily or hourly with relevant information; the chief advantage of the dice over the gourmetoscope—aside from price—is that they require no maintenance. They give you *an* answer every time you ask, and who cares if it's "right"?)

---

your *particular* pseudo-random or random search pattern will also be invisible, but precisely because of the (presumed, attempted) extreme irregularity in your search sequence, the likelihood of a similarly irregular "pattern" in the phenomena being studied mirroring your "pattern" perfectly is infinitesimal. With regular patterns—periodic patterns, in particular—there *can* be many different ways to superimpose them so that they are (partially) in phase.

31. Jaynes (1976) suggests that in prehistoric times the discovery of something like coin flipping was a major technological breakthrough, the acquisition of a valuable cognitive technique. People were then not sophisticated problem solvers, he speculates, and often found themselves in practical dilemmas whose outcomes were imponderable to them. To get such a person out of the predicament of Buridan's ass (who died from indecision, equidistant between food and water and unable to budge), what was needed was what Jaynes calls "exopsychic methods of thought and decision-making" (p. 245): sortilege or the casting of lots, the examination of entrails ("extispicy" or "haruspicy"), and similarly apparently superstitious practices. It is interesting that we still feel the need, at times, of such arbitrary tie-breaking strategems.

6. "Let Yourself Go"

Not any self-control or self-limitation
for the sake of specific ends,
but rather a carefree letting go of oneself:
not caution, but rather a wise blindness;
not working to acquire silent,
slowly increasing possessions, but rather
a continuous squandering of all perishable values.
—Rilke, "Uber Kunst"
(translation from Brown 1959, p. 67)

Once the demands of acting—and hence deciding—in a time-pressured world are factored into our vision of rational thought, we get a model of the mind vastly unlike the model typically (and dimly) imagined by rationalists in the great tradition of Descartes, Leibniz and Kant.[32] For instance, a certain amount of arbitrariness, of informational insensitivity (which from the wrong vantage point would look like sphexishness) is an essential feature of time-pressured rationality; otherwise there is no breaking out of the vicious regress of deciding to decide to decide (on various incomplete grounds) . . . to terminate deliberation and act. We *never* choose a course of actions as the best course *all things considered*; it would be insane to try to consider all things. (See also chapter four.)[33]

I noted at the beginning of chapter two that counterbalancing the perennial persuasiveness of the ideal of freedom as *obeying the dictates of reason* is the subterranean *un*attractiveness of the selfsame idea. There seems in it no room for spontaneity, for whim, for individuality, for art. It is tempting to say: "If I let my acts be dictated by reason alone, I would be bereft of *personality,* a mere conduit for Truth and Doing the Right Thing, not a unique and idiosyncratic actor on the world's stage."

The mistaken model of rationality lying behind this concern is easily seen if we apply it to a much simpler domain than the world's stage: chess. "If I let my moves in chess be dictated by reason alone, I would always play exactly the same game, for there is one Best Game of chess to play." Perhaps there is, but who can find it? There is in fact an algorithm for determining the optimal line of play in chess. Since chess is a finite game, in principle one can plot all legal games in a gigantic decision tree of moves and then, starting at winning last moves, work backwards

32. As has been proposed, for instance, by Simon (1957), in his concept of "satisficing." For further philosophical discussion of the relevance of Simon's concept, see Nozick 1981, and Cherniak 1983.

33. Designing a wise and workable method of ignoring things has proven to be one of the deepest and most intractable problems in Artificial Intelligence. See Dennett forthcoming-a.

inspecting all the pathways until one arrives back at the best first move. But this decision tree, though finite, has more nodes in it than could be explored by the fastest computer in billions of years. The most rational course any finite, macroscopic intelligence could take (knowing itself to be finite) will have to involve "heuristic" decision procedures, in which a risky, limited amount of analysis is terminated *in some arbitrary way* in the interests of conserving time on the game clock.

Under those constraints, the most rational course over a series of games would not dictate always playing the same game (though it might well stabilize on a highly successful stock opening). This would be true for several reasons. First, always trying to use the same game plan creates a pattern for opponents to exploit; they can concentrate their off-hours analysis efforts on breaking that particular attack, confident that their efforts will not be wasted. Second, "shuffling" one's middle game decisions somewhat produces more "genetic variation," in effect, from which novel and highly successful strategies can be discovered and selected. Third, such freewheeling strategies may be favored simply because the agent has been *designed* to favor them, to enjoy them in themselves, and hence to derive pleasure from them. There is surely a powerful rationale (free-floating or not) in support of designing a rational agent to be in general disposed to prize variety, to be bored by repetition—but, in counterbalance, to be charmed by pattern.

In chess we find several quite crisp distinctions that can also be discerned rather more problematically in the larger game of life. There are, for instance, the "forced moves" in chess. Moves are occasionally forced by the rules of chess: in these instances one finds oneself so boxed in that one and only one legal move is available. (If no legal move is available, and one is not in check, one has achieved a draw, of course.) More interesting, from our present point of view, are the forced moves on those occasions when there is more than one legal move, but only one non-"idiotic," non-"suicidal" move, which is said for that reason to be forced. It is forced not by the rules of chess, and not by the laws of physics, but by the dictates of reason. It is obviously the only rational thing to do, given one's interest in winning (or just not losing) the game.

One is always somewhat desperate when faced with an opportunity in which there is obviously only one rational thing to do. Sometimes we are put in such binds by other agents: "I made him an offer he couldn't refuse." Sometimes Nature impersonally fences us in so that our very survival depends on our managing to follow a very particular (and foreseeable) trajectory: for example, you will freeze to death if you don't get to warm shelter within the hour; the only accessible shelter is on the other side of the chasm; the only way across the chasm is the rope bridge, and so on. We rightly dread such confining circumstances, where our (sane) options are reduced to one. More generally, we prefer more options to less—up to the point where we become so swamped with options that we do not have time to consider them all. We prefer to find ourselves in circumstances where we can indulge in a modicum of spontaneous exploration, and while this preference for spontaneity is perhaps a genetically encouraged or even strongly hard-wired part of our characters, it is also dictated by reason.

So the apparent conflict (expressed by Rilke) between the ideal of spontaneity and the ideal of rational deliberation is an illusion. While no one of sound mind would choose a totally chaotic policy of decision and deliberation, it is equally true that the purest devotee of reason will be led, by that very devotion, to a policy that includes a fair measure of "letting yourself go." And as we shall see in later chapters, this policy has other manifestations in our model of ourselves as free agents—in the "idea of freedom" under which we act and in our policy of *not looking too closely* when looking at ourselves and each other as agents.

There is more of importance to be said about self-control and our concepts of our selves, but we have come far enough in our examination of the concept of control to make a few reassuring points. Contrary to the familiar vision that opened this chapter, *determinism does not in itself "erode control."* The Viking spacecraft is as deterministic a device as any clock, but this does not prevent it from being able to control itself. Fancier deterministic devices can not only control themselves; they can evade the attempts of other self-controllers to control them. If we are also deterministic devices, we need not on that account fear that we cannot be in control of ourselves and our destinies.

Moreover, *the past does not control us.* It no more controls us than the people at NASA can control the space ships that have wandered out of reach in space. It is not that there are no causal links between the Earth and those craft. There are; reflected sunlight from Earth still reaches them, for instance. But causal links are not enough for control. There must also be feedback to inform the controller. There are no feedback signals from the present to the past for the past to exploit. Moreover there is nothing in the past to foresee and plan for our particular acts, even if it is true that Mother Nature—gambling on our general needs and predicaments—did, in effect, design us to fend quite well for ourselves. Far from it being the case that we are completely under the control of our ancestors or our evolutionary past, it is rather the case that that heritage has tended to set us up as *self*-controllers—lucky us.

What begins to emerge from this exploration of the concept of control is a sketch of an ideal: how we would like to be. We would like to be as immune as possible from manipulation and dirty tricks and as sensitive as possible to harbingers of future vicissitudes that might cause us to alter course in the right ways—so that we can face the world with as much elbow room (as large a margin for error and as little relevant uncertainty) as we can get.

This implies that we would also like the world to be a certain way: full of variety, certainly, and with lots of sustenance and delight—but more important in this context: not so savagely demanding (given our needs and abilities) as to constrain our options to a bare minimum. If we must live on a desert island, make it fertile and rich with opportunity, not so barren and unyielding that all our moves would be like forced moves in chess.

The thesis of determinism carries no implications, of course, about how in particular the world will arrange itself, but it sometimes seems as if we respond to the prospect of determinism as if it were just such a limiting future—as if the pilot in the airplane had just said to us over the intercom "I'm afraid we're in for a long stretch of *determinism* just ahead; we'll be *powerless* and *have no room to maneuver;* we'll be very lucky to survive intact!" That is certainly not the right way to look at the issue, but we have not yet canvassed and dismissed all the compelling reasons for thinking there is some grain of truth in it.

4

Self-Made Selves

For my part, when I enter most
intimately into what I call *myself*,
I always stumble on some
particular perception or other,
of heat or cold, light or shade,
love or hatred, pain or pleasure.
I never can catch *myself* at any time
without a perception, and never can
observe anything but the perception.
—Hume, *Treatise,* I, VI, iv

Some souls one will never discover,
unless one invents them first.
—Nietzsche, *Thus Spake
Zarathustra,* Part I

1. The Problem of the Disappearing Self

The first day I was ever in London, I found myself looking for the nearest
Underground station. I noticed a stairway in the sidewalk labeled "SUB-
WAY," which in Boston is our word for the Underground, so I
confidently descended the stairs and marched forth looking for the
trains. After wandering about in various galleries and corridors, I found
another flight of stairs and somewhat dubiously climbed them to find
myself on the sidewalk on the other side of the intersection from where I
had started. I must have missed a turn, I thought, and walked back
downstairs to try again. After what seemed to me to be an exhaustive
search for hitherto overlooked turnstiles or side entrances, I emerged
back on the sidewalk where I had started, feeling somewhat cheated.
Then at last it dawned on me; I'd been making a sort of category mistake!
Searching for the self or the soul can be somewhat like that. You enter
the brain through the eye, march up the optic nerve, round and round
the cortex, looking behind every neuron, and then, before you know it,

you emerge into daylight on the spike of a motor nerve impulse, scratching your head and wondering where the self is.[1]

So far our discussion of self-control has been silent about just what a self is, and where it is, and what, if anything, it is made of. Is there any sense in which selves are among the things that really exist?[2] Hume's famous failure to find his self by introspection is paralleled by other expeditions that seem to end empty-handed: Mozart's search for the central font of his creative genius (See chapter one, p. 13), and the search for the *inner culprit* when there is blame to be assigned. Nagel observes:

> If one cannot be responsible for consequences of one's acts due to factors beyond one's control, or for antecedents of one's acts that are properties of temperament not subject to one's will, or for the circumstances that pose one's moral choices, then how can one be responsible even for the stripped-down acts of the will itself, if *they* are the product of antecedent circumstances outside of the will's control?
>
> The area of genuine agency, and therefore of legitimate moral judgment, seems to shrink under this scrutiny to an extensionless point. (Nagel 1979, p. 35)

This extensionless point or singularity is theoretically unpromising—to say the least—as a model of the moral agent. In this passage Nagel relies on several assumptions about the conditions under which one can be in control of things that were shown to be false in chapter three. But since control is only part of the story about responsibility, even a more circumspect causal account of control may leave the *self* threatened with dissolution "through the gradual erosion of what we do by the subtraction of what happens," as Nagel puts it. (Nagel 1979, p. 38) Do we *do* anything? What is it to be an agent, as opposed to a mere thread in the fabric of causation?

> But you had taken on a greater, and more harmful, illusion. The illusion of control. That A could do B. But that was false. Completely. No one can *do*. Things only happen. . . . (Spoken by a

---

1. Some writers seem to think that there really are secret doors in the brain's labyrinth, through which, with the help of a very special and mysterious sort of key, the self's messengers can pass. See, for example, Popper and Eccles 1977. That is not the way to locate the self.

2. *The Mind's I* (Hofstadter and Dennett 1981) is devoted to this search for the self; hence my very brief remarks on this important topic here. On the particular question of whether selves *exist*, see my "Introduction" (pp. 3–16) and "Reflections" on Borges (pp. 348–352). See also Dennett forthcoming-b.

character in Thomas Pynchon's novel, *Gravity's Rainbow*, 1973, p. 34.)

On the one hand, we have the image of the agent, the do-er, the locus and source of action rather than mere reaction. We think of our-selves as such agents. As Rawls notes, "citizens think of themselves as *self-originating sources* [my italics] of valid claims." (Rawls 1980, p. 543) We want to be able to say of ourselves, as Harry Truman famously said, "the buck stops here." On the other hand we have the image of the physical human being as no more salient, really, than domino number 743 in a chain of a million dominoes. If we are mere conduits of causa-tion, it seems, we cannot also be agents.

This leads almost irresistibly to the doctrine of "agent-causation." As Reid put it, "In the present case, either the man was the cause of the action, and then it was a free action, and justly imputed to him; or it must have had another cause, and cannot justly be imputed to the man." (Reid 1788, p. 329) Agent causation is a rather mysterious doctrine, however traditional. Chisholm, the most forthright exponent of the doctrine, puts it this way (See also Chisholm 1976, esp. chapter 2.):

> If we are responsible . . . then we have a prerogative which some would attribute only to God: each of us, when we act, is a prime mover unmoved. In doing what we do, we cause certain events to happen, and nothing—or no one—causes us to cause those events to happen (Chisholm 1964b, reprinted in Watson 1982, p. 32)

Can we find a naturalistic account of the self or agent that avoids this "obscure and panicky metaphysics"[3] while distinguishing agents suf-ficiently within the causal fabric? That is the task of this chapter.

It is clear that if such a positive account can be given, it will have to declare the intuitions that support Chisholm's vision of the self as un-moved mover to be a sort of cognitive illusion. If such a declaration is to be anything better than theory-driven name-calling, it will have to be supported by a convincing diagnosis of the cause of this illusion. It does *seem* somewhat as if we must be unmoved movers; if it *only* seems to be so, what makes it seem to be so? Not one factor, I would say, but several.

First, there is something like an illusion of scale caused by magnification of effects by the nervous system. Whatever else we are, we are information-processing systems, and all information-processing sys-tems rely on amplifiers of a sort. Relatively small causes are made to yield relatively large effects. In particular, the expenditure of large amounts of

---

3. Strawson (1962) was referring to the metaphysics of "libertarianism," but I for one would extend the epithet to the metaphysics of agent causation.

stored energy is controlled by modulation of lower-energy events. An information-processing system is essentially an organization of *switches* or *triggers*. The switches that control the output effectors—the arms, legs, mouths, wheels, projectiles, rockets—use very little input energy to initiate, modulate, and terminate processes or activities that expend dramatic amounts of energy in clearly observable ways.

Moreover, such a system's input switches—the transducers that form the perceptual organs—are also amplifiers. The "firing" of a retinal neuron, for instance, may be "triggered" by the arrival of a single photon on a retinal receptor. Vast amounts of information arrive on the coattails of negligible amounts of energy, and then, thanks to the amplification powers of systems of switches, the information begins to do some work—evoking other information that was stored long ago, for instance, transmuting it for the present occasion in a million small ways, and leading eventually to an action whose pedigree of efficient (or triggering) causation is so hopelessly inscrutable as to be invisible.[4] We see the dramatic effects leaving; we don't see the causes entering; we are tempted by the hypothesis that there are no causes.[5]

This invisibility of causal paths is not just a matter of the invisibility

4. In such an inscrutable tangle of microcausation, one can postulate, without fear of experimental contradiction, the possible contribution of quantum-level indeterministic events. The mere ubiquity of microscopic quantum effects in the world, and hence in our brains, would not ensure any *macroscopic* indeterminism of human action, however, unless there happen to be internal transducers that are, in effect, miniature natural Geiger counters, capable of amplifying the electron's effect to the scale at which control switching occurs in the nervous system. Otherwise, random perturbations at the subatomic level would just be absorbed as background noise, having no effect on the switching dispositions of the information-processing system. Describing such mechanisms is easy: the difficult task is finding a point for them (in light of the discussion of the uses of mere pseudorandomness in chapter three).

5. Aristotle, in *Nicomachean Ethics* (Book III, 1110a), characterizes a voluntary act as one whose source is within the agent, and an involuntary act as one "of which the moving principle is outside." In *Physics* (Book VII), he asserts that everything in motion is moved either by itself or by something else, suggesting that an agent capable of voluntary acts must be in the class of self-movers. But Thorp (1980) shows that Aristotle's analysis of the concept of a self-mover arrives eventually at the conclusion that any self-mover is actually not simple, but composed of parts, some of which move other parts and derive motion from outside. For Thorp, this is "disappointing" for it shows the "utter inadequacy, for the libertarians, of Aristotle's account of self-movement." (p. 99) On Aristotle's account, "self-movement is not a strict category but a sort of cheat" (p. 98); one of its defects, in Thorp's eyes, is that a remote-controlled airplane could count as a self-mover (p. 99).

(to us) of other minds. From our own first-person "introspective" vantage point the causal paths are equally untraceable.[6] Consider decisions themselves, presumably the focal events in the mental life of a genuinely free agent. Are decisions voluntary? Or are they things that happen to us?[7] From some fleeting vantage points they seem to be the preeminently voluntary moves in our lives, the instants at which we exercise our agency to the fullest. But those same decisions can also be seen to be strangely out of our control. We have to wait to see how we are going to decide something, and when we do decide, our decision bubbles up to consciousness from we know not where. We do not witness it being *made;* we witness its *arrival.* This can then lead to the strange idea that Central Headquarters is not where we, as conscious introspectors, are; it is somewhere deeper within us, and inaccessible to us. E. M. Forster famously asked "How can I tell what I think until I see what I say?"—the words of an outsider, it seems, waiting for a bulletin from the interior.

But why should we interpret our imperfect self-knowledge (our "underprivileged access" in Gunderson's fine phrase) in this way, as a literal *eccentricity* of our vantage point on our own self-control? Why must there be a center at all? The illusion of such an ultimate center arises, I think, from our taking a good idea, the idea of the self as a unitary and cohering point of view on the world (Dennett, forthcoming-b), and pushing it too far under the pressure of preoccupations with our responsibility (moral, but also artistic and intellectual, as in the case of Mozart). We ask ourselves "Did *I* do *that?*" and our attempt to answer the question produces something like a geometrical construction in search of an interpretation.

According to our traditional understanding of responsibility, we are

6. Hume is particularly acute about the misleading phenomenology of decision: "We feel that our actions are subject to our will on most occasions, and imagine we feel that the will itself is subject to nothing; because when by a denial of it we are provok'd to try, we feel that it moves easily every way, and produces an image of itself even on that side, on which it did not settle." *Treatise,* II, III, ii, Selby-Bigge ed., p. 408)

7. Ryle, in "The Myth of Volitions" (Ryle 1949, pp. 62–68), offers a *reductio ad absurdum:* if voluntary actions are those produced by an agent's *volitions* (whatever they might be) then are volitions themselves voluntary? If so, we get an infinite regress; if not, we get voluntary acts as the result of involuntary (or nonvoluntary) events—"a conclusion which might embarrass those moralists who use volitions as the sheet-anchor of their systems." (p. 67) One may join Ryle in scoffing at volitions as ill-favored theoretical entities for psychology and still suppose that *decisions* are sufficiently well-behaved and familiar items for theorists to rely on; I am raising problems about the everyday category of decisions.

primarily or directly responsible for our "voluntary" actions, the things we *do,* and (at most) only indirectly responsible for the things that happen to us. It is held, for instance, that "I can't help" the surge of anger (or lust, say) that I feel when objects in the environment present themselves to my senses in certain ways; however, I am supposed to govern my subsequent thoughts and activities regarding these objects by the force of my will. When we look inside ourselves with the goal of sorting our mental events into these two morally important categories something peculiar happens. Events near the input and output "peripheries" fall unproblematically into place. Thus *feeling pain in my foot* and *seeing the desk* are clearly not acts "in my control," but things that happen to me as a result of impingements from the world. And *moving my finger* or *saying these words* are obviously things that I do—voluntary actions par excellence.

But as we move away from those peripheries towards the presumptive center, the events we try to examine exhibit a strange flickering back and forth, like the illusion drawing of a transparent cube. It no longer seems so clear that perception is a passive matter. Do I not voluntarily contribute something to my perception, even to my recognition or "acceptance" of the desk as a desk? For after all, can I not *suspend judgment* in the face of any perceptual presentation, and withhold conviction? And on the other side of center, when we look more closely at action, is my voluntary act really *moving* my finger, or is it more properly *trying* to move my finger? A familiar intuition pump about someone willing actions while totally paralyzed attests that I am not in control of all the conditions in the world (or in my body) that are necessary for my finger actually to move.

Moving in still further, is it so obvious after all that either *accepting* or *trying* are voluntary? Is it not perhaps an illusion that I can grant or withhold acceptance of some proposition "at will"?[8] And aren't there conditions under which I am unable even to try to do this or that? And aren't those conditions themselves outside my control?

Faced with our inability to "see" (by "introspection") where the center or *source* of our free actions is, and loath to abandon our conviction that we really do things (for which we are responsible), we exploit the cognitive vacuum, the gaps in our self-knowledge, by filling it with a rather magical and mysterious entity, the unmoved mover, the active self.

8. The presumed voluntariness of accepting or rejecting propositions plays a large and problematic role in decision theory and related normative disciplines. See, for instance, Eells 1982, chapter 2.

This theoretical leap is nowhere more evident than in our reaction to our failures of "will power." "I'm going to get out of bed and get to work right *now!*" I say to myself, and go right on lying drowsily in bed. Did I or did I not just make a decision to get up? Can't I tell when I've really made a decision? Perhaps I just seem to myself to have made a decision. Once we recognize that our conscious access to our own decisions is problematic, we may go on to note how many of the important turning points in our lives were unaccompanied, so far as retrospective memory of conscious experience goes, by *conscious* decisions. "I have decided to take the job," one says. And very clearly one takes oneself to be reporting on something one has done recently, but reminiscence shows only that yesterday one was undecided, and today one is no longer undecided; at some moment in the interval the decision *must have happened,* without fanfare. Where did it happen? At Central Headquarters, of course.

But such a deduction reveals that we are building a psychological theory of "decision" by idealizing and extending our actual practice, by inserting decisions where theory demands them, not where we have any first-hand experience of them. I must have made a decision, one reasons, since I see that I have definitely made up my mind, and hadn't made up my mind yesterday. The mysterious inner sanctum of the central agent begins to take on a theoretical life of its own, and paves the way for doctrines of agents as unmoved movers.[9]

Such simple sorts of misdirection could hardly sustain the doctrine of "agent causation" all by themselves, but they could certainly contribute, spuriously, to the attractiveness of that doctrine when supplemented by the conviction that no positive naturalistic account can be given of what we hold dear when we contemplate "the dear self." The way to

---

9. Schneewind (1981) notes that John Stuart Mill's autobiography is wonderfully consistent with his determinist-compatibilist view of agency.

> Mill gives us a fascinating example of . . . a determinist effort to portray oneself from inside without either abandoning the philosophical theory or losing all sense of a lived individual life. . . . The famous "crisis" in Mill's "mental history" is plainly the "experience of the painful consequences of the character [he] previously had"; and the love for Harriet Taylor is the "strong feeling of admiration of aspiration accidentally aroused." Mill's language presents both of these events—the critical turning points in the life Mill shows us—in ways that avoid any suggestion of choice or decision or willing (p. 1234)

It is not that a compatibilist must deny that we ever make decisions—and Mill, Schneewind notes, alludes to various "trivial decisions and choices"—but that a compatibilist like Mill is under no theoretical pressure to attach a special metaphysical trigger to every morally relevant episode in his life.

undercut that conviction is to attempt such a positive account, a task to which I now turn.

2. *The Art of Self-Definition*

One thing is needful—
to "give style" to one's character—
a great and rare art!
—Nietzsche, *The Gay Science*

First I will examine some generally overlooked features of the process by which we become selves, features that, properly appreciated, might save us from one of the most deeply entrenched fears that motivate the free will problem. In particular, I will look at the contribution of *luck* in the development of self, an examination that will require a brief preliminary analysis of the concept of luck—a treacherous concept that lures us into many traps. This will yield an account of our accession to full-fledged moral personhood, but it must be protected from a familiar philosophical tug-of-war that threatens to pull it apart: oversimplification on the one hand, which naturally breeds the skepticism that attacks such diminished visions, and compensatory exaggeration on the other hand, the promulgation of absolutist doctrines to "protect" the idea of self from encroaching mechanism.

A self is, above all, a locus of self-control. How do you know, when you look in a mirror, that the person whose reflection you see is you? Not just by noting the resemblance, for how do you know what you look like right now?[10] You determine that you are looking at yourself by using the same tests you use to determine that you are controlling the model airplane. You see if you control the motions of the person you see. Can you wave *that* hand? If you can, it's yours.[11] The epistemological problem of such self-identification is normally trivial, but in contrived cases it can be difficult. In a suitably disguised and complicated tangle of arms and legs—say, a group wrestling match in identical costumes and

10. Most animals, presumably, have no knowledge at all about what their own faces look like—unless it is innate knowledge! But some animals, notably certain apes, can come to recognize themselves in mirrors. And when they do, the order of their reasoning is clear: since that image is of me, I must look like that (I must have a smudge of paint on my forehead). See Gallup 1977.

11. The relationship between self-control and "indexical" reference emerges (but is not discussed) in the host of examples that illuminate the recent literature on that topic. See, for example, Boër and Lycan 1980 for a useful discussion and an extensive bibliography of other recent work. See also Hofstadter and Dennett 1981, passim, and esp. pp. 20–22, 265–268, 471.

gloves—the question "Which of these hands are mine?" can become an occasion for careful experimentation and reflection.[12] Control is the ultimate criterion: I am the sum total of the parts I control directly.

Are all self-controllers selves? Each organism is, in some regards, a self-controller. That is, its behavior is controlled, not (normally) controlled by any other controller, and controlled in the main for the benefit of the organism.[13] Organisms have been designed to take care of themselves. But even if this endows each of them with a sort of self, our first intuition is that such selves are at best quite rudimentary and shallow, compared to the selves we take ourselves to be.

Once again it would help us understand the difference between ourselves (our *selves*) and lesser creatures if we had some developmental story to tell about the critical features in the intervening process that led from those lesser creatures to us. Surely part of that developmental story is to be found in the evolutionary story already sketched about how *homo sapiens* emerged once the environment began to include the social complications that were created by the ancestors of *homo sapiens*. But it is also clear that a large and important part of the development of a person occurs in the individual. Infants, intuitively, are scarcely more selves and maybe even less selves than dogs or cats are. Some process of learning and maturation turns infants into the self-conscious moral adults we take ourselves to be.

The idea that a full-fledged self or *person* must be the outcome of processes of social interaction has been ably and persuasively explored by others, and I will not take the time to review their reasoning.[14] Instead I will look at this process of the acquisition of selfhood from the simplified perspective of strategies of control.

12. Some years ago New York Harbor experimented with a shared radar system for small boat owners. A single powerful radar antenna formed a radar image of the harbor which could then be transmitted as a television signal to boat owners who could save the cost of radar by simply installing a small television set. But what good would this do? If you were lost in the fog, and looked at the television screen, you would know that one of those many blips on the screen was you—but which one? Perform a simple test. Turn your boat quickly in a tight circle; then your blip is the one that traces the little "O" on the screen—unless several boats in the fog try to perform the same test at the same time.

13. See Dawkins 1982, chapters 11–14, for the surprising fruits of adopting the perspective of looking at some animal behaviors as under the control of, and working for the benefit of, others (other animals and other genes).

14. See Strawson 1959 for a particularly abstract and ingenious philosophical analysis of this claim, and see Jaynes 1976 for an imaginative reconstruction of the historical forces and pressures that could have shaped this sociobiological evolution. Also very useful is Campbell 1975, and A. Rorty 1976.

An individual human being starts life with a problem: learning how to control himself or herself. As in all problems, one starts in a certain position with certain limited resources, and must then bootstrap those resources somehow into a solution. This may sound trivial, but it flies in the face of a very influential—if ultimately incoherent—vision of self-choosing: Sartre's idea that one chooses oneself *completely* by a "radical choice" that brings none of yesterday's baggage along. In Sartre's view, it is as if one could create oneself *ex nihilo;* as if, to borrow another familiar bit of philosophers' Latin, the self at birth were a *tabula rasa* or blank slate. We know better.

Sartre knew better, too, of course, but unfortunately chose this extravagant metaphor to express his view.[15] It is not a helpful metaphor. It postulates a magical power none of us could have, and encourages people to believe that if science shows they cannot have it, they cannot be free. Not only do we know, empirically, that a newborn child is very far from being a blank slate, but we also know, by a priori reasoning as compelling as any, that we have to start that way if we are to be capable of learning or developing at all. It is not hard to see, however, why a philosopher (such as Sartre) would want to hold out for the absolute, for there is an argument that often bubbles up to the surface to the effect that unless one were absolutely responsible for oneself, one could not be responsible at all.

"Compatibilists" or "soft determinists"—those who believe that free will and responsibility are compatible with determinism—typically claim in one way or another that one acts freely and responsibly just so long as one does what one decides, based on what one believes and desires. But "hard determinists" and other skeptics see this as a mere postponement of the difficulty. Edwards provides a clear expression of the basic argument:

> Let us suppose that both *A* and *B* are compulsive and suffer intensely from their neuroses. Let us assume that there is a therapy that could help them, which could materially change their character structure, but that it takes a great deal of energy and courage to undertake the treatment. Let us suppose that *A* has the necessary energy and courage while *B* lacks it. *A* undergoes the therapy and changes in the desired way. *B* just gets more and more compulsive and more and more miserable. Now it is true that *A* helped form his own later character. But his starting point, his desire to change, his

15. I do not know how to do exegetical justice to two passages on a single page in Sartre: "Thus in a certain sense I *choose* being born." and "I am responsible for everything, in fact, except for my very responsibility, for I am not the foundation of my being." (Sartre 1956, p. 555)

energy and courage, were already there. They may or may not have been the result of previous efforts on his own part. But there must have been a first effort, and the effort at that time was the result of factors that were not of his making (Edwards 1961, p. 121)

This is a subtler challenge than our earlier worry about being controlled by the past. I may not be controlled by the past, but my current capacity to make decisions and control myself is not, it seems, something I can take credit for. How could any deterministic process of "character transformation" beginning with a being that was *not* responsible for any of its "decisions" ever yield a being who was not only responsible for its decisions, but responsible for having the sort of character that would make those decisions? For that matter, how could an *in*deterministic process from the same starting point yield anything better?

Unless we can find a way of making a responsible self out of initially nonresponsible choices, so that there is a gradual acquisition of responsibility by the individual, we will be stuck with an unpalatable alternative. We will either have to deny that anyone ever is the sort of responsible self we all want to be, or we will have to follow Sartre's—or Chisholm's—way out and espouse a frankly mysterious doctrine of something like *absolute agenthood*.[16] It is certainly part of common wisdom that responsibility is gradually acquired—indeed earned—but unless we can find a fatal flaw in Edwards' argument, that common wisdom is in jeopardy, and unsupported allegiance to it will be nothing better than wishful thinking.

Before turning to the positive account of the acquisition of responsible selfhood, we can reassure ourselves a little by noting that Edwards' argument looks suspiciously like an instance of the well-known but ill-understood fallacy, the *sorites*. (A classical example: you can never make a man who isn't bald into a bald man by plucking just one hair from his head; so do it; now do it again, and again; by our first premise he'll never get bald, no matter how many times you do it!) No matter how many steps of character formation one has engaged in, Edwards says, there has to have been a first step, and if it was a decision over which the agent had no control, its product cannot be anything the agent is responsible for. The second step, from this base, will have the same properties as the first, so such a process never will yield a decision by an agent responsible for his own character.

But by parity of reasoning, there couldn't really be any mammals, since every mammal must have a mammal for a mother, and if you go

---

16. Van Inwagen (1983, p. 150) acknowledges the bind: "I must choose between the puzzling and the inconceivable. I choose the puzzling." I on the other hand choose to stretch the boundaries of what we find conceivable.

back far enough in the family tree of any apparent mammal, you must find a manifestly nonmammalian ancestor, whose offspring just couldn't themselves be mammals, and so forth.[17] Since we know perfectly well that we are mammals, we take this argument seriously only as a challenge to discover whatever fallacy it is that is lurking within it. It is tempting to dismiss Edwards' argument outright, as nothing but an application of the fallacious strategy of argument (whatever it is) exhibited by the mammal argument. But on such a controversial issue as our selfhood, this might well be seen as begging the question. It would be better to have an analysis of the error, or errors, in the argument.

Perhaps the error is this: it presupposes that one could not take full responsibility for something unless it was entirely of one's making. But of course nothing is ever entirely of one's making, unless one is God, so this is an extravagantly strong premise with which to begin an argument. Can the artist not claim full credit for a creation that incorporates, as a proper part, an *objet trouvé?* Does a resourceful exploitation of serendipity count *against* the authorship of the exploiter?

I *take* responsibility for any thing I make and then inflict upon the general public; if my soup causes food poisoning, or my automobile causes air pollution, or my robot runs amok and kills someone, I, the manufacturer, am to blame. And although I may manage to get my suppliers and subcontractors to share the liability somewhat, I am held responsible for releasing the product to the public with whatever flaws it has. Common wisdom has it that much the same rationale grounds personal responsibility; I have created and unleashed an agent who is myself; if its acts produce harm, the manufacturer is held responsible. I think this common wisdom is indeed wisdom, and can be supported against Edwards' suspiciously strong *reductio,* which, one should note, makes no essential use of any premise about determinism, and can be just as compellingly constructed on the hypothesis of an indeterministic world. *NB*

In what ways are we the products of acts of self-creation then? In the previous chapter I sketched some examples of meta-level decisions in a self-controller: what course should the airplane pilot take to maximize his elbow room, and hence to maximize his chances for maintaining control? Should the game player adopt a patterned strategy of play or opt for as much patternlessness as possible? These are relatively easy meta-level decisions to reach, for the set of apparently relevant considerations pro and con is manageably small and salient. To such problems we can often work out a standard solution, the best solution, the solution "by the book." For children growing up and learning to control themselves

17. The example, somewhat altered, comes from Sanford 1975. See also Sher 1979 and Zaitchik 1977.

there are similarly easy meta-level problems of control, with familiar "by the book" answers: look before your leap, a stitch in time saves nine, don't cry wolf. But one eventually graduates from such simple issues to much more imponderable questions.

Among the questions facing a sophisticated self-controlling agent are: could I revise my basic projects and goals in such a way as to improve my chances of satisfaction? Are there grand strategies or policies that are better than my current ones? Is there a style of operation that would suit my goals better than my current style? Will my current policies tend to lead me into tight quarters with little room to maneuver and great risk of disaster? What should my general policy regarding risk be? What kind of an agent do I want to be or become? (Some of these questions may strike one as objectionably amoral, but I am deliberately keeping explicitly moral questions at bay here, for I want to show how much of the structure of "free will" is fixed before the issue of morality arises.) There are in general no "book" answers to these questions and so, as in the mid-game in chess, one must abandon the book openings and strike boldly out into the territory of risky, heuristic reasoning.

In order to engage in this process of meta-level reasoning, the aspirant to a high order of self-control must have the capacity to represent his current beliefs, desires, intentions, and policies in a detached way, as objects for evaluation. As Locke noted, such an agent has "a power to *suspend* the execution and satisfaction of any of its desires" and hence is "at liberty to consider the objects of them, examine them on all sides, and weigh them with others." (*Essay.* II, XXI, 48) But once this examination extends beyond the mere resolution of immediately conflicting goals (for example, I can't go to the theater and the concert at the same time)[18] the "weighing" can invoke an indefinitely large and unstructured set of further considerations. One must limit one's reflections and take a few relatively blind leaps—or else postpone resolution forever.

However much one considers and evaluates and reflects, there is always logical room for more. Since we are thus inevitably confronted with the need for a limited and incomplete survey of considerations, it becomes important to us that the "right" considerations occur to us *early* in the deliberation process. But we cannot directly control this ordering; we cannot play parade marshal for the queue of considerations-to-be-

---

18. See Frankfurt 1976 on two different kinds of conflict between desires: conflicts where the desires "belong to the same ordering" so that if one cannot be satisfied, the other is automatically a candidate for satisfaction, and conflicts the resolution of which involves the agent *rejecting* the losing desire. Taylor 1976 draws the same distinction in different terms: "qualitative" and "non-qualitative" evaluation (p. 282ff).

reviewed, putting each in its proper place in line. For such control takes time and effort, and we are rushed. We must relinquish control over the very process that generates the incomplete set of considerations on which we act, and hence we are always somewhat at the mercy of that process. However, knowing that we are and always will be at the mercy of that process, we can take steps to improve—if not guarantee—its reliability. As Hampshire notes, "What a man will *think* of trying to do is narrowly circumscribed and may sometimes be predictable with almost perfect accuracy." (Hampshire 1959, p. 183) That being the case, we can take steps of self-improvement (and help others to take these steps) to make it more likely in the future that we will think the right sorts of things at the right times.

But even this process of reflective self-criticism and meta-level control reasoning must have its limits. If a complacent or sphexish rejection of all opportunities for reflection would be ill-advised, it would clearly also be irrational to embark on a limitless round of self-evaluation. The unexamined life may not be worth living, but the overexamined life is nothing to write home about either.[19] Moreover, there is almost certainly no "book" answer to the question of how much moderation is the right amount of moderation.

Why are we inclined to think, then, that further levels of reflection, further bouts of self-evaluation, *tend* to lead to improvements in the "character" of the agent? Suppose there are two agents, A and B, born to similar circumstances and with similar endowments, except that agent A engages in considerably more self-reflection and subsequent self-choosing than agent B. Is there any reason to suppose that A will tend to be a "better" agent? There is, it seems, if A and B are both members of the class of learners, that is, beings designed to have a propensity for gathering truths. For then their bouts of self-evaluation will *tend* to create self-knowledge, and how could more self-knowledge fail to be better than less?

One can see that up to some ill-defined point, the acquisition of self-knowledge must be a good thing, for as we saw in chapter three (page 63), our anticipation of future constraints that we may encounter should include any constraints we carry with us.[20] But it is always possible to overload the system with too much self-knowledge. A necessary feature

19. I believe Kurt Baier once made a remark to this effect. Ryle (1949) has useful observations on the limits of reflection and the "eternal penultimacy" of self-admonition in "The Systematic Elusiveness of 'I'," pp. 195–198.

20. Frankfurt (1971) has stressed the importance, for the sort of free will that might give us responsibility, of higher order desires: desires about which desires should move us. (This is discussed in Dennett 1976.)

of this task of self-evaluation is that it has no objective upper bound but at the same time gets more difficult the higher up the evaluation proceeds.

> Evaluation is such that there is always room for re-evaluation. But our evaluations are the more open to challenge precisely in virtue of the very character of depth which we see in the self. For it is precisely the deepest evaluations which are least clear, least articulated, most easily subject to illusion and distortion. It is those which are closest to what I am as a subject, in the sense that shorn of them I would break down as a person, which are among the hardest for me to be clear about. The question can always be posed: ought I to re-evaluate my most basic evaluations? Have I really understood what is essential to my identity? Have I truly determined what I sense to be the highest mode of life? . . . A re-evaluation of this kind, once embarked on, is of a peculiar sort. It is unlilke a less than radical evaluation which is carried on within the terms of some fundamental evaluation, when I ask myself whether it would be honest to take advantage of this income-tax loophole, or smuggle something through customs. These latter can be carried on in a language which is out of dispute. In answering the questions just mentioned the term 'honest' is taken as beyond challenge. But in radical re-evaluations, the most basic terms, those in which other evaluations are carried on, are precisely what is in question. . . . How then can such re-evaluations be carried on? There is certainly no meta-language available in which I can assess rival self-interpretations. If there were, this would not be a radical re-evaluation. (Taylor 1976, p. 296–297)

We have returned to the vertigo of Nietzsche's revaluation of all values, and it now appears that the price we pay for our open-ended capacity for reflection is entrance, on occasion, into domains where we can no longer reside any faith in our benign tendency to self-*improvement.*[21] In general, no doubt, the self-reflective agent is more mature and more responsible. That is, if one is thinking of *giving* someone responsibility for something—for example, leaving one's children in someone's care—one will in general do better to choose the more self-reflective agent. But some of the virtuosos of self-reflection seem to get in over their heads. Nietzsche, notoriously, was one; Charles Manson was another.

---

21. "We live in a buzzing cloud of whys and wherefores, the purposes and reasonings of our narratizations, the many-routed adventures of our analog 'I's. And this constant spinning out of possibilities is precisely what is necessary to save us from behavior of too impulsive a sort." (Jaynes 1976, p. 402)

The reason for this unreliability at the highest levels is clear enough; finite agents must use heuristic methods when faced with large problems and limited time (and other resources). The larger the search space[22] of a problem, the larger and messier the haystack in which the needle must be found, the more risky any heuristic method (with its inevitably blind leaps) must be.

Are these blind leaps the "radical choices" of Sartre's existentialism? Taylor sheds light on this question in his examination of Sartre's famous example (Sartre 1946) of the young man who is torn between caring for his ailing mother and going off to join the Resistance. This is a genuine moral dilemma, Taylor notes, for there are powerful moral claims in favor of each alternative; one cannot simply declare, by "radical choice," that the claim not heeded is worthless. "The real force of the theory of radical choice comes from the sense that there are different moral perspectives, that there is a plurality of moral visions . . . between which it seems very hard to adjudicate." (Taylor 1976, pp. 293–294)

There is a real question of what one ought to do, a question that may well have an objective, "definitive" answer; there is, nevertheless, no feasible "decision procedure" for determining what this answer, if there is one, might be. And time rushes on; one must act. Later, in retrospect, one may learn that one made the wrong decision—wrong by virtue of considerations that one values now *and valued then,* and (perhaps) would have heeded then, had matters been put in those terms at the time. On Taylor's reading, Sartre emerges recommending self-knowledge and acknowledgment:

> Granted this is the moral predicament of man, it is more honest, courageous, self-clairvoyant, hence a higher mode of life, to choose in lucidity, than it is to hide one's choices behind the supposed structure of things, to flee from one's responsibility at the expense of lying to oneself, of a deep self-duplicity. (Taylor 1976, p. 294)

---

22. Or *apparent* search space. Hofstadter (1983) describes a "one-shot prisoner's dilemma" experiment he conducted, in which participants had to choose between "cooperating" and "defecting" under rather unusual conditions. He insists that the problem faced by the participants had a unique best solution (one should cooperate)—a solution dictated by reason. But how could he be right that there is a clear, uncontroversial "by the book" solution in favor of cooperating, when a lot of quite rational people didn't see it that way? They saw an open-ended stack of considerations looming; so far as they could see, the prisoner's dilemma is an *uncertainty magnifier,* which could thus be expected to provoke a nonuniform set of solutions from a group of agents. They seem to have been right, and Hofstadter seems to have been wrong; the prisoner's dilemma does not seem to be like a problem of addition, in which each agent can rely on the others to arrive at the same answer.

But Taylor claims this is not enough. What reason could one have, on this view of radical choice, for not just shrugging off one's hard choices the way a chess player, in retrospect, shrugs off his mistakes? "The time clock was running, and I took a stab in the dark; wrong stab, as it turns out. Pity." The chess player acknowledges authorship for his choices (how could he not—save by claiming to have been under the remote control of another?), but that sort of authorship is, while necessary, not sufficient for moral responsibility.

The further ground of responsibility, Taylor suggests, comes from the particular nature of the way in which we accomplish radical re-evaluation. There is no meta-language, as he says, in which to conduct such an inquiry:

> The re-evaluation is carried on in the formulae available, but with a stance of attention, as it were, to what these formulae are meant to articulate. . . . Anyone who has struggled with a philosophical problem knows what this kind of enquiry is like. In philosophy typically we start off with a question, which we know to be badly formed at the outset. We hope that in struggling with it, we shall find that its terms are transformed, so that in the end we will answer a question which we couldn't properly conceive at the beginning.

When the question is one of radical self-evaluation,

> our attempts to formulate what we hold important must, like descriptions, strive to be faithful to something. But what they strive to be faithful to is not an independent object with a fixed degree and manner of evidence, but rather a largely inarticulated sense of what is of decisive importance. (Taylor 1976, p. 123)

But then if we succeed in this attempt at resolution, our success amounts to more than just an authored act, for we define ourselves in the process, by making "articulate" and more definite that which had been inchoate and ill-formed. This, Taylor thinks, is the way we create our values while creating ourselves.

Other writers have expressed similar views. Kant's famous claim in *Foundations of the Metaphysics of Morals* that the law we *give ourselves* does not bind us suggests that the selves we become in this process are not constrained by the laws we promulgate because these selves are (partly) constituted by those very laws, partly created by a fiat that renders more articulate and definite something hitherto underdone or unformed. Mill describes the outcome of a moral crisis in language that, in another writer, would conjure up extravagant metaphysical theses:

> But it is obvious that "I" am both parties in the contest; the conflict is between me and myself; between (for instance) me desiring a

pleasure, and me dreading self-reproach. What causes Me, or, if you please, my Will, to be identified with one side rather than with the other, is that one of the Me's represents a more permanent state of my feelings than the other does. After the temptation has been yielded to, the desiring "I" will come to an end, but the conscience-stricken "I" may endure to the end of life. (Mill 1867, p. 452)

Nozick finds still another analogy for these cumulative moments of self-definition: the measurement or observation in quantum mechanics that "'collapses the wave packet', reducing the superposition [of different possible states] to a particular state. . . ." (Nozick 1981, p. 298) This may be a seductive analogy to many, but it is of dubious value. For one thing, the collapse of the wave packet as described in quantum mechanics is itself notoriously hard to comprehend, so we run the risk of "explaining" one mystery in terms of a darker one. (Philosophers sometimes enjoy committing this sin in the very act of accusation: this is the fallacy of *obscurum per obscurius*.) For another thing, it invites being taken too seriously, as a speculation about the ultimate microphysics of human choice, although Nozick himself is careful to forestall this reading.[23]

This vision of self-formation represents the gradual development of self to be importantly unlike other processes of material transformation that might seem to be appropriate metaphors to those hylephobes[24] with lazy imaginations: crystal formation, erosion, ripening, the formation of scar tissue. Self-formation, unlike these, is informationally sensitive, amenable to indefinitely many levels of meta-level criticism, and "creative" in a way that art is: the forms that emerge contribute to the constitution of the canons by which they are judged.

But the position, for all its persuasiveness, seems just as vulnerable as ever to a version of Edwards' skeptical challenge: if I happen to have defined myself so as to be able to listen to the voice of reason (on occasion) that is just my good luck, and if another person is unlucky enough to start life with a character tainted by ancestral shortcomings, his misdeeds are similarly only a product of his bad luck. Neither of us was responsible for being who we were the day we were born, and neither of us is, or could be, responsible for anything we subsequently do, so long as our characters today are deterministic outgrowths, how-

---

23. "The purpose of this comparison is not to derive free will from quantum mechanics or to use physical theory to prove free will exists, or even to say that nondeterminism at the quantum level leaves room for free will. Rather, we wish to see whether quantum theory provides an analogue. . . ." (p. 298) See also his discussion of the self as "an artifact of self-synthesis," pp. 105–114.

24. *Hylephobia* is my term for the fear of materialism. I discuss humanistic hylephobia in Dennett 1978b, p. 252.

ever constructive or creative, of our characters yesterday and the day before.

Is it "just luck" that some of us were born with enough artistic talent, in effect, to have developed "good" characters while some of us have turned out less well? The concept of luck, and its role in arguments about free will and responsibility, has received surprisingly little attention from philosophers.[25]

3. Trying Our Luck

And how many there are who may
have led a long blameless life,
who are only *fortunate* in having
escaped so many temptations.
—Kant, *Metaphysical Elements of Ethics*

Luck is a curious concept. When we are told that something that happened was just luck, we should ask ourselves: luck as opposed to what? We know it would be superstitious to believe that "there actually is such a thing as luck"—something a rabbit's foot might or might not bring—but we nevertheless think there is an unsuperstitious and unmisleading way of characterizing events and properties as *merely* lucky. The contrast can be brought out with a thought experiment.

Suppose the United States and Russia were to agree that henceforth they would settle all disagreements and conflicts by tossing a coin in Geneva. Each country was to designate a contestant for the great international toss-up. Who should represent us? I expect someone would hit upon the idea, both democratic and grandiose, of a national coin-tossing tournament, engaging every man, woman and child in a systematic elimination. The winner, of course, would be the ideal representative to send to Geneva: America's luckiest citizen, someone who had just won twenty-eight consecutive coin tosses without a single loss! Surely that person would stand a much better chance of winning in Geneva than some citizen just chosen at random? If there were such a thing as luck— that is, if luck were a projectible property of people or things—then this imagined tournament would be a fine luck distiller or amplifier. But of course (unless we are very much mistaken) luck isn't like that; luck is *mere* luck, not a genuine, projectible endowment.

The winner of the imagined tournament would be lucky indeed (in

---

25. Nagel (1979) and Williams (1981) have drawn philosophers' attention to the curious role of luck in questions of moral responsibility, but both take the concept of luck itself more or less for granted.

the "safe," unsuperstitious sense). "I guess I was just lucky," the winner ought to say, but not: "I guess I am just a lucky person." For there is really no such thing (we think) as being lucky in general, being reliably lucky; there is only being lucky on particular occasions. But the winner would probably find it very difficult not to feel chosen or special or in some other way magically singled out for favor. The lucky survivors of disasters—shipwrecks and mining accidents—typically cannot forego drawing extravagant conclusions from the fact they *they* survived while others perished. The winner of our tournament, then, would be strongly tempted to believe that luck was something real, a force in nature that was running his way.

Someone might even feel *responsible* for winning the tournament—as if he had actually done something to deserve all the attention. Suppose, just to heighten the illusion, that the winner was unaware of the existence of the tournament. So far as he knew, he had simply started calling coin tosses a few weeks ago and had had an almost unbelievable string of wins—twenty-eight in a row without a loss. He would no doubt either begin to wonder about the fairness of the coins used or become devoutly superstitious.[26] Of course those of us in the know would not be tempted by that line of thought; we would know that even if there is no such thing as luck, such a tournament is guaranteed to produce a winner (some winner or other) just so long as it takes place.

Now is there an illusion of personal responsibility in those of us who take ourselves to be the captains of our destiny analogous to the illusion of responsibility or prowess engendered in our tournament winner? Surely anyone who, winning such a tournament, takes credit for it, or anticipates future success on the basis of past experience, is simply mak-

---

26. This thought experiment is inspired by one of the most elegant and insidious of the classic con games; it probably already has a name, but not knowing it, I call it the touting pyramid. You obtain a mailing list of serious gamblers, divide it in half, and send one half the prediction that team A will win the championship next week, and the other half the prediction that team A will lose. A week later half your mailing list has received a true prediction from you—free of charge. Discard the other half of the mailing list; divide the remainder in half again, and send them a second brace of complementary predictions; this cuts down your pool of suckers, but now they have two "proofs" of your clairvoyance. After a few more "successes," you announce that the free trial period is over; for your next prediction they will have to pay. And as Skinner would tell you, the beauty of the scheme is that one does not have to stick to such a rapidly diminishing group. Some people are suckers for "random schedules of reinforcement." Try offering a "discount" on the next prediction to those for whom your success rate is slightly tarnished—say, one out of four predictions was false—and you will find many takers.

ing a mistake. Might we similarly be just wrong in thinking we—some of us, in any case—are genuinely responsible for our acts?[27]

There is a sense in which we are all, like the winner of the coin-tossing tournament, extraordinarily lucky to be here in the winner's circle. Not a single one of *our* ancestors suffered the misfortune of dying childless! When one thinks of all the millions of generations of predecessors knocked out in the early rounds of the natural selection tournament, it must seem that the odds against *our* existing are astronomical.[28]

The big difference between us and the winner of the coin-tossing tournament is that while we cannot take personal credit for the success of our ancestors, our genes can. The contest our genes have won was a test of genuine prowess. You have to be good at something (in fact, good at things in general) to get through to the round that is playing today. The person who wins a selective tournament in a game of skill *is* likely to do much better than the randomly chosen person in subsequent contests; skill, unlike luck, is projectible. And since the skills of self-control and deliberation have been put to a fairly severe test over the eons, there is a real basis in fact for our having high expectations about the deliberative skill, and more generally the capacity for self-control, of our fellow human beings. If you weren't very well equipped in that department, you wouldn't have made it to this round of the tournament. Of course some unfortunates, though born of skilled self-controllers, are defective, through no fault of their own. We do not consider them responsible. They are excused. But we do expect a lot from the rest of us, and for good reason. We are not just lucky; we are skilled.

The relation between skill and luck is complex. It is a maxim of athletes that the luck tends to average out, and that the best players are those who are well equipped to capitalize on lucky opportunities. After all, if you are not even capable of throwing a basketball seventy feet, you cannot ever avail yourself of the occasional desperate opportunities to heave a lucky, game-winning toss. Moreover, the better you are, the less luck you need, and the less your successes count as merely lucky. Why? Because the better you are, the more control you have over your performance.[29] When the star basketball player shoots ten consecutive baskets

27. Compare the discussion of this issue in Hospers 1961 and Hook 1961b.

28. And speaking of astronomy, think how fortunate we are that *our* planet just happened to get formed out of heavy elements (which are a great rarity in the universe)—so we have something solid and comfortable to stand on! Whether or not we are lucky to be here, from the fact that we *are* here we may be able to deduce surprising facts about the "laws of nature." See Gale 1981.

29. Alex Bird (a famous British "punter" who made a fortune betting on horse races) once said, "I've never thought of myself as lucky. I'm a coward. That's why

in a game, we don't call it luck; if I were to get ten in a row, we would certainly call it luck.[30] The star is not so good as to be beyond the reach of luck altogether, but for him, the threshold for what counts as luck is considerably higher. We expect more of him. Similarly then, if someone is skilled at self-improvement, such success in this line as he may achieve is not attributable to his luck on each occasion, but to his skill. We expect more of him. *Noblesse oblige,* as the saying goes.

But still, one may be tempted to say, there are two sorts of differences in an agent's circumstances that are merely matters of luck: how much initial strength or talent or character one is lucky enough to be born with, and how many lucky breaks one encounters during one's period of self-creation. One way or the other, it seems, these factors must conspire to defeat any self-styled agent's claim of personal responsibility for his own character. Let us look at these one at a time.

Suppose—what certainly seems to be true—that people are born with noticeably different cognitive endowments and propensities to develop character traits; some people have long lines of brilliant (or hot-blooded, or well-muscled) ancestors, for instance, and seem to have initial endowments quite distinct from those of their contemporaries. Is this "hideously unfair"—to use a phrase of Williams (1981, p. 228)—or is this bound to lead to something hideously unfair? Not necessarily.

Imagine a footrace in which the starting line was staggered: those with birthdays in January start a yard ahead of those born in February, and eleven yards ahead of those born in December. Surely no one can help being born in one month rather than another. Isn't this manifestly unfair? Yes, if the race is a hundred yard dash. No, if it's a marathon. In a marathon such a relatively small initial advantage would count for nothing, since one can reliably expect other fortuitous breaks to have even greater effects. In fact, in a large marathon the best runners are typically seeded and given a considerable head start, but I have never heard anyone complain that this is unfair. A good runner who starts at the back of the pack, if he is really good enough to deserve winning, will probably have plenty of opportunity to overcome the initial disadvantage. Some may doubt that this is fair, in spite of its current acceptance. They must agree, however, that the arbitrary birthday system just described is fairer. Is it fair enough not to be worth worrying about? Of course. After all, luck averages out in the long run.

I can't be a gambler. But I work very hard. The harder I work, the luckier I get!" (*Sunday Observer,* London: April 24, 1983)

30. See Wimsatt 1980 on the relationship between skill, chance, and tolerance for error.

Do we have any reason, however, to believe that the process of moral development or acquisition of agenthood is more like a marathon than a sprint? Yes, we have such evidence in abundance. For one thing, moral development is not a race at all, with a single winner and everyone else ranked behind, but a process that apparently brings people sooner or later to a sort of plateau of development—not unlike the process of learning your native language, for instance. Some people reach the plateau swiftly and easily, while others need compensatory effort to overcome initial disadvantages in one way or another.[31]

But everyone comes out more or less in the same league. When people are deemed "good enough" their moral education is over, and except for those who are singled out as defective—retarded or psychopathic, for instance—the citizenry is held to be composed of individuals of roughly equivalent talents, insofar as the demands of such citizenship are concerned. Both initial differences and variations in subsequent luck are commonly held to average out. Is this, the common wisdom, a big mistake? We can address the question by trying to envisage better policies, again in the simpler domain of sports.

Imagine trying to change the rules of basketball in the following way: if the referees decide that a particular basket was just a lucky shot, they disallow the points, and if they notice that bad luck is dogging one of the teams, they give that team compensatory privileges. A perfectly pointless effort at reform, of course, which would not appeal to anybody's sense of fairness. In sports we accept luck, and are content to plan and strive while making due allowance for luck—which is, after all, the same for everyone; no one actually *has more luck* than anyone else, even though some *have been* lucky enough to start off with more talent. But that is fair too, we think. We don't suppose that the only fair contest is between perfectly matched opponents; the strength of one may defeat the finesse of the other, or vice versa. Roughly comparable overall prowess is all we demand. And if on some particular occasion the particular strengths of one count for more than the particular strengths of the other, that is "too bad" for the latter, but not at all unfair.

When the talented succeed, it is not because they are lucky, but because they are talented.[32] Ah, but they are lucky to be talented in the

31. See Sher 1979. See also Hampshire 1959, p. 186: "Human beings can identify their own limitations, as one feature of the world among others to be self-consciously accepted, or, if possible, deliberately changed, rather than simply responded to."

32. Suppose our coin-toss tournament winner receives a million dollar prize. Now he can say that he not only was lucky to win, but is lucky to have a million dollars (he didn't earn it). But then henceforth he isn't lucky; he's rich. If you're

first place! Not always. Some talented performers are made, not born; some have diligently trained for hours every day for years on end to achieve their prowess, and in the process have denied themselves many delights and opportunities that we less skilled performers have enjoyed. Ah, but they were lucky to be born with the gumption and drive required to develop their skill in training themselves. Not always. Some aren't born with that temperament, but learn it from a wise teacher or coach. Ah, but then they are lucky to have the intelligence required to comprehend the lesson of that good coach. (After all, not all the players are capable of being inspired by him.) And, of course, they are lucky to have been born in the town where that fine coach works his miracles. Moreover, they are lucky not to have been born blind, and lucky not to have been struck by lightning on their way to school. In fact, as already remarked, they are astronomically lucky to have ever been born at all!

As this petulant little dialogue exhibits, there is a tendency to treat "lucky" and "unlucky" as complementary and exhaustive, leaving no room for skill at all. On this view nothing in principle could count as skill or the result of skill. This is a mistake. Once one recognizes that there is elbow room for skill in between lucky success and unlucky failure, the troubling argument that seems to show that no one could ever be responsible evaporates. Luck averages out and skill will tell in the end. Once in a while, to be sure, luck plays too large a role, but anyone who thinks that all losses are explicable *in the end* as due to bad luck, and all victories as due to good luck, simply misuses the concept of luck.

This is clear enough in the domain of sports I have used for my examples. What happens when we shift the topic of discussion from the easy realm of sports to the more serious realm of moral decisions? Will the intuitions about luck that seemed so secure just now travel well? The discussion of luck and prowess in sports was just a warm-up, not the main event. So with the warm-up behind us, what should we say about that poor chap, B, in Edwards' example, who was described as not having had the good fortune to be born with the courage and strength of character required to endure the cure?

It seems compelling to some—for instance, Nagel (in "Moral Luck," 1979)—that we should always excuse people like B, since it was just B's bad luck that explains B's failure to endure the cure. Sometimes, no doubt, but why always? We don't know enough about B to know whether to attribute his problem to hard luck or B's own failure on a task

---

rich, you don't need to be lucky! If luck were something like an endowment that someone could have, it would be truly unfair to give a million dollars to the winner, who had already been proved to have plenty of advantage in this world: all that luck.

we had every reason to expect him to succeed at. Was he like the star player who "blew" the easy shot and will have to live it down for years, or like the second-stringer who missed on the desperate gamble but who walks into the locker room a near hero just for trying so hard? Why shouldn't the distinctions we find so comfortable in the sports arena be applied in the larger world as well?

Because—comes the answer—when we say "we have every reason to expect" an agent to do well on something, we are actually not speaking correctly. If determinism is true, it is only because we never have all the information that is in principle relevant to such questions that we ever expect anyone to do other than what they end up doing. If we knew the fine-grained details we would always be able to see that the person "couldn't help" doing what he did in fact do on that occasion. That this line of argument is a mistake will be shown in chapters five and six. (To some, this is the very heart of the free will issue, and they may have been waiting with growing impatience for me to address it. I hope to show them that it cannot be properly addressed without these preliminaries.)

We are all the "gifted" ones. That is, I take it that all my readers are members, like me, in the community of reason-givers and considerers. We are all gifted with the powers of deliberation, or we wouldn't be here (in the adult world of books and readers). Some of our friends and relations aren't here; some of them are infants, and some of them are, through no fault of their own, infantile or otherwise incapable of reason. A few of them *may* be culpable for their unfortunate state—for instance, a few may have quite knowingly ruined their brains with drugs or alcohol, but now that they are incapacitated, they are excused from further responsibility. We take steps to keep them out of circumstances where they might do serious mischief to themselves or to others.

We gifted ones are good at deliberation and self-control, and so we expect a good deal of each other in these regards. On the basis of those expectations we place gifted ones in positions of trust and responsibility, and then we *count on them* to do the right thing. And since they are gifted, when they do the right thing we don't call it luck. The better they are, in fact, the less of a role there is for sheer luck in the outcome of their deliberations.

We are not totally responsible for being responsible, of course, any more than the star player is totally beyond luck. After all, a mugger might leap out of an alley and brain me tomorrow. I would then be unlucky enough to lose my status as a responsible citizen through no fault or error of my own. But if that would be most unlucky, my not having met with a mugger to date is not just a matter of luck; I am quite good at staying out of trouble. The fact is that all of us responsible agents are well enough designed so that we tend to avoid circumstances where the odds are high that we will lose our prowess and hence our status as responsible citizens. We take care of ourselves. We are systematic status-preservers, but of course sometimes we fall on hard times. Sometimes the unexpectable and unavoidable happens. Then we are unlucky.

We can imagine (just barely, I think) a being who went through a lifetime of "correct" decision making, but always just by sheer luck, never thanks to skill. At every turn, this being just happened to turn the right way, away from the gallows, away from calumny and disgrace. One unlucky misstep, and boom—condemned to a lifetime of disgrace. But that is not the way we are.

"There but for the grace of God go I." (John Bradford (1510?–1555) A very curious sentiment. It is often repeated in our own times with an even more curious meaning: indeed I could be so unlucky; I may yet suffer some such misfortune. But it would take an extraordinarily unlikely conspiracy of accidents (see chapter six) to turn *me* into (say) a murderer—while quite a likely, normal, everyday turn of events could make all the difference to a tough young hoodlum who has so far stayed out of serious trouble only by the skin of his teeth. The day someone happens to make the mistake of insulting him is the day his life of violent crime begins. If the sort of temptation that would turn him into a mur-derer were to flash before my eyes, however, I would almost certainly resist it. If I failed to resist it, I would have no one but myself to blame. I am supposed to be good at resisting such temptations—and in fact most of them are child's play. I'm so good at them, *I don't even notice them as opportunities.* Consider fine chess players, who never even notice the stupid move opportunities. (See Hofstadter 1979, p. 286ff. on "implicit pruning.") It is not just luck that keeps them from making the "patzer" plays.

If the hoodlum is a patzer at life (and he is), this is too bad for him, and it *may* be just his bad luck that he is so bad at decision making. We do make allowances, however. We set the threshold of expectations lower for patzers. For children, for instance. We keep them out of situations in which their juvenile powers of deliberation might lead them into horri-ble, regrettable errors. What counts as luck for them is something that would not count as luck for us adults.

That is all very well—comes the objection—but what of those un-fortunates who look like adults, and wander onto the adult playing field and into difficult circumstances where they make extremely regrettable decisions? If we can identify them, we ought to. And then we ought to treat them like children and excuse them. But if we do that job right, will there be anyone left to blame? Even if some of these folk are willing to blame themselves, will they be right to do so? For that matter, when I blame myself for some lapse that I think I cannot attribute to mere bad luck, why do I give my *self* such a large domain? This, once again, is a question I will address in the last three chapters.

4. *Overview*

What has been accomplished by our examination so far? Almost nothing has been settled; no part of our statue is "finished." We had a partial, sketchy account of our rationality in chapter two, and some of the points left untouched there have received further work in chapters three and four, but there are still some nagging problems about rationality postponed until chapter five. We had a first, rough pass over the topic of control and self-control in chapter three, augmented in chapter four, but in need of further refinement, promised in chapters five and six. This chapter has presented a naturalized vision of the gradual process of self-definition and our emergence as agents, adding details on a different time scale to the evolutionary account given in chapter two. We have seen (but in something of a blur) the looming presence of randomness and luck in several different areas, and further work must be done on those surfaces of the statue in the next two chapters.

The fear that this chapter has focused on is the fear that no naturalistic theory of the self could be given that sufficiently distinguished it from a mere domino in a chain. We do not want to be mere dominoes; we want to be moral agents. Let us review what has been found to be special about naturalistically conceived selves. Only some of the portions of the physical universe have the property of being designed to resist their own dissolution, to wage a local campaign against the inexorable trend of the Second Law of Thermodynamics. And only some of these portions have the further property of being caused to have reliable expectations about what will happen next, and hence to have the capacity to control things, including themselves. And only some of these have the further capacity of significant self-improvement (through learning). And fewer still have the open-ended capacity (requiring a language of self-description) for "radical self-evaluation." These portions of the world are thus loci of self-control, of talent, of decision making. They have projects, interests, and values they create in the course of their own self-evaluation and self-definition. How much less like a domino could a portion of the physical world be?

5

Acting Under the Idea of Freedom

Time does not really exist without
unrest; it does not exist for dumb
animals who are absolutely without
anxiety.
—Kierkegaard

And one of the deepest, one of
the most general functions of
living organisms is to look ahead,
to produce future as Paul Valery
put it.
—François Jacob (1982, p. 66)

1. How Can You Go On Deliberating at a Time Like This?

We all take deliberation seriously, and would hate to learn that we are
deluded to do so. We plan for the future; we lie awake nights gnawing at
the bones of indecision, worrying about what to do and why; we promise
ourselves that we will be more circumspect in the future. If we find
ourselves on a jury, we try especially hard to pay close attention to the
evidence presented, so we can render a responsible verdict. Is all this
worry and work wasted? Is it somehow a sham or delusion? Many people
are afraid that it is, if determinism is true.

Suppose we begin with a God's-eye view of the universe. We imagine the entire fabric of causation from the dawn of creation (on the left)
to the heat death of the universe (on the right) laid out before us along
the time line. And we suppose, with Laplace, that its entire history is
determined. We see that right in the middle, at time *t,* sits Alice, trying
to decide whether or not to go to London "tomorrow." *We* see that there
are no branch points to the future of *t* that would make it the case that it
was still possible at *t* for Alice to go to London the next day. For we
would see that even though she had not yet—at time *t*—decided not to

go, it was already determined that she was going to reach that decision. If *she* thinks, at *t,* that the possibility of her going to London the next day is a genuine possibility, a "live" option her decision will eventually either kill or embrace, she is wrong; it is only her narrow perspective, her limited knowledge, that permits her to think this.

If she could see the world from our vantage point, she would see that there wasn't really any possibility of her going to London tomorrow, that there never had been any such possibility, and that the "possibility" she saw at time *t* was just a figment of her imagination, given free reign to occupy the space left blank by her ignorance. From her perspective, her past looks unitary and fixed, while her future looks "open" and rich with branches of opportunity and possibility; from our imagined perspective her future looks precisely as fixed as her past. In fact from our perspective there is no real *now,* zipping up the spreading future into the thin line of the past.

If determinism were true, wouldn't our imagined perspective be the right way to view the world, the Alice's way be mistaken? The fact that we, like Alice, cannot actually adopt the God's-eye view and see our own futures would not make the view from that inaccessible perspective any less true. It seems that we can conclude that *if* determinism is true, then any belief we ever have about there being more than one possible future for us is false. If determinism is true, then only the actual is possible; whatever did happen was the only thing that could have happened, and whatever will happen will be the sole possibility the future ever held in store for us. But then, since deliberation surely presupposes that there are multiple possibilities to be decided amongst, determinism and deliberation are incompatible.

But what could this supposed incompatibility come to? If we are to do justice to this suspicion we must first clear away some of the jostling crowd of bad ideas that are easily confused with the best version. Then we will be able to see that even the best version is mistaken; there is no incompatibility at all between determinism and deliberation.

If determinism were true, people sometimes say, deliberation would be impossible. But this cannot be right. People deliberate every day. What is actual is possible, but this manifest actuality of deliberation hardly shows that determinism is false. (If it could show this, physics would be a much easier science!)

A second pass: if determinism were true, the deliberation that people engage in wouldn't be *effective* deliberation, wouldn't "make any difference." If we think of making a difference as simply *being efficacious,* this must also be false. (Later in the chapter we will explore in more detail what it might mean to "make a difference.") Even in a perfectly determined world there is plenty of room for a distinction between bouts of deliberation that contribute importantly to the causation of an event deliberated about and bouts of deliberation that are without important issue. The prisoner who spends his days and nights concocting vengeful schemes but dies in his chains has engaged in deliberations whose only effects are, let us say, to deepen the furrows in his brow and to exacerbate his high blood pressure. His cellmate engages in similar deliberations, and acting on them, escapes his cell and puts all his plans into tumultuous effect. If this is what "making a difference" comes to, then some of the deliberation in a deterministic world will make a big difference and some of it will not. There will be cases of premeditated murder, for instance, of which one can truly say: had the premeditation not occurred, the victim would still be alive.

Third pass: however effective such determined deliberation might be in contributing to a causal chain, it wouldn't be *real* deliberation, since its outcome would be just as determined as its inauguration. But why is this the mark of phony, unreal deliberation? (Wouldn't a determined thunderstorm be a real thunderstorm? Wouldn't a determined traffic accident be a real traffic accident?) It begs the question to declare, without support, that determined deliberation is not real deliberation. But—comes the reply—in real deliberation, there is a genuine *opportunity* for the agent, with both branches "open to the agent." The agent's deliberation closes off one of these as it selects the other. If the outcome of the deliberation were itself determined, then it would have been determined "all along"—so there wouldn't have been a real opportunity in the first place, but only an apparent opportunity.

This third pass, finally, presents a worthy challenge. It is clear, familiar, compelling—and utterly fallacious. In this chapter I will show that this line of argument rests on misapprehensions about the nature of deliberation, about what an opportunity is *or could possibly be,* about what it would be to avoid something, and hence about what "unavoidable" must mean (even when it is thinly disguised in its apparently metaphysical and impersonal form as "inevitable"). But before turning to the diagnosis of the mis-steps in the familiar argument, I want to pause to draw attention to how very peculiar and unstable its conclusion is.

Suppose for the moment that a believer in determinism were to accept the conclusion of this argument. She comes to believe, then, that no *real* deliberation is possible, that no *real* opportunities could come her way in the future. But what then ought to be her attitude in the wake of this discovery? Resignation? Apathy? Of course if determinism is true then she is caused to adopt whatever attitude she adopts. It may still be that she is not caused to adopt her attitude in a sphexish way; she may be caused to adopt her attitude by a consideration of the most cogent reasons. In any case, which attitude would be the *right* one to adopt? It is typically supposed that if she is rational, she will be constrained to abandon deliberation because it is a demonstrably futile *modus operandi*.

I can never decide whether this is a tragic or comic vision: the deterministic world unfolds over the eons, eventually producing creatures who gradually grow in rationality and curiosity to the fatal point where they can be caused, inexorably, thanks to their very rationality, to see the futility of their frantic, scheming ways. And so they pass, in a final self-annihilating spasm of ratiocination, into complete stolidity. Perhaps that's what happened to trees! Perhaps in the olden days trees scampered about, preoccupied with their projects, until the terrible day when they saw the light and had to take root and "vegetate"![1]

To suppose that such a verdict of futility must follow on the heels of the confirmation of determinism is to confuse our third pass with our second pass. Our second pass, the claim that determinism implied the causal impotence of deliberation, was seen to be a manifest error—it is in fact the error of confusing determinism with *fatalism*. Fatalism is the rather mystical and superstitious view that at certain checkpoints in our lives, we will necessarily find ourselves in particular circumstances (the circumstances "fate' has decreed) *no matter what the intervening vagaries of our personal trajectories.* (Remember the parents of Oedipus, whose very efforts to elude their prophesied fate created the circumstances that "sealed" it.) It is widely agreed that this sort of fatalism has absolutely nothing to recommend it—aside from its considerable power to create creepy effects in literature. Determinism does not imply fatalism, and there are no reasons from other quarters for thinking fatalism to be true in general.

But there are genuine instances of what we might call *local fatalism,* and it is from an appreciation of these cases that we derive the idea that deliberation might be just so much futile body English. Consider the man who has thrown himself off the Golden Gate Bridge and who thinks to himself, as he plummets, "I wonder if this is really such a good idea." Deliberation has indeed become impotent for this man. We can plot his future destination without bothering to factor in his intervening efforts at problem solving; whatever they are, they will not yield a causal chain that will deflect him from the trajectory we have already plotted for him. But this case is precisely unlike ordinary cases of deliberation in having this feature.

A variety of local fatalism that is less obviously unlike our normal

---

1. According to van Inwagen 1983 (p. 157), if one didn't deliberate, one "would either move about in random jerks or scuttles, or would withdraw into catatonia."

circumstances is found in the well-worn intuition pump, the Invisible Jail. Here is an instance:

> The man who is locked in a room and who does not know it. He may certainly make a choice about staying, despite the fact that he has no choice about staying. (van Inwagen 1983, p. 239)

Why is the Invisible Jail a more popular example than the Golden Gate Bridge? Because it is less obvious that this is not the situation we find ourselves in. These things do happen, on rare occasions. And when they do we can plot the future trajectories of the room's inhabitant without factoring in his deliberation; for whatever it is, it will be impotent, a gear that turns without engaging any other gears. When one learns that one's deliberation is bound to be detached in this way from the critical causal paths, one does indeed discover grounds for despair, apathy, or resignation. But discovering that one is caught in such an eddy of local fatalism must not be confused with discovering that one is living in a deterministic stream.

Here is an instance of yet another variety of local fatalism: the man who is madly and helplessly in love, but who sets out, with paper and pencil, to make a list of his beloved's shortcomings—as an aid to helping him decide whether or not to propose marriage to her. (Charles Darwin attempted this, for one.) We know this fellow is just going through the motions; we already know the outcome of his pathetic effort at deliberation. This is not because the outcome is determined, but because of the way it is determined: a simple, informationally insensitive way. Just as we can ignore the thought processes of the plummeter in calculating his trajectory, so we can ignore the particular content of the thought processes of the lover in calculating what his verdict will be, since there is a compensating mechanism at work that will convert any supposed blemish into a virtue: she's not stupid, she's down-to-earth; she's not selfish, she's spirited. Does she have a face like a Dover sole? Well, you either like Picasso or you don't. Our lover will arrive at a positive verdict no matter what evidence is placed before him.[2] But in this case, too, precisely the feature that warrants the fatalistic interpretation—the deliberator's deafness to the voice of reason (he is, remember, "madly and helplessly" in love)—distinguishes the case from ordinary cases of deliberation.

---

2. The relevant set of counterfactuals we would deem true of him have a common consequent. That is, we suppose that with negligible exceptions, we get true statements when we substitute different propositions for "p" in "If it were drawn to his attention that p, he would (still) decide to propose to Lulu."

The lover's capacity for self-deluded deliberation is an extreme case, of course, and we all succumb to his temptation on occasion—to varying degrees and with varying frequency. This universal pathology, mild or severe, presents itself in a variety of guises that array themselves between the two poles of *self-deception* and *weakness of will* (what Aristotle called *akrasia*). Consider the smoker: to the extent that she devises no end of disingenuous and convoluted arguments to convince herself that all things considered, smoking is a relaxing, mind-focusing, low-risk, stylish, flavorful pastime, her pathology is self-deception; to the extent that she sees through all that sophistry and persuades herself of the manifest stupidity of smoking—and goes right on smoking—her pathology is weakness of will. When there is a strain between inclination and manifest interest of this sort, there seems to be a trade-off between the integrity of operation of the reasoning machinery and the degree to which it engages the gears that control behavior. People have different "driving" styles in different circumstances: sometimes we "ride the clutch" and reason beautifully but ineffectually; sometimes we "lug the engine" and our deliberation degrades, our standards of thought disintegrate under the load of yearning.

This crude metaphor does not do justice to the intricacy and perplexity of the phenomenon, which has received intense philosophical scrutiny (for example, Davidson 1970, de Sousa 1970, A. Rorty 1972, Schiffer 1976). There is scant consensus on its correct analysis beyond the one point of direct concern to us here: although it does seem that no one is immune to this condition, severe (truly disabling) cases—like the affliction of our lover, or, at the other pole, the addict with an urge so overpowering as to put him completely out of control—are recognizably abnormal. We need not fear that the human condition is *beset* with this variety of local fatalism.

We know from cases like these, cases of actual local fatalism, that there are indeed conditions under which deliberation is futile. But we also know that it is our good fortune that these conditions are abnormal in our world. So when we put our second pass, the doctrine of global or universal fatalism, firmly behind us, we must also relinquish the moral that holds only if (or when) fatalism is true. Deliberation *is* (in general) effective in a deterministic but nonfatalistic world. How could you rationally conclude that it was futile to deliberate in a circumstance in which you have every reason to believe that if the outcome of your deliberation is a decision to do *A*, then *A* is what you will do, and if the outcome of your deliberation is a decision to do *B*, then *B* is what you will do, and, moreover, the outcome of your deliberation is more likely than not to be the rational thing to do under the circumstances?

But still there is a feeling that there must be something absurd about soldiering on with one's deliberating after reaching the opinion that that very deliberating is determined, both in its process and in its ultimate product.[3] There is a feeling that anyone who happened to continue deliberating under such circumstances would have to be deluded about *something*. Hence, once the nature of the case was presented to him, he would either have to reveal a sphexish blind spot—an inability or refusal to accept the appalling truth—or have to do the honorable and rational thing: commit intellectual *hara kiri*. But suppose the person went blithely on deliberating, and shrugged off the charge of irrationality with the familiar retort: "If I'm so stupid, how come I'm so successful?" This reply is certainly a tempting one, but it may just be wishful thinking. How could we decide?

Recall the golfer in chapter one who assiduously kept his head down during the follow-through, after the ball had left the club face. One can present quite a compelling argument to the effect that this must be a superstitious and irrational policy, since the trajectory of the ball is already determined before the follow-through commences. But in fact the policy has, on reflection, a sound rationale. We can explain why looking ahead in this way and resisting distractions should tend to ensure that the right, desirable sorts of things happen at the crucial time in the swing. Might there be a similar rationale in defense of the policy of looking ahead in a certain way (and resisting distractions) while deliberation is in full swing?

2. Designing the Perfect Deliberator

Life can only be understood
backwards; but it must be lived
forwards.
—Kierkegaard

---

3. The overstatement of our first pass is often repeated here; what *might* be absurd or irrational if it happened is instead declared flat impossible: "If one does not know what he is going to do, but knows that conditions already exist sufficient for his doing whatever he is going to do, then he cannot deliberate about what to do, even though he may not know what those conditions are." (Taylor 1964) This is obviously false—unless it is saved by interpreting "deliberate" in such a way that nothing could count as irrational or deluded deliberation, in which case it is still false, but not so obviously.

> Yet while it is part of our nature
> to produce a future, the system is
> geared in such a way that our
> predictions have to remain
> dubious. We cannot think of
> ourselves without a following
> instant, but we cannot know what
> this instant will be like.
> —François Jacob (1982, p. 67)

We cannot help acting under the idea of freedom, it seems; we are *stuck* deliberating as if our futures were open. But is there anything to criticize or regret in this irresistible proclivity of ours? We may be able to assess the rationality or wisdom behind our way of deliberating by taking Mother Nature's view of us—or what comes to the same thing: by asking what constraints there are on the design of a finite, physical deliberator. In order to test the hypothesis that determinism is compatible with (good, rational) deliberation, we will assume determinism to be true, and see if anywhere we have to deny it to make sense of our enterprise. If one were to design the perfect deterministic deliberator, then, what features would it have?

As we saw in the previous chapter, it must have the capacity to be caused by current features of its environment to foresee the causal milieu into which it will soon pass. And it must foresee this reliably, swiftly, and accurately. There is a trade-off, however, among these desiderata. If this is to be genuine foresight, and not hindsight, a price must be paid: the device must simplify its information-handling tasks.[4] It must throw away or ignore data it could in principle obtain, for the costs (in time and effort) of carrying along too much information will frustrate real time prediction.[5] And it cannot jettison just any data; if it is to maintain some modicum of reliability of prediction, it must make the "right" simplifications, throw away the "right" data.

The optimum balance of these factors in the trade-off is an idiosyncratic matter that can vary from species to species, depending on their circumstances and talents. Thus the anteater, unlike the insectivorous

---

4. The price is in fact not very great. As Simon (1969, p. 110) notes, in his philosophically rich discussion of these issues: "for a tolerable description of reality only a tiny fraction of all possible interactions needs to be taken into account."

5. "To predict the future of a curve is to carry out a certain operation on its past. The true prediction operator cannot be realized by any constructible apparatus; but there are certain operations which bear it a certain resemblance, and are in fact realizable by apparatus we can build." (Wiener 1948, p. 12)

bird, does not devote its cognitive energies to tracking individual insects, sampling their trajectories, and making a fine-grained prediction of their future locations; it just averages over the ant-infested area, and lets its tongue take up the slack.[6] A philosopher might say that "ant" is a *mass noun* in the anteater's language of thought; some regions have more ant in them than others.[7]

Whatever particular trade-off of these factors is dictated by the circumstances of a species, it will involve making certain distinctions. In each deliberator some line or other will be drawn, marking off those features of its environment that it "considers"

(1) *fixed*—so reliably fixed that it needn't waste any effort checking up on them;

(2) *beneath notice*—so irrelevant to the system's interests that they can be safely ignored whether they are fixed or not; or

(3) *changing (and worth caring about)*.

The changing features must be further distinguished into those changes that are

(3a) *trackable* at least under some conditions—and hence efficiently and usefully predictable under those conditions; or

(3b) *chaotic* or capricious or "random"—unpredictable but relevant and worth caring about. (In this case "unpredictable" means *practically* unpredictable, of course: unpredictable via the resources that can be spared.)[8]

The changing events worth caring about—both those that are sometimes predictable and those that are not—must be specially accommodated. They must not be just averaged over, like the anteater's chaotically swarming ants, since their particular actual trajectories count

6. The example, like many of the ideas in this section, comes from Wimsat 1980, see esp. p. 296.

7. Roughly, mass nouns are contrasted with sortals or count nouns: you ask *how many* chairs in the room, stars in the sky, minutes in an hour; but you ask *how much* sugar in the bowl, water under the bridge, time until lunch. Some words can go either way, depending on context. Quine's (1960) example: Mary had a little lamb, [a little gravy, and some mashed potatoes . . .]. For the finer details and problems, see Cartwright 1970.

8. See the pioneering exploration of these ideas in Wiener 1948, pp. 43ff., on "Newtonian and Bergsonian time." For an example of a built-in assumption about a *fixed* feature, consider the "rigidity assumption" that is apparently hardwired into the operation of our visual system (Ullman 1979). The term "capricious" is due to Richard Lewontin. See Wimsatt 1980, p. 289.

for too much in the system's calculus of well-being. But they cannot always be tracked, and some of them cannot be tracked at all.

This uncertainty must itself be kept track of; the range of different spatiotemporal coordinates the untracked or untrackable things might occupy, for all the predictor knows, must be broken down into a set of "possible" alternatives, and distinguished from the background of excluded coordinates, the "impossible" states. Moreover, to save cognitive effort, this set of alternatives must be partitioned in a relatively coarse-grained way into a manageably small number of different possible *states,* with the intrastate micro-differences averaged over like so many negligibly swarming ants. As Wimsatt observes: "In the context of such models, even an omniscient and omnipotent organism would not be a Laplacean demon. It would neither require nor seek total knowledge of the universe, but only knowledge of those factors affecting fitness." (1980, p. 293)[9] The variety of possibility thus introduced into the conceptual scheme of any well-designed deliberator is a variety of *epistemic possibility,* of course. It distinguishes the states of things that are possible-for-all-the-deliberator-knows-or-cares. But it gives birth to a concept whose epistemic ancestry is typically overlooked: the concept of the *potentialities* of a thing.[10] Dogs *can bark,* but where or when they are going to bark is not practically predictable in most circumstances. For some deliberators, but not all, whether or not a nearby dog barks at time *t* can be as non-negligible as it is indeterminable. As Ryle (1949, pp. 125–135) puts it, what it means to say a dog can bark is that one may not rely on its silence. These same deliberators, to whom barks are so important, may not care much just how a dog barks when it does. When you've heard one bark you've heard them all, as far as they are concerned. So such deliberators will for these purposes partition dogs as systems with a two-state degree of freedom: the barker is either ON or OFF. This simplified conception of dogs—oversimplified for some purposes, of

9. Wimsatt is injudicious in speaking of an "omniscient and omnipotent" organism, for such an infinite being can ignore the constraints that spawn *any* rationales, but one can see what he means: a well-designed finite organism would not find its circumstances improved in the slightest by being granted Laplacean powers. A case in point is the value, indeed the practical necessity, of adopting the intentional stance toward oneself and other agents (Dennett 1981b). Other paths to this point, with important variations, can be found in Simon 1969 and in the discussion of "level-chunking," "sealing off" (Simon's term) and related concepts in Hofstadter 1979.

10. See Hofstadter 1979, and also his discussion of what he calls "the implico-sphere" (the implicit counterfactual sphere) and "axes of slippability" in Hofstadter 1982c.

course, but not for all—permits these deliberators to formulate a potentially solvable problem in control theory: can I drive this barker into its OFF state and keep it there?

So a particular *type* of deliberator-agent—a species, for instance— will always be equipped with a somewhat idiosyncratic way of gathering and partitioning information about its world; it will have its way of "conceiving" the world so it can act effectively in it. Extending somewhat a concept of Sellars', we may call this "conceptual scheme" of a species its *manifest image* (Sellars 1963, see esp. pp. 6–14). In its manifest image some features are standing, background conditions, and some are "possible" states of things in the world. Among these possible states of things, some are simply unpredictable, some are reliably predictable by their various harbingers, some are indirectly controllable by (the effects of) actions of the deliberator, and some—the actions themselves[11]—are directly controllable by the deliberator.

The point of all this prudent information management is to enable the deliberator to make good (reliable, useful) control decisions before it is too late. And these decisions must be based not only on the deliberator's goals (or desires), but also on reliable expectations of several sorts:

(1) what will happen soon no matter what the deliberator does;

(2) what will happen soon *if* the deliberator does A or *unless* the deliberator does B.

If the deliberator has as a particular goal the preservation or protection of x, then x's likely future states and circumstances under various circumstances will figure importantly in its calculations, especially if x is the deliberator itself. So as we saw already for other reasons in the previous chapter, self-prediction is an essential component in the competence of a self-controlling deliberator. A self-controlling deliberator has to have a good idea of what it is getting itself in for. But self-prediction itself breaks down into a variety of categories, and has its limits. There are expectations about:

---

11. It would be closer to the truth to call these the "basic actions" of the deliberator (following Danto 1965), but it should be borne in mind that which set of actions are basic for an agent or deliberator can change as a result of training or other experience. One must be careful to avoid any sort of foundationalism resting on a bed of "basic" actions, for while it is the case that at any time (any instant, really) the distinction can be drawn between what the agent can decide to do "directly" and what the agent can decide to (try to) bring about by doing something *else* "directly," the easily shifting membership of the classes makes them poor foundation stones for a foundationalist theory.

(1) what will happen soon to the deliberator no matter what the deliberator does;

(2) what will happen to the deliberator if the deliberator does *A* or unless the deliberator does *B*; and

(3) what the deliberator will decide to do soon.

Expectations of the first two sorts are no harder—though not particularly easier—to obtain than the parallel expectations about other things. But expectations about what the deliberator will decide to do next are another matter (Ryle 1949, p. 188, Popper 1951, MacKay 1960, Pears 1964). Any attempt to track its own process of deliberation with an eye to making an accurate projection of its trajectory must be self-defeating, threatening an infinite regress of self-monitoring. But that does not mean that no progress at all can be made on narrowing down the likely range of future decisions (Pears 1964). The deliberator can foresee that, barring unforeseen interference, it will decide to follow one of, say, two or five or twelve courses (roughly individuated—ignoring microvariations within courses). Which of these courses will actually emerge as the adopted course remains practically unforeseeable by the deliberator, to whom they must all count as "possibilities."

Thus there must always be two important varieties of events that are unpredictable by the deliberator: events concerning other things in its world that are unpredictable in practice (given whatever constraints on "expenditure" prevail) and events concerning the outcomes of its own deliberations that are beyond its prognosis machinery in a way that no further investment in cognitive machinery could possibly overcome. These are inescapable categories of future events that are epistemically possible or epistemically open so far as the agent is concerned. Our own decisions must be systematically unpredictable by us—even if others can predict them.[12] We necessarily get diminishing returns from any increased expenditure of tracking and calculating in that area of prediction.

So of course the wise moral for any deliberator—or deliberator-designer—to draw is don't even try; it's self-defeating. Just "keep your head down" (like the golfer) and keep on deliberating; it's your best chance of arriving at the decisions you'd like to arrive at. (This is good advice to anyone who wants to reap the benefits of deliberation. But some agents "may not care." If some agent would actually prefer to play

---

12. And what if some other tries to tell me his prediction before I have decided? He must either confound his prediction of me with his own self-unpredictability (what will I tell him, and just when and how?), or (if he attempts to circumvent this problem by "leading his target") frame a prediction whose warrant depends on my believing it when I am told. In either case my uncertainty about my own future is ineliminable. See the discussions in Popper 1951 and MacKay 1960.

Tristram Shandy with his own mental states, spiraling down an infinite regress of self-observations, and letting the world deal him whatever blows it may, that is another matter.)

So the manifest image of any deliberator will include a partitioning of things into some that are to emerge as the results of the deliberator's deliberation—things that are thus "up to" the deliberator—and things, predictable or not, fixed or not, that are not up to the deliberator. It is this *epistemic* openness, this possibility-for-all-one-knows, that provides the elbow room required for deliberation. Even if one knew one's decision was determined, but did not know what decision one was determined to make, one would be in a position in which there would be a sound rationale in favor of the policy of deliberating.

This central feature of the world view or attitude of a deliberator, often noted by philosophers but seldom analyzed, has begun receiving a different sort of theoretical analysis at the hands of workers in Artificial Intelligence. In his interesting article, "A Temporal Logic for Reasoning about Processes and Plans," McDermott (1982) discusses a simple example of a planning problem—presented "in the first person," but intended as an exercise to aid in designing robots that solve such problems. (I mix my own observations with McDermott's in what follows.)

Suppose I want to paint my ceiling and my stepladder. Which should I do first? *That* is up to me. But it is not up to me whether or not to open the paint can before I dip the brush in or whether to use the stepladder when painting the ceiling. Yes, of course, I *could* conceivably dream up some other way of reaching the ceiling, or for that matter, getting the paint out of the can, but the important thing is that I don't. I don't even try to dream up "all possible" ways of solving the problem (or of replacing it with another problem); I take certain constraints as given, as not up to me on this occasion, and get on with the planning.

It is also not up to me whether or not to risk dripping paint on the walls when I paint the ceiling. (Which direction gravity works in is never up to me.) Of course if I were painting a chair, its orientation would be up to me. I should recognize that I may turn the chair upside down before painting it, precisely in order to get a helping hand from gravity in the drip-prevention department. Now I *could* arrange to turn the room upside down before painting it. That is (officially) one possible way of doing it, but not one I would or should ordinarily take seriously or consider at all; far better, for the most part, to ignore it as impossible (as belonging to the category of things that are fixed and not worth thinking about).[13]

13. See Levi 1980, pp. 2–3, on the related concept of *serious possibility* for an agent.

Getting the best scope for the range of what is up to me, getting neither too broad nor too narrow a class of "possibilities" on which to invest some precious deliberating effort, is a critical, and nontrivial problem for any deliberator or deliberator-designer. If on the one hand we are well off if we don't normally think of turning rooms upside down before painting their ceilings, on the other hand without the capacity for some such leaps of imagination, we will be stuck in sphexish ruts. Sartre sees the importance of this, and with his customary cool understatement defines a free agent as "a being who can realize a nihilating rupture with the world and with himself." (Sartre 1956, p 435) "It is on the day that we can conceive of a different state of affairs that a new light falls on our troubles and our suffering and that we *decide* that these are unbearable." (Sartre 1956, p. 439)

A creature with a particularly hidebound and unadventurous policy of imagination management in its manifest image would no doubt never run the risk of encountering, let alone being bothered by, the problem of free will. But we human beings have proven too clever for that. The manifest image of human beings is the everyday world of colored things (not swarms of molecules); our eyes are macroscopes, not microscopes. We also perceive only "middle-sized" rates of change; things that happen faster or slower are imperceptible to our naked eyes and ears. But unlike any other species, we have in addition to our manifest image what Sellars calls the scientific image. With our natural equipment we may not be able to see, or track, electrons, but we understand that while "water" is a mass noun for us, water is also a swarm of countable molecules, whose trajectories are trackable in principle, and sometimes even in practice (with the aid of prosthetic extensions of our senses).

Given our extended purposes and circumstances, it even becomes in our interests, in special circumstances, to abandon the wise economies of our manifest image and reconceive portions of our world at a different, more fine-grained level of description. It is then that we discover the incompleteness of the conceptual scheme of our manifest image, and begin to reconceive it as a limited, biased, defeasible perspective on the world. We have seen that our capacity to engage in real-time deliberation—including the deliberation required to engage in scientific research—depends on our manifest image, but it still seems to be a sort of illusion born of cognitive miserliness.

We come, then, to an apparent dilemma, wavering back and forth between a practical—even, perhaps, optimally practical—way of thinking of the world, and an impractical but still rationally endorsed vision. We have made some progress, however. We have found some reasons supporting our parochial hunch that the way *we* think about our place in the universe is not only the only way *we* can think of it (on a day-to-day basis), but the only way *to* think of it—the only way for a finite, rational deliberator to think, whether or not determinism is true. If you want to deliberate, and deliberate well, it is rational for you to *act as if* the world really does have an open future, with real opportunities.

But isn't that to say that it is rational to *keep yourself under the illusion that* the future is open and contains real opportunities? Not necessarily. I have assumed for the sake of argument that we have been discussing deterministic deliberators in a deterministic world, but I did not assume for the sake of argument that these were deliberators operating in a world with no real opportunities. It may seem as if determinism rules out opportunity, but a closer look at the concept of opportunity may convince us otherwise.

3. *Real Opportunities*

What is an opportunity? Are the opportunities we seem to have merely apparent opportunities if determinism is true? Would real opportunities be possible if determinism were false? What would a real opportunity be? An opportunity is supposed to be a "chance" for an agent to "do something" that will "make a difference." In America you "take your turn"; in England you "have to go." Are these chances we all want to have real *chance* chances, occasions on which determinism is suspended (if it ever is in force), or could there be opportunities in a perfectly determined world containing perfectly determined deliberators (or "deliberators")?

Let us look at such a world, stipulated to be deterministic, to see what sense could be made of opportunities in it. Once again we will take the world of the robot explorer, for then we can know just what we are stipulating in saying that its control system is completely deterministic: we design it to be deterministic, to be highly resistant to micro-level noise and random perturbation. (It has no built-in Geiger counters to propagate random effects; it is designed instead to damp out such effects.) Moreover, the alien, uninhabited planet on which it trundles around can easily be supposed to be entirely uninhabited, and hence uncontaminated by any genuine agents' actions—which might be indeterministic macro-events that could introduce large-scale indeterminism to the environment in which the robot is to operate. (A further reason for looking at the case of the robot: we won't care as much if a robot turns out not to have real opportunities—so we will be slightly less likely to engage in wishful thinking.)

Suppose, then, that our robot, the Mark I Deterministic Deliberator, is well designed for its mission. One way of putting this would be to say that it is designed to make the most of its opportunities. What

are these robot-opportunities? The robot has interests (if somewhat contrived and artificial interests), in the sense developed in chapter two. So
events bearing on those interests can be, and should be, recognized as
having a special interest for the robot. Then it is clear what a robot-
opportunity would be:

> *The robot has a robot-opportunity* whenever it is caused by such spe-
> cial-interest events to "consider," and if it so decides, to plan and
> execute, a timely project designed by it to further its interests in the
> light of those events.

In our everyday world, whether it is deterministic or not, we take
ourselves to have two main ways of denying people opportunities. The
first, and most effective, is brute force: we erect some barrier or restraint
so that the person cannot do something or other *even if he wants to.*
Sometimes this is for a person's own good; in factories where workers
must reach into the maws of huge cutting machines to place articles to be
shaped, they are often required to wear handcuffs of sorts attached to
strong chains that are attached in turn to a lever that is part of the
working machine. As the machine's knives descend, they automatically
raise the lever, and the chains are just short enough so that the worker's
hands are forcibly pulled out of harm's way if he happens not to have
removed them already "of his own free will." So even if he wants to, even
if he decides (for some strange reason) to insert his hands in the machine
at the wrong time, he cannot.

Brute force restraints of this sort overwhelm deliberations and
create islands of local fatalism, in which an agent's deliberations are
virtually guaranteed to be ineffective. Similarly, a prison keeps its prisoners in a state such that their decisions, the fruits of their deliberations,
cannot then or there be executed (except of course for their trivial
decisions—about where in their cells to sit, and so forth).

But suppose a whimsical jailer were to adopt the practice, once a
month, of waiting till late at night when all the prisoners were sound
asleep, and then silently unlocking all the cell doors and opening the
gate. He would be deliberately creating an opportunity, it seems, for
them to escape. That is certainly how the prison's board of governors
would see it as they relieved the jailer of his job. "But," he might protest,
"they didn't *really* have an opportunity to escape, because I always waited
until they were sound asleep before opening the doors. I always concealed from them the information that the so-called opportunity existed." And this is the other way of denying people an opportunity:
keeping them in the dark about it. We might call such an unrecognized
and unimagined opportunity a *bare opportunity.* If I walk by a row of trash

cans, and one of them happens to contain a purse full of diamonds, then I pass up a bare opportunity to become wealthy. It makes no difference that I had no reason to suspect there were any jewels there for the taking, or that my normal behavior has never included checking out trash cans for valuables.

Bare opportunities are in great abundance, but they are not enough; when we say we want opportunities, or chances to improve our lots, we don't want just bare opportunities. We want to detect our opportunities, or be informed of them, in time to act.[14] Thus we rightly object if an "open fellowship competition" is not properly advertised; only those who were enabled to learn of the competition well before its application deadline had any real opportunity to compete for it.

There is an important similarity between the case of the cutting machine, which has been designed to *eliminate* a particular opportunity systematically, and the jailer, who is diabolically systematic in his *presentation* of the opportunity. The factory worker, in the regular course of his duties, often has the desire to put his hands into the machine—in order to insert or remove a workpiece. But there are times, predictable in advance, when *if* he were to have this desire, he would be most unfortunate to act on it. So the machine has been designed to override his desires only in those circumstances when they would be inappropriate. The prisoners, on the other hand, can be assumed to have a practically constant desire to escape, and here the jailer has arranged that the opportunity to escape is made to exist only when it cannot be recognized and thence acted on.

We can imagine "improvements" on both devices. The cutting machine could have a brain monitor that checked the worker's current state of desire; the machine only yanks the chains when it detects a seriously mistimed desire in the worker. Similarly, the jailer could have had a much more secure system for airing out the prison at night if he made the locks controllable by electronic links to the sleeping EEG's and REM's of the prisoners; at the first sign of waking, the locks would close.[15]

---

14. "Looking back to an age and a culture remote from our own, we allow that possibilities of action, based on discriminations then unrecognized, were not genuine possibilities of action for those who lived at that time." (Hampshire 1959, p. 184)

15. This science fiction could quite readily be made into fact. An even stranger real-time anticipator is already in operation at the University of Illinois. I call it the Berkeley machine (Dennett 1982b). A subject sits in front of a computer screen reading text that appears on it. An extraordinarily sophisticated optical device continuously tracks the agent's rapid eye movements or *saccades*. A sac-

What is important about these cases is precisely that they are cases of one agent controlling some facet of the world of another agent to deny him an opportunity by systematically linking conditions so that all the conditions that are necessary for the opportunity to be acted upon (or, one might say, risen to) are never jointly satisfied. But in the absence of devious counteragents of this sort, the environment, in its indifferent way, does not systematically hide opportunities from agents. Nature does not play hide-and-seek; it is, as Einstein said of God, subtle, but not malicious.

So a real opportunity is an occasion where a self-controller "faces"— is informed about—a situation in which the outcome of its subsequent "deliberation" will be a decisive (as we say) factor. In such a situation more than one alternative is "possible" so far as the agent or self-controller is concerned; that is, the critical nexus passes through its deliberation. That is what we mean when we say that the outcome is up to the agent. (Once the robot is far away on its uninhabited planet, and we can no longer intervene, it is on its own. What it does when confronted with problems is up to it.)

I have described the robot as in general rising to its occasions, and making the most of its opportunities. It will do this so long as no malicious robot-predictors start arranging things in phase with the robot's patterns of exploration. But what of those perhaps infrequent occasions when the robot is in the right position to act on some information it has received, but simply fails to? Even if it is highly reliable, it will not be perfect, and when it fails, it will have been determined to fail, because *ex hypothesi* it is always determined. Will it have had an opportunity, a *real* opportunity, in those instances? If one of our fellow human beings were to fail on such an occasion we would be inclined to say he blew it; he had the opportunity all right, and simply failed to capitalize on it. It might be inappropriate for us to speak of each other in these terms, but is it not obvious that our robot, in virtue of its deterministic predicament, is inappropriately described in such terms?

Let us look closely at such a case, a case in which the robot fails to arrive at the correct solution to its problem because it has failed to find the right way of thinking about the problem, or has failed to give the

---

cade is a "ballistic" motion, and its trajectory can be plotted shortly after lift-off, just like a rocket's trajectory. This machine does just that, and in real time the computer calculates where on the page the eye will alight and, quicker than any magician, erases the word that appears there and replaces it! The reader sees no change. The page might be carved in marble for all the reader can tell, but another reader, looking over his shoulder and saccading to a different drummer, sees the page as aflutter with word changes.

right weight to some information it has. The robot is finite (like us) so it cannot follow a policy of considering everything that might be relevant to its interests all the time. And it is deterministic. But as a well-designed, real-time self-controller it makes use of heuristic procedures, and hence is designed to "take chances" by relying on some "random" generation of considerations. The standard way of achieving this design feature in a deterministic system is to equip it with a perfectly deterministic subroutine that generates a virtually patternless sequence of digits on demand. Almost every computer today comes equipped with one of these "random number generators," but the sequence generated by such a device is pseudo-random, not random. It is not the effect of a quantum-indeterministic process and it is not mathematically random in the sense of informational incompressibility (Chaitin 1976).

If we look microscopically at the robot's program on the occasion of its failure to arrive at the correct solution, we see that *if* the pseudo-random number generating program had spewed up a 5 or a 6, the program would then have taken one more round of deliberation-generation and would have found the item in its memory that would have altered its decision in just the right way. But on the actual occasion a 3 was delivered by the pseudo-random number generator—and of course it was determined (alas) that the number generated would be that 3. So the robot never really had a chance!

Well, what do you say? Does that seem right to you? What intuition is pumped in you? Perhaps you are inclined to declare that the robot really never did have an opportunity. Suppose then that we turn a knob on our intuition pump and try a variation or mutation: in the Mark II Random Deliberator the pseudo-random number generating program is replaced, as it easily can be, by a genuine radium randomizer (basically a built-in Geiger counter listening to the decay of a bit of radium) so that even Laplace's infinite predictor could not have known, in advance of the instant, whether or not the robot would rise to the occasion. Would that be fairer to the robot, or better in some way? In any way? Would the robot "really have had a chance" under these altered circumstances?

If your intuitions tell you that this is indeed so, then we have made some fine progress. Not only can we greatly improve the existential predicament of the robot by installing a radium randomizer or other quantum-effect amplifier, but we can pin our own hopes for free will on the discovery of similar, organically based hardware in our brains (Lucas 1970). The Mark II Random Deliberator will not perform to higher standards, of course, either in the long run or in the short run. It will not have any survival advantage over its deterministic cousin, the Mark I Deterministic Deliberator—provided there aren't any malicious Laplace demons in the environment. But, by your lights, it will at least be situated better *metaphysically:* its opportunities will be real opportunities, unlike those of its cousin.

But let us look more closely at the grounding of such intuitions. Why, exactly, would the "chance" be more real in the Geiger-counter-equipped robot than in the robot with the pseudo-random number generating program? The intuition that suggests this is, I submit, an illusion, and its false credentials can be brought out if we consider it in a slightly different context. Compare the following two lotteries for fairness. In Lottery A, after all the tickets are sold, their stubs are placed in a suitable mixer, and after suitable mixing (involving some genuinely—quantum-mechanically—random mixing if you like), the winning ticket is blindly drawn. In Lottery B, this mixing and drawing takes place *before* the tickets are sold, but otherwise the lotteries are conducted the same. Many people think the second lottery is unfair. It is unfair, they think, because the winning ticket is determined before people even buy their tickets. One of those tickets is *already* the winner; the other tickets are so much worthless paper, and selling them to unsuspecting people is a sort of fraud. But in fact, of course, both lotteries are equally fair. Everyone has an equal chance of winning; the timing of the selection of the winner is an utterly inessential feature.

The reason the drawing in a lottery is typically postponed until after the sale of the tickets is to provide the public with firsthand eyewitness evidence that there have been no shenanigans. No sneaky agent with inside knowledge has manipulated the distribution of tickets, because the knowledge of the winning ticket did not (and could not) exist in any agent until after the tickets were sold. (In effect, this practice is designed to show that the lottery is bogeyman-proof.) It is interesting that not all lotteries follow this practice. *Publishers' Clearing House* and *Reader's Digest* mail out millions of envelopes each year that say in bold letters on them "YOU MAY ALREADY HAVE WON"—a million dollars, or some other prize. Surely these expensive campaigns are based on market research that shows that in general people do think lotteries with pre-selected winners are fair so long as they are honestly conducted. But perhaps people go along with these lotteries uncomplainingly because they get their tickets for free. Would many people *buy* a ticket in a lottery in which the winning stub, sealed in a special envelope, was known to be deposited in a bank vault from the outset? I suspect that most ordinary people would be untroubled by such an arrangement, and would consider themselves to have a real opportunity to win. I suspect, that is, that most ordinary people are less superstitious than those philosophers (going back to Democritus and Lucretius) who have convinced themselves that without a continual supply of genuinely random *cruces* to break up the fabric of causation, there cannot be any real opportunities or chances.

If our world is determined, then we have pseudo-random number generators in us, not Geiger counter randomizers. That is to say, if our world is determined, all our lottery tickets were drawn at once, eons ago, put in an envelope for us, and doled out as we needed them through life. "But that isn't fair!" some say, "for some people will have been dealt more winners than others." Indeed, on any particular deal, some people have more high cards than others, but one should remember that the luck averages out. "But if all the drawings take place before we are born, some people are *destined* to get more luck than others!" But that will be true even if the drawings are not held before we are born, but periodically, on demand, throughout our lives. Even in a perfectly random and unbiased drawing, a genuinely undetermined drawing, it is still *determined* that some people will get more winners than others. Remember, even in a perfectly fair, perfectly random, coin-tossing tournament, it is determined that someone (or other) will win. The winner cannot properly claim it was his "destiny" to win, but whatever advantages accrue to winning are his, destiny or not, and what could be fairer than that? Fairness does not consist in everybody winning.

The concept of *opportunity* has been explicated here with reference to the exploits of agents (or self-controllers), because that is the home territory (in some obscure sense I cannot elaborate further) of the concept. But in fact it has a much broader role to play in science. Some philosophers have thought otherwise, and have insulated the free will issue, and its nuclear family of concepts, from these other issues. For example:

> *Opportunity* is a notable example of a concept closely related to *possibility,* but that can have nothing but a wildly metaphorical application outside a personal sphere. (Ayers 1968, p. 9)

But this is not so. Consider, for instance, Dawkins' entirely non-metaphorical use of the concept:

> The distinction that I wish to emphasize is that between germ-line cell devision (reproduction) and somatic or 'dead-end' cell division (growth). A germ-line cell division is one where the genes being duplicated *have a chance* [my emphasis] of being the ancestors of an indefinitely long line of descendants, where the genes are, in fact, true germ-line replicators . . . (Dawkins 1982, p. 255)

This usage cannot be discarded in favor of talk about logical possibility or quantum-mechanical possibility, for instance. Opportunities play a role, as we shall see in chapter six, not only in our conception of the biological world but also in our conception of the lifeless world of physics and chemistry. But the particularly human sort of opportunities, the chances to make informed choices, have been our concern here. And our conclusion is that the question of whether or not any of us has any real opportunities is entirely independent of the question of whether or not determinism is true.

The idea that the opportunities we see for ourselves might be only apparent, might not be real (if determinism is true) is not only metaphysically ill-founded; it is politically retrograde and morally dubious in a way we should acknowledge. If there were no real opportunities, then there might be no real, important difference between the person who is agonizing over whether to accept admission at Harvard, Stanford or Swarthmore, and the person who is *not* agonizing over whether or not to go to work today in the factory. Some may pretend to wonder whether either agent has any *real* opportunities—but with which agent would any sane person trade places? We do not advance the cause of freedom by supposing that the truly important and ultimate question is a largely imponderable question that hinges on abstruse implications of doctrines and discoveries in subatomic physics. The opportunities that matter to people hinge on everyday-sized features of their manifest images, and some people have more opportunities than others.

The variation is not just a matter of position on the socioeconomic scale, of course. Lack of freedom, "having one's hands tied," is not the exclusive province of the poor and disenfranchised. Consider the bank president, to whom the idea of quitting his job (which is killing him with ulcers and hypertension) and becoming a gardener (which he would love) is all but unthinkable: his wife would go gray (or mad) overnight, his children would have to drop out of college, his friends would be appalled and uncomprehending. We who are not tied by a thousand strings of affection and commitment to those acquaintances of his may scoff at his quandary, but which of us could carry off a similarly radical break? There is more than a kernel of truth in Kris Kristofferson's lyric: "Freedom's just another word for nothing left to lose." ("Me and Bobby McGee") Those who are wise (and lucky) anywhere on the socioeconomic spectrum "keep their options open." The freedom of the hobo is a genuine sort of freedom, and a sort the bank president might quite reasonably envy; it is something the hobo has, and the wage slave does not have, even though neither has any economic or political power. This is all common knowledge of course. It is worth bearing in mind when we take ourselves to be asking a gripping question about our place in the scheme of things.

4. "Avoid," "Avoidable," "Inevitable"

I'm an old man,
and I've seen many troubles,
but most of them never happened.
—Mark Twain

The Mark I Deterministic Deliberator teaches us an important lesson about the nature of opportunities, but still—comes the objection—even if this deterministic robot has genuine opportunities, and genuinely rises to them in ways that are (on the whole) wise, its decisions, being determined, are still *inevitable*—and that's not good. If determinism is true, all our acts are inevitable, because they are the inevitable effects of events in the past that are themselves quite beyond revision.

This line of reasoning is as familiar as it is incoherent. It involves an entirely illicit slide from "determined" or "causally necessary" to "inevitable." It is commonly thought that there is nothing illicit in this slide. Thus Ayers (1968, p. 5) sees nothing wrong in speaking of what is "necessary or unavoidable;" Wiggins (1973, pp. 42–43) proposes to "abbreviate" the expression of "causal or historical tensed modality" as *"inevitable* at *t*,*"* thus helping himself to all the connotations of inevitability for the price of an abbreviation; and Chisholm (1961, p. 158) espouses (as one horn of a dilemma) the claim that if acts "have sufficient causal conditions they are not avoidable." We shall see that this last claim, with its air of complete obviousness, is—at best—a harmless tautology, irrelevant to our concerns when we deliberate. It looks dangerous, however, for it apparently implies that

> if determinism is true, then (since all our acts will have sufficient causal conditions) no act of ours is avoidable,

which looks for all the world as if it licenses an inference to the effect that if determinism is true, no agent can do anything about anything. But this is just fatalism, and we must not confuse determinism with fatalism.

It is mildly surprising that in the intense and acute attention that has been paid to the modal logic of necessity and so-called historical inevitability, so little attention has been paid to what the word "inevitable" actually means (Slote 1982). It means *unavoidable* of course, and that suggests that when one speaks of something as inevitable *tout court* one means it is unavoidable *by* someone or other, or maybe, in the default case, unavoidable by anyone or everyone. But if we are to know what it means for something to be unavoidable by anyone, we had better first come to see what it means to say something is (or was) avoidable. And getting clear about that requires knowing what it is to avoid something.

"Avoid" belongs to a family of verbs we use to discuss the goals and outcomes of deliberation: "foresee," "anticipate," "prevent," "avoid," "avert," "bring about," "ensure," "protect," "preserve," "foster," "hinder," "help," "thwart," . . . These are the preeminent verbs of agency, the terms we use to describe the deeds of those movers and shakers who "change the course of history" or "disturb the universe" or "make a difference." We all aspire to this. We want, perhaps more than anything else in life, to "make a difference."

But if we want to change the course of history we are in for a big disappointment. For no one can change the course of history—for reasons that have nothing to do with determinism. At the beginning of the chapter we imagined all of space and time, past, present and future, laid out before us (*"sub specie aeternitatis"* in philosophical parlance: under the aspect of eternity). If the scene we thereby imagine is supposed to be the *actual* course of history through eternity, then—look, and see—the image has no branchings. Only one actual thing can happen[16] whether or not what happens is determined to happen, so the part of our image we label "Future" consists of the events that actually happen—happen to happen—in the fullness of time. The image we should have when we imagine this universe to be nondeterministic ought to be indistinguishable from the image we imagine when we conjure up a deterministic universe throughout time. Today's future is tomorrow's history: the sequence of events that actually happen (this is the "timeless" present tense).

What would it be to change the course of history? From what to what? Would it be to replace one future event with another? The idea is, in this undoctored form, incoherent. It is often said that no one can change the past. This is true enough, but it is seldom added that no one can change the future either. If the past is unchangeable, the future is unavoidable—on anyone's account. The future consists, timelessly, of the sequence of events that will happen, whether determined to happen or not, and it makes no more sense to speak of avoiding those events than it does to speak of avoiding the events that have already happened.

What is it to avoid something? We speak of avoiding *things*—the bee avoids the tree when it swerves around it—but more relevantly to our purposes, we speak of avoiding events, particularly regrettable events: calamities, misfortunes, disasters. With most "-able" words, such as "soluble" or "inflatable" or "fragile," we can satisfy ourselves that something has or had the power or dispositional property in question by

16. Unless we adopt the "many-worlds interpretation" of quantum mechanics proposed by Hugh Everett. See Hofstadter and Dennett 1981, pp. 44–46.

pointing to real cases of the thing—or something like it—dissolving, inflating, or breaking. But we cannot point to any real event that was ever avoided. No event that actually has happened, is happening, or will happen is an event that was, is being, or will be avoided. But if you want examples, here are some calamities that were avoided: the Great London Earthquake of 1981, the Riot and Massacre at Barry Goldwater's Inauguration Parade in 1964, the Great London Earthquake of 1982. "But these imaginary events were never going to happen in the first place!" Of course not, but then no event that ever was really going to happen—no event, determined or not, that ever belonged to the set of future events—could ever be avoided.

We noted in chapter three that one's control of a situation is threatened not by "causal forces" outside one's control, but by *unexpected* causal forces, and by causal forces that, even if expected, are insuperable. It is the latter sort of case that gives us our model—our chilling vision— of *inexorability*. Suppose astronomers discover a huge comet and calculate its trajectory: it will land on North America in exactly one week, and *there's nothing anyone can do about it.* Faced with this horrible vision, we can imagine people casting about frantically for stratagems; they ask themselves over and over, "Is there *nothing* that can be done?" People begin praying for a miracle, and then, on the eve of destruction, another comet appears in just the right place to deflect the doomsday comet from its path, *preventing* the death of millions. Was it a miracle? No, as it turns out; the second comet did not just miraculously materialize. It, too, had been heading on its foreordained route for millions of years; the astronomers had just not noticed it before. But a careful scrutiny of old observatory photos shows that it was out there, exactly on track to save us. So there was never really any emergency at all. Had the astronomers had better data—or had they put the data they already had to better use—they would never have alarmed us.

Did the second comet really *prevent* a catastrophe? Which catastrophe did it prevent? There was never going to be a catastrophe. One might as well say that a variety of astronomical forces combine once a day (or every millisecond) to prevent the awful catastrophe of Mars colliding with Earth. That collision isn't in the cards, and in spite of first appearances, the dreaded comet crash wasn't either. What gives us the appearance of impending catastrophe, staved off at the last minute, is the unreliable *projection* by the astronomers of a certain trajectory into the future. Against the background of that anticipated future (that misanticipated future) we see the events that happen as an instance of prevention.

All of the verbs of "making a difference" involve a tacit comparison between the way the world was *apparently* going to go, and the way it turned out to go.[17] To "change the course of history" is to be the agent whose acts (and before that, whose deliberations) make a *salient* ("pivotal") contribution to the actual trajectory of the world—as judged by contrast with the projected or anticipated (or retrospectively judged) likely trajectory of the world. The use of the concept invokes something like a principle of the inertia of the normal; it relies on the existence of a tacit background of the way things are expected to go "other things being equal," against which an agent's act, being a case of some other thing not being equal, "makes all the difference."

So entrenched are our habits of expectation—our Humean habits of expectation—that it takes major intellectual leaps of scientific imagination to see what needs explaining and what doesn't. It was only when Newton could think to ask what prevented the apple from wandering off into space, or hanging in midair, that the need for a gravitational force was noticed. Only some sorts of events require explanation in Newtonian physics: the accelerations. The rest is just business-as-usual, motion in a straight line. And once the basic forces are in place, we raise the threshold for what requires *further* explanation. We ask what prevents an apparently unsupported stone from falling with gravitational acceleration; we don't ask what prevents it from bursting into flames or turning into a teacup.

Like the concept of an opportunity, the concept of prevention (and its kin) is best explicated by considering its role in the deliberative life of human beings (and other self-controllers), but this does not mean that it has no application outside the narrow compass of human projects. Consider the following familiar fatalistic dialogue:

Why do you bother putting a lock on your door?

To prevent unauthorized people from passing through it, of course.

But if it is already determined that no unauthorized person will ever enter your house, you might just as well leave the door wide open, and if on the other hand it is already determined that some unauthorized person will enter your house, a lock won't (can't, by sheer logic!) prevent him!

We are as wise to turn a deaf ear to this argument as Mother Nature was when she designed and installed all manner of prevention and avoidance devices in organisms. Why bother having antibodies, or eyelids, or thick hide, or heavy fur? One simply cannot make sense of any aspect of the evolved, living world without helping oneself to large amounts of pre-

---

17. A good example of someone *almost* making this point (but overlooking the epistemic twist) is von Wright 1974, pp. 42ff.

vention and avoidance. If determinism showed that no *one* could prevent anything, it could do this only by showing that there is not an ounce of prevention anywhere: *nothing* can prevent anything. The sound of Niagara Falls cannot prevent a nearby bird from hearing an approaching cat's footsteps, and the Earth's gravity cannot prevent the escape into space of the atoms that compose the Earth's atmosphere.

The first, but by no means last, observation to make about this family of concepts is that they are tied somehow to what is normal or expectable—that is, expectable by expecters like us. What is the difference between the Great London Earthquake of 1982 and the Melt-Down at Three Mile Island? Neither event occurred, but the latter event was narrowly *averted*. What is the difference between the Goldwater Inauguration Day Riot and the Conviction of Lee Harvey Oswald? Neither event occurred, but the latter was *prevented* by Jack Ruby's highly successful attempt to disturb the universe. That is to say, Oswald's trial and conviction, like the melt-down at Three Mile Island, was projected, anticipated, expected, planned about, as part of the way things would or might normally go.

Roger Schank (in conversation) notes that our use of the definite article can be a dead giveaway. We don't balk at "He sat down in the restaurant and the waitress brought him a menu," but we do balk at "He sat down in the restaurant and the hunchback asked him for a light." *What* hunchback? (But we don't feel obliged to ask: *what* waitress?) What this gives away is our *commitment* in thought to various merely projected entities—not in the sense in which philosophers speak of "ontological commitment" but in the sense in which basketball coaches speak of getting your opponent to commit himself before you choose your own course.

We view the world, when we are deliberating and planning, always in terms of those features of the world that are going to continue "normally" and those that might change or will change or that we plan to change or hope to change. (This fact is at the heart of the "frame problem" of Artificial Intelligence. See Dennett forthcoming-a.) We categorize some of those projected things as things that will happen *unless* we take certain steps, and others as things that will happen *because* we will take certain steps, and some of them as things that will happen *no matter what steps we take*. We call the latter "inevitable," because nothing *we do* makes any difference to them, and hence it is pointless to deliberate about them.[18]

18. Berlin (1954) does a fine debunking of the pernicious idea of historical inevitability, but he does not get entirely clear on the distinction between *inexor-*

Now that is what "inevitable" means. It does not mean "causally necessary" or "determined," and it is not implied by those terms. One can see the dim recognition of this gap in a curious instability of perspective that often bedevils philosphers' treatments of the issue. In discussing (and typically deploring) the implications of determinism, authors often seem to want to have it both ways. On some occasions they seem to want to include the agent and all his deliberating motions as part of the great fabric of causation envisaged by determinism. But then on other occasions they seem to want to consider that deterministic world minus the hapless agent, to exclude some small—perhaps tiny—part of the agent's history from the determining web (Greenspan 1976).

This dual way of thinking is found in many quarters—aside from philosophy. When scientists think of conducting some experiment on the world, they set themselves apart from that world, imagine themselves hovering to the side, and completely independently reaching into the world to pluck at the fabric of causation. Then they add, more or less parenthetically: we ourselves are really just parts of that fabric, of course. As we saw in chapter three, this radical polarity of perspectives is not required. The two visions can be merged with the realization that for the scientists' probes of nature to be epistemologically potent, they need not be absolutely and metaphysically independent of the causal stream they are examining; they need only to be highly unlinked with features of that causal stream. The demand for the absolute is clearly expressed by Lucas:

> We have to be agents, not just spectators. And the reason is this: we believe that as free agents we can introduce an arbitrary disturbance into the universe and thus destroy any pre-arranged harmony; under the transformations that our arbitrary interventions produce, only real regularities will be preserved, and coincidental and pre-arranged ones will be destroyed. (1970, p. 63)

But the goal of forcing "real regularities" in the world to show themselves can be achieved (as we saw in the discussion of the uses of disorder in chapter three) if our exploratory activities "at will" are neither inadvertently in phase with any regularity, nor tracked by any demon. So long as they hinge on chaotic or pseudo-random processes,

---

able historical forces (like our comet, or a tidal wave), forces that might sweep aside any agent's deliberations and projects in a temporary onslaught of local fatalism, and forces that determine historical events by operating through the deliberations of the agents involved. He seems not to see that he need have no quarrel with the latter supposition, which is consistent with his vigorous dismissal of the pernicious form of historical determinism: historical inevitability.

they will give exploratory leverage to those who use them—not absolute leverage, not leverage always guaranteed to be out of phase with what is being studied, but good enough leverage for human science. For absolute, Cartesian certainty, no doubt, our exploratory activities should not only not be tracked, but should also not be trackable in principle. Hence the appeal—to absolutists—of perfect randomness. (See also Nozick 1981, pp. 310ff and von Wright 1974, p. 39ff.)

When the reliance on such link-breaking strategies is brought together with the studied blindness to one's own causal processes that reason dictates, it takes just the slightest exaggeration to create the illusion of "absolute agenthood." And then the supposed exemption of the agent from the general causal stream creates the opportunity for fatalistic reflections. This in turn invites the false elision of determinism and inevitability. In order to get any of the right (depressing) flavor of inevitability, one must image a moment, however fleeting, when one sees that deliberation is pointless. At that moment one "sees" that one is falling, falling, and watching, horrified; one's deliberative machinery is disengaged, wheels spinning futilely as the relentless, inexorable drama plays itself out. In this imagined scenario one's thought processes are temporarily *and tacitly* detached from nature, permitting the imaginer a relatively stationary viewpoint from which to experience the brute flow of causation—the sort of detachment with which one can contemplate the local fatalism of an impending sneeze or ejaculation.

But all this imagery of local fatalism is misplaced in such a discussion. It is only on those relatively rare occasions of local fatalism that one's deliberative machinery is actually disengaged from the trajectories that matter to us. Typically one's current, up-to-the-last-instant thinking is critical to the end result. As Hobart[19] says, "the past cannot determine the event, except through the present. And no past moment determined it any more truly than does the present moment." (Hobart 1934) The depressing imagery of local fatalism does not belong in the background of anyone's thought about *what it would be like* to be a deterministic thinker in a deterministic world. And to the extent that one's distaste for determinism is colored by such imagery, one is simply failing to think carefully about the matter at hand.

In this chapter we set out to confront the suspicion that, if determinism is true, our manifest image of opportunities seized and tragedies averted is just an illusion. The only illusions we found, however, were those induced by philosophical distraction, inattention to detail, and the

19. "R. E. Hobart" was the pseudonym of Dickinson S. Miller, 1868–1963.

abuse of intuition pumps. The apparent incoherence of the idea of a deterministic deliberator dissolves on closer examination. It looks for all the world as if there could be no real opportunities if determinism were true, but this is also an illusion. And in spite of first appearances, something can be "causally necessitated" but not inevitable. We haven't solved all the problems or answered all the questions about the relation between our manifest image and our scientific image, but we have seen that the traditional grounds for alarm are the products of hasty examination, not deep insight.

6

"Could Have Done Otherwise"

1. Do We Care Whether We Could Have Done Otherwise?

In the midst of all the discord and disagreement among philosophers about free will, there are a few calm islands of near unanimity. As van Inwagen notes:

> Almost all philosophers agree that a necessary condition for holding an agent responsible for an act is believing that the agent *could have* refrained from performing that act. (van Inwagen 1975, p.189)

But if this is so, then whatever else I may have done in the preceding chapters, I have not yet touched the central issue of free will, for I have not yet declared a position on the "could have done otherwise" principle: the principle that holds that one has acted freely (and responsibly) only if one could have done otherwise. It is time, at last, to turn to this central, stable area in the logical geography of the free will problem. First I will show that this widely accepted principle is simply false. Then I will turn to some residual problems about the meaning of "can"—Austin's frog at the bottom of the beer mug (see chapter one, page 19).

The "could have done otherwise" principle has been debated for generations, and the favorite strategy of compatibilists—who must show that free will and determinism are compatible after all—is to maintain that "could have done otherwise" does not mean what it seems at first to mean; the sense of the phrase denied by determinism is irrelevant to the sense required for freedom. It is so obvious that this is what the compatibilists *have* to say that many skeptics view the proffered compatibilist "analyses" of the meaning of "could have done otherwise" as little more than self-deceived special pleading. James (1921, p.149) called this theme "a quagmire of evasion" and Kant (*Critique of Practical Reason*, Abbot translation 1873, p.96) called it a "wretched subterfuge."

Instead of rising to the defense of any of the earlier analyses—many of which are quite defensible so far as I can see—I will go on the offensive. I will argue that *whatever* "could have done otherwise" actually means, it is not what we are interested in when we care about whether some act was freely and responsibly performed. There is, as van Inwagen notes, something of a tradition of simply assuming that the intuitions favoring the "could have done otherwise" principle are secure. But philosophers who do assume this do so in spite of fairly obvious and familiar grounds for doubt.

One of the few philosophers to challenge it is Frankfurt, who has invented a highly productive intuition pump that generates counterexamples in many flavors: cases of overdetermination, where an agent deliberately and knowingly chose to do. something, but where—thanks typically to some hovering bogeyman—if he hadn't so chosen, the bogeyman would have seen to it that he did the thing anyway (Frankfurt 1969, but see also van Inwagen 1978 and 1983, and Fischer 1982). Here is the basic, stripped-down intuition pump (minus the bells and whistles on the variations, which will not concern us—but only because we will not be relying on them):

> Jones hates Smith and decides, in full possession of his faculties, to murder him. Meanwhile Black, the nefarious neurosurgeon (remember him?), who also wants Smith dead, has implanted something in Jones' brain so that *just in case Jones changes his mind* (and chickens out), Black, by pushing his special button, can put Jones back on his murderous track. In the event Black doesn't have to intervene; Jones does the deed all on his own.

In such a case, Frankfurt claims, the person would be responsible for his deed, since he chose it with all due deliberation and wholeheartedness, in spite of the lurking presence of the overdeterminer whose hidden presence makes it the case that Jones couldn't have done otherwise.

I accept Frankfurt's analysis of these cases (that is, I think they can be defended against the objections raised by van Inwagen, Fischer, and others), and think these thought experiments are useful in spite of their invocation of imaginary bogeymen, for they draw attention to the importance, for responsibility, of the actual causal chain of deliberation and choice running through the agent—whatever may be happening elsewhere.

But Frankfurt's strategy seems to me to be insufficiently ambitious. Although *he* takes his counterexamples to show that the "could have done otherwise" principle—which he calls the principle of alternate possibilities—is irremediably false, his counterexamples are rather special and unlikely cases, and they invite the defender of the principle to try for a patch: modify the principle slightly to take care of Frankfurt's troublesome cases. Exotic circumstances do little or nothing to dispel the illusion that in the normal run of things, where such overdetermination is lacking, the regnant principle is indeed that if a person could not have refrained (could not have done otherwise), he would not be held responsible. But in fact, I will argue, it is seldom that we even *seem* to care whether or not a person could have done otherwise. And when we do, it is often because we wish to draw the opposite conclusion about responsibility from the one tradition endorses.

"Here I stand," Luther said. "I can do no other." Luther claimed that he could do no other, that his conscience made it *impossible* for him to recant. He might, of course, have been wrong, or have been deliberately overstating the truth. But even if he was—perhaps especially if he was— his declaration is testimony to the fact that we simply do not exempt someone from blame or praise for an act because we think he could do no other. Whatever Luther was doing, he was not trying to duck responsibility

There are cases where the claim "I can do no other" is an avowal of frailty: suppose what I ought to do is get on the plane and fly to safety, but I stand rooted on the ground and confess I can do no other— because of my irrational and debilitating fear of flying. In such a case I can do no other, I claim, because my rational control faculty is impaired. But in other cases, like Luther's, when I say I cannot do otherwise I mean I cannot because I see so clearly what the situation is and because my rational control faculty is *not* impaired. It is too obvious what to do; reason dictates it; I would have to be mad to do otherwise, and since I happen not to be mad, I cannot do otherwise. (Notice, by the way, that we say it was "up to" Luther whether or not to recant, and we do not feel tempted to rescind that judgment when we learn that he claimed he could do no other. Notice, too, that we often say things like this: "If it were up to me, I know for certain what I would do.")

I hope it is true—and think it very likely is true—that it would be impossible to induce me to torture an innocent person by offering me a thousand dollars. "Ah"—comes the objection—"but what if some evil space pirates were holding the whole world ransom, and promised not to destroy the world if only you would torture an innocent person? Would that be something you would find impossible to do?" Probably not, but so what? That is a vastly different case. If what one is interested in is whether *under the specified circumstances* I could have done otherwise, then the other case mentioned is utterly irrelevant. I claimed it would not be possible to induce me to torture someone *for a thousand dollars*. Those who hold dear the principle of "could have done otherwise" are always insisting that we should look at whether one could have done otherwise in *exactly* the same circumstances. I claim something stronger; I claim that I could not do otherwise even in any roughly similar case. I would *never* agree to torture an innocent person for a thousand dollars. It would make no difference, I claim, what tone of voice the briber used, or whether or not I was tired and hungry, or whether the proposed victim was well illuminated or partially concealed in shadow. I am, I hope, immune to all such offers.

Now why would anyone's intuitions suggest that if I am right, then if and when I ever have occasion to refuse such an offer, my refusal would not count as a responsible act? Perhaps this is what some people think: they think that if I were right when I claimed I could not do otherwise in such cases, I would be some sort of zombie, "programmed" always to refuse thousand-dollar bribes. A genuinely free agent, they think, must be more volatile somehow. If I am to be able to listen to reason, if I am to be flexible in the right way, they think, I mustn't be too dogmatic. Even in the most preposterous cases, then, I must be able to see that "there are two sides to every question." I must be able to pause, and weigh up the pros and cons of this suggested bit of lucrative torture. But the only way I could be constituted so that I can always "see both sides"—no matter how preposterous one side is—is by being constituted so that *in any particular case* "I could have done otherwise."

That would be fallacious reasoning. Seeing both sides of the question does not require that one not be overwhelmingly persuaded, in the end, by one side. The flexibility we want a responsible agent to have is the flexibility to recognize the one-in-a-zillion case in which, thanks to that thousand dollars, not otherwise obtainable, the world can be saved (or whatever). But the general capacity to respond flexibly in such cases does not at all require that one "could have done otherwise" *in the particular case*, but only that under some variations in the circumstances—the variations that matter—one would do otherwise.

It might be useful to compare two cases that seem quite different at first, but belong on a continuum.

1. Suppose I know that if I ever see the full moon, I will probably run amok and murder the first person I see. So I make careful arrangements to have myself locked up in a windowless room on several nights each month. I am thus rendered *unable* to do the awful things I would do otherwise. Moreover, it is thanks to my own responsible efforts that I have become unable to do these things. A fanciful case, no doubt, but consider the next case, which is somewhat more realistic.

11. Suppose I know that if I ever see a voluptuous woman walking unescorted in a deserted place I will probably be overcome by lust and rape her. So I educate myself about the horrors of rape from the woman's point of view, and enliven my sense of the brutality of the crime so dramatically that if I happen to encounter such a woman in such straits, I am *unable* to do the awful thing I would have done otherwise. (What may convince me that I would otherwise have done this thing is that when the

occasion arises I experience a considerable inner tumult; I discover myself shaking the bars of the cage I have built for myself.) Thanks to my earlier responsible efforts, I have become quite immune to this rather more common sort of possession; I have done what had to be done to render certain courses of action *unthinkable* to me. Like Luther, I *now* can do no other.

Suppose—to get back all the way to realism—that our parents and teachers know that if we grow up without a moral education, we will become selfish, untrustworthy and possibly dangerous people. So they arrange to educate us, and thanks to their responsible efforts, our minds recoil from thoughts of larceny, treachery and violence. We find such alternatives unthinkable under most normal circumstances, and moreover have been taught to think ahead for ourselves and to contribute to our own moral development. Doesn't a considerable part of being a responsible person consist in making oneself unable to do the things one would be blamed for doing if one did them? Philosophers have often noted, uneasily, that the difficult moral problem cases, the decisions that "might go either way," are not the only, or even the most frequent, sorts of decisions for which we hold people responsible. They have seldom taken the hint to heart, however, and asked whether the "could have done otherwise" principle was simply wrong.

I grant that we do indeed often ask ourselves whether an agent could have done otherwise—and in particular whether or not we ourselves could have done otherwise—in the wake of some regrettable act. But we never show any interest in trying to answer the question we have presumably just asked! Defenders of the principle suppose that there is a sense of "could have done otherwise" according to which, if determinism is true, no one ever could have done otherwise than he did. Suppose they are right that there is such a sense. Is it the sense we intend when we use the words "could he have done otherwise?" to inaugurate an inquiry into an agent's responsibility for an act he committed? It is not. In pursuing such inquiries we manifestly ignore the sort of investigations that would have to be pursued if we really were interested in the answer to that question, the metaphysicians' question about whether or not the agent was completely determined by the state of the universe at that instant to perform that action.

If our responsibility really did hinge, as this major philosophical tradition insists, on the question of whether we ever could do otherwise than we in fact do *in exactly those circumstances,* we would be faced with a most peculiar problem of ignorance: it would be unlikely in the extreme, given what now seems to be the case in physics, that anyone would ever know whether anyone has ever been responsible. For today's orthodoxy is that indeterminism reigns at the subatomic level of quantum mechanics, so in the absence of any general and accepted argument for universal determinism, it is possible for all we know that our decisions and actions are truly the magnified, macroscopic effects of quantum-level indeterminacies occurring in our brains. But it is also possible, for all we know, that even though indeterminism reigns in our brains at the subatomic quantum mechanical level, our macroscopic decisions and acts are all themselves determined; the quantum effects could just as well be self-canceling, not amplified (as if by organic Geiger counters in the neurons). And it is extremely unlikely, given the complexity of the brain at even the molecular level (a complexity for which the word "astronomical" is a vast understatement), that we could ever develop good evidence that any particular act was such a large-scale effect of a critical subatomic indeterminacy. So if someone's responsibility for an act did hinge on whether, at the moment of decision, that decision was (already) determined by a prior state of the world, then barring a triumphant return of universal determinism in microphysics (which would rule out all responsibility on this view), the odds are very heavy that we will never have *any* reason to believe of any particular act that it was or was not responsible. The critical difference would be utterly inscrutable from every macroscopic vantage point, and practically inscrutable from the most sophisticated microphysical vantage point imaginable.

Some philosophers might take comfort in this conclusion, but I would guess that *only* a philosopher could take comfort in it. To say the very least it is hard to take seriously the idea that something that could matter so much could be so magnificently beyond our ken. (Or look at the point another way: those who claim to know that they have performed acts such that they could have done otherwise in exactly those circumstances must admit that they proclaim this presumably empirical fact without benefit of the slightest shred of evidence, and without the faintest hope of ever obtaining any such evidence.)[1]

Given the sheer impossibility of conducting any meaningful investigation into the question of whether or not an agent could have done otherwise, what can people think they are doing when they ask that question in particular cases? They must take themselves to be asking some other question. They are right; they are asking a much better question. (If a few people have been asking the unanswerable metaphys-

---

1. Raab (1955) claims that the metaphysical question about "the absence of causality" is "untestable," and notes the peculiarity of taking such an unanswerable question seriously. Raab's reason for declaring such questions unanswerable rests on the claim—true, no doubt—that no agent has any privileged access to whether or not his action was caused. All this shows is that such questions ought not to be addressed exclusively to the agent. My point is that *no* investigation could shed any reliable light on this.

ical question, they were deluded into it by philosophy.) The question people are really interested in asking is a better question for two reasons: it is usually empirically answerable, and its answer matters. For not only is the traditional metaphysical question unanswerable; its answer, even if you knew it, would be useless.

What good would it do to know, about a particular agent, that on some occasion (or on every occasion) he could have done otherwise than he did? Or that he could not have done otherwise than he did? Let us take the latter case first. Suppose you knew (because God told you, presumably) that when Jones pulled the trigger and murdered his wife at time *t*, he could *not* have done otherwise. That is, given Jones' microstate at *t* and the complete microstate of Jones' environment (including the gravitational effects of distant stars, and so on) at *t*, no other Jones-trajectory was possible than the trajectory he took. If Jones were ever put back into exactly that state again, in exactly that circumstance, he would pull the trigger again. And if he were put in that state a million times, he would pull the trigger a million times.

Now if you learned this, would you have learned anything about Jones? Would you have learned anything about his character, for instance, or his likely behavior on merely similar occasions? No. Although people are physical objects which, like atoms or ball bearings or bridges, obey the laws of physics, they are not only more complicated than anything else we know in the universe, they are also designed to be so sensitive to the passing show that they never can be in the same microstate twice. One doesn't even have to descend to the atomic level to establish this. People learn, and remember, and get bored, and shift their attention, and change their interests so incessantly, that it is as good as infinitely unlikely that any person is ever in the same (gross) *psychological* or *cognitive* state on two occasions. And this would be true even if we engineered the surrounding environment to be "utterly the same" on different occasions—if only because the second time around the agent would no doubt think something that went unthought the first time, like "Oh my, this all seems so utterly familiar; now what did I do last time?" (see chapter two, page 33)

There is some point in determining how a bridge is caused to react to some very accurately specified circumstances, since those may be circumstances it will actually encounter *in its present state* on a future occasion. But there would be no payoff in understanding to be gained by determining the micro-causation of the behavior of a human being in some particular circumstance, since he will certainly never confront that micro-circumstance again, and even if he did, he would certainly be in a significantly different reactive state at the time.

Learning (from God, again) that a particular agent was *not* thus determined to act would be learning something equally idle, from the point of view of character assessment or planning for the future. As we saw in chapter five, the undetermined agent will be no more flexible, no more versatile, no more sensitive to nuances, no more reformable, than his deterministic cousin.

So if anyone is interested at all in the question of whether or not one could have done otherwise in *exactly* the same circumstances (and internal state), this will have to be a particularly pure metaphysical curiosity— that is to say, a curiosity so pure as to be utterly lacking in any ulterior motive, since the answer could not conceivably make any noticeable difference to the way the world went.[2]

Why, though, does it still seem as if there ought to be a vast difference, somehow visible from the ordinary human vantage point, between a world in which we could not do otherwise and a world in which we could? Why should determinism still seem so appalling? Perhaps we are misled by the God's-eye-view image, "*sub specie aeternitatis*," in which we spy our own life-trajectories in space and time laid out from birth to death in a single, fixed, rigid, unbranching, four-dimensional "space-time worm," pinned to the causal fabric and unable to move. (Causation, in Hume's fine metaphor, is "the cement of the universe" (Mackie 1974), so perhaps we see our entire lives as *cast in concrete*, trapped like a fossil in the unchanging slab of space-time.)

What we would like, it seems, is for someone to show us that we can *move about* in that medium. But this is a confusion; if we feel this yearning it is because we have forgotten that time is one of the dimensions we have spatialized in our image. Scanning from left to right is scanning from past to future, and a vertical slice of our image captures a single moment in time. To have elbow room in that medium—to be able to wiggle and squirm in between the fixed points of birth and death for instance—would not be to have the power to choose in an undetermined way, but to have the power to choose two or more courses *at one time*.

Is that what we want—to have our cake and eat it too? To have chosen *both* to marry and to remain unmarried, *both* to pull the trigger

---

2. Nozick (1981, p. 313) claims that we all want "originative value," but the only conditions under which we would have this are (on his analysis) conditions that apparently demand the metaphysical reading of "could have done otherwise": "We want it to be true that in that very same situation we could have done (significantly) otherwise, so that our actions will have originative value." Once again, is it plausible at all that something we care so much about (if Nozick is right) is something we could never know to be the case? Put another way, if originative value requires this, why would anyone care about having originative value?

and to drop the gun? If that is the variety of free will we want, then whether or not it might be worth wanting, we can be quite confident that it must elude us—unless, perhaps, we adopt Everett's many-worlds interpretation of quantum mechanics, in which case it just might follow that we do lead a zillion lives (though our many alter egos, alas, could never get together and compare notes)!

If we let go of that fantasy and ask what we really, soberly want, we find a more modest hope: while there are indeed times when we would give anything to be able to go back and undo something in the past, we recognize that the past is closed for us, and we would gladly settle for an "open future." But what would an open future be? A future in which our deliberation is effective: a future in which if I decide to do *A* then I will do *A*, and if I decide to do *B* then I will do *B*; a future in which—since only one future is possible—the only possible thing that can happen is the thing I decide in the end to do.

2. What We Care About

If it is unlikely then that it matters whether or not a person could have done otherwise (when we look microscopically closely at the causation involved) what is the other question that we are really interested in when we ask "but could he have done otherwise?"

Once more I am going to use the tactic of first answering a simpler question about simpler entities. Consider a similar question that might arise about our deterministic robot, the Mark 1 Deterministic Deliberator. By hypothesis, it lives its entire life as a deterministic machine on a deterministic planet, so that whatever it does, it could not have done otherwise, if we mean that in the strict and metaphysical sense of those words that philosophers have concentrated on. Suppose then that one fine Martian day it makes a regrettable mistake; it concocts and executes a scheme that destroys something valuable—another robot, perhaps. I am not supposing, for the moment, that it can regret anything,[3] but just that its designers, back on Earth, regret what it has done, and find themselves wondering a wonder that might naturally be expressed: *could it have done otherwise?*

They know it is a deterministic system, of course, so they know better than to ask the metaphysical question. Their question concerns the design of the robot; for in the wake of this regrettable event they may

---

3. Just because, for *this* purpose, I can consider a relatively simple robot. A robot that was self-made in the manner of the self-made selves of chapter four would be capable (I would claim) of regret.

wish to redesign it slightly, to make this *sort* of event less likely in the future.[4] What they want to know, of course, is what information the robot was relying on, what reasoning or planning it did, and whether it did "enough" of the right sort of reasoning or planning. Of course in one sense of "enough" they know the robot did not do enough of the right sort of thing; if it had, it would have done the right thing. But it may be that the robot's design in this case could not really be improved. For it may be that it was making optimal use of optimally designed heuristic procedures—but this time, unluckily, the heuristic chances it took didn't pay off. Put the robot in a *similar* situation in the future, and thanks to no more than the fact that its pseudo-random number generator is in a different state, it will do something different; in fact it will usually do the right thing. It is tempting to add: it *could* have done the right thing on this occasion—meaning by this that it was well enough designed, at that time, to have done the right thing (its "character" is not impugned). Its failure depended on nothing but the fact that something *undesigned* (and unanticipatable) happened to intervene in the process in a way that made an unfortunate difference.

A heuristic program is not guaranteed to yield the "right" or sought-after result. Some heuristic programs are better than others; when one fails, it may be possible to diagnose the failure as assignable to some characteristic weakness in its design. But even the best are not foolproof, and when they fail, as they sometimes must, there may be no reason at all for the failure: as Cole Porter would say, it was just one of those things.

Such failures are not the only cases of failures that will "count" for the designers as cases where the system "could have done otherwise." If they discover that the robot's failure, on this occasion, was due to a "freak" bit of dust that somehow drifted into a place where it could disrupt the system, they may decide that this was such an unlikely event that there is no call to redesign the system to guard against its recurrence.[5] They will note that, in the micro-particular case, their robot could not have done otherwise; moreover, if (by remotest possibility) it ever found itself in *exactly* the same circumstance again, it would fail again.

---

4. "We are scarcely ever interested in the performance of a communication-engineering machine for a single input. To function adequately it must give a satisfactory performance for a whole class of inputs, and this means a statistically satisfactory performance for the class of inputs which it is statistically expected to receive." (Wiener 1948, p. 55)

5. Strictly speaking, the recurrence of an event *of this general type;* there is no need to guard against the recurrence of the particular event (something logically impossible), or against the recurrence of an event of *exactly* the same type (something nomologically impossible).

But the designers will realize that they have no rational interest in doing anything to improve the design of the robot. It failed on the occasion, but its design is nevertheless above reproach. There is a difference between being optimally designed and being infallible. (See chapter seven.)

Consider yet another sort of case. The robot has a ray gun that it fires with 99.9 percent accuracy. That is to say, sometimes, over long distances, it fails to hit the target it was aiming at. Whenever it misses, the engineers want to know something about the miss: was it due to some *systematic* error in the controls, some foible or flaw that will keep coming up, or was it just one of those things—one of those "acts of God" in which, in spite of an irreproachable execution of an optimally designed aiming routine, the thing just narrowly missed? There will always be such cases; the goal is to keep them to a minimum—consistent with cost-effectiveness of course. Beyond a certain point, it isn't worth caring about errors. Quine (1960, pp. 182 and 259) notes that engineers have a concept of more than passing philosophical interest: the concept of "don't-cares"—the cases that one is rational to ignore. When they are satisfied that a particular miss was a don't-care, they may shrug and say: "Well, it could have been a hit."

What concerns the engineers when they encounter misperformance in their robot is whether or not the misperformance is a telling one: does it reveal something about a pattern of systematic weakness, likely to recur, or an inappropriate and inauspicious linking between sorts of circumstances and sorts of reactions? Is this *sort* of thing apt to happen again, or was it due to the coincidental convergence of fundamentally independent factors, highly unlikely to recur? To get evidence about this they ignore the micro-details, which will never be the same again in any case, and just average over them, analyzing the robot into a finite array of *macro*scopically defined states, organized in such a way that there are links between the various degrees of freedom of the system. The question they then ask is this: are the links the right links for the task?[6]

---

6. Shaler Stidham has pointed out to me that in queuing theory, a branch of operations research, there is a method called the common random numbers technique, used on occasion in running simulations of queuing systems to see how well they respond to "random" variation in their operating conditions. In the technique one tests different settings of the design parameters *on the very same sequence of pseudo-random numbers*. This is, in effect, an experimental investigation in "possible worlds," where one test drives slightly different systems in *exactly* the same worlds, and compares their performances. For some purposes this is a provably more sensitive test of relative strengths and weaknesses than the more realistic simulation, in which the different models are test driven on what are "microscopically" different, but "practically" indistinguishable batches of random or pseudo-random numbers. In theoretical work in queuing theory, the assump-

This rationale for ignoring micro-determinism (wherever it may "in principle" exist) and squinting just enough to blur such fine distinctions into probabilistically related states and regions that can be *treated as* homogeneous is clear, secure, and unproblematic in science, particularly in engineering and biology, as we have seen. (See Wiener 1948 and Wimsatt 1980.) That does not mean, of course, that this is also just the right way to think of people, when we are wondering if they have acted responsibly. But there is a lot to be said for it.

Why do we ask "could he have done otherwise?" We ask it because something has happened that we wish to interpret. An act has been performed, and we wish to understand how the act came about, why it came about, and what meaning we should attach to it. That is, we want to know what conclusions to draw from it about the future. Does it tell us anything about the agent's character, for instance? Does it suggest a criticism of the agent that might, if presented properly, lead the agent to improve his ways in some regard? Can we learn from this incident that this is or is not an agent who can be trusted to behave similarly on similar occasions in the future? If one held his character constant, but changed the circumstances in minor—or even major—ways, would he almost always do the same lamentable sort of thing? Was what we have just observed a "fluke," or was it a manifestation of a "robust" trend—a trend that persists, or is constant, over an interestingly wide variety of conditions?[7]

When the agent in question is oneself, this rationale is even more plainly visible. Suppose I find I have done something dreadful. *Who cares* whether, in exactly the circumstances and state of mind I found myself, I could have done something else? I didn't do something else, and it's too late to undo what I did.[8] But when I go to interpret what I did, what do I

---

tion of such matched random worlds is known as the assumption of stochastic coupling. For an introductory account, see Fishman 1973.

7. We are interested in trends and flukes in both directions (praiseworthy and regretted). If we had evidence that Luther was just kidding himself, that his apparently staunch stand was a sort of comic-opera coincidence, our sense of his moral strength would be severely diminished; "He's not so stalwart," we might say, "he could well have done otherwise."

8. I sometimes wonder if part of the subliminal appeal of "radical freedom" or "contra-causal" freedom of choice is this: "I can't change the past (dammit), but I'd feel better about myself if I thought I could *almost* change it, *or*, I'd feel better about myself if I learned that it was a sort of cosmic slip for which I was *not* responsible." It has often been claimed that responsibility and indeterminism are incompatible (for example, Hobart 1934 and Ayer 1954). The argument typically offered is fallacious, as I show in Dennett 1978a, chapter 15. But might it be

learn about myself? Ought I to practice the sort of maneuver I botched, in hopes of making it more reliable, less vulnerable to perturbation, or would that be wasted effort? Would it be a good thing, so far as I can tell, for me to try to adjust my habits of thought in such sorts of cases in the future?

Knowing that I will always be somewhat at the mercy of the considerations that merely happen to occur to me as time rushes on, knowing that I cannot entirely control this process of deliberation, I may take steps to bias the likelihood of certain sorts of considerations routinely "coming to mind" in certain critical situations. For instance, I might try to cultivate the habit of counting to ten in my mind before saying anything at all about Ronald Reagan, having learned that the deliberation time thus gained pays off handsomely in cutting down regrettable outbreaks of intemperate commentary. Or I might decide that no matter how engrossed in conversation I am, I must learn to ask myself how many glasses of wine I have had every time I see someone hovering hospitably near my glass with a bottle. This time I made a fool of myself; if the situation had been quite different, I certainly would have done otherwise; if the situation had been virtually the same, I might have done otherwise and I might not. The main thing is to see to it that I will jolly well do otherwise in similar situations in the future.

That, certainly, is the healthy attitude to take toward the regrettable parts of one's recent past. It is the self-applied version of the engineers' attitude toward the persisting weaknesses in the design of the robot. Of course if I would rather find excuses than improve myself, I may dwell on the fact that I don't *have* to "take" responsibility for my action, since I can always imagine a more fine-grained standpoint from which my predicament looms larger than I do. (If you make yourself really small, you can externalize virtually everything.)

In chapter seven I will say more about the rationale for being generous with one's self-ascriptions of responsibility. But for now I will just draw attention to a familar sort of case in which we hover in the vicinity of asking whether we really could have done otherwise, and then (wisely) back off. One often says, after doing something awful, "I'm terribly sorry; I simply never thought of the consequences; it simply didn't occur to me what harm I was doing!" This looks almost like the beginning of an excuse—"Can I help it what occurs to me and what doesn't?"—but healthy self-controllers shun this path. They *take* responsibility for what might be, very likely is, just an "accident," just one of those things. That

---

that this presumed incompatibility of responsibility and "contra-causal freedom" is, secretly, just what attracts some people to contra-causal freedom?

way, they make themselves less likely to be "accident" victims in the future.

3. The Can of Worms

The chance of the
quantum-theoretician is not the
ethical freedom of the
Augustinian, and Tyche is as
relentless a mistress as
Ananke.—Norbert Wiener (1948,
p 49)

These edifying reflections invite one final skeptical thrust: "You paint a rose picture of self-controllers doing the best they can to improve their characters, but what sense can be made of this *striving*? If determinism is true, then whatever *does* happen is the only thing that *can* happen." As van Inwagen (1975, pp. 49–50) says, "To deny that men have free will is to assert that what a man *does* do and what he *can* do coincide." In a deterministic world what sense could we make of the exhortation to do the best we can? It does seem to us that sometimes people do less well than they are able to do. How can we make sense of this? If determinism is true, and *if* this means that the only thing one can do is what one does in fact do, then without even trying, everyone will always be doing his very best—and also his very worst. Unless there is some room between the actual and the possible, some elbow room in which to maneuver, we can make no sense of exhortation. Not only that: retrospective judgment and assessment are also apparently rendered pointless. Not only will it be true that everyone always does his best, but every thing will be as good as it can be. And as bad. Dr. Pan-gloss, the famous optimist, will be right: it is the best of all possible worlds. But his nemesis, Dr. Pang-loss the pessimist, will sigh and agree: it *is* the best of all possible worlds— and it couldn't be worse![9] As the philosophers' saying goes, "ought" implies "can"—even in domains having nothing whatever to do with free will and moral responsibility.

Even if we are right to abandon allegiance to the "could have done otherwise" principle as a prerequisite of responsible action, there is the residual problem (according to the incompatibilists) that under determinism, we can never do anything but what we in fact do. As Slote observes, "this itself seems a sufficient challenge to deeply entrenched and cherished beliefs to make it worthwhile to see whether the recent

9. The wandering "g" in "Pangloss" was pointed out to me by Hofstadter (who also noted that "elbow room" is *almost* "more wobble" backward).

arguments can be attacked at some point *before* the conclusion that all actions are necessary." (Slote 1982, p. 9). But the challenge is even more unpalatable than Slote claims.

If the incompatibilists were right about us, it would be because they were right about everything: under determinism *nothing* can do anything other than what it in fact does. The conclusion must be that in a deterministic world, since an atom of oxygen that never links up with any hydrogen atoms is determined never to link up with any hydrogen atoms, it is physically *impossible* for it to link up with any hydrogen atoms. In what sense, then, could it be true that it, like any oxygen atom, *can* link up with two hydrogen atoms?

Ayers calls this threatened implication of determinism "actualism"—only the actual is possible. (Ayers 1968, p. 6) Something is surely wrong with actualism, but actualism is so wrong that it is highly unlikely that its falsehood can be parlayed into a *reductio ad absurdum* of determinism. The argument would be disconcertingly short: this oxygen atom has valence 2; therefore it can unite with two hydrogen atoms to form a molecule of water (it *can* right now, whether or not it does); therefore determinism is false. There are impressive arguments from physics that lead to the conclusion that determinism is false—but this isn't one of them.

Hume speaks of "a certain looseness" we want to exist in our world. (*Treatise*, II, III, 2, Selby-Bigge ed., p. 408) This is the looseness that prevents the possible from shrinking tightly around the actual, the looseness presupposed by our use of the word "can." We need this looseness for many things, so we need to know what "can" means, not just for our account of human freedom, and for the social sciences, but for our account of biology, engineering (see chapter three), and in fact any field that relies significantly on statistics and probability theory.

What could the biologist mean, for instance, when speaking of some feature of some species as *better* than some other "possible" feature? If the generally adaptive trend of natural selection is to be coherently described—let alone explained—we must often distinguish a design selected as better (or as *no* better) than other "possible" designs that selection has spurned.[10] Biologists assure us that unicorns are not only not actual; they are impossible—as impossible as mermaids. (It has some-

---

10. See, for instance, Sober's interesting article, "The Evolution of Rationality" (Sober 1981, p. 110), where he speaks of "a selection process in which many possible endowments were simply not represented." Note that the *denial* of adaptationism, just as much as its assertion, presupposes the coherence of assumptions about possibility. (On the risks and benefits of adaptationism, see Dennett 1983b.)

thing to do with the violation of bilaterality required for a single, centered horn, I gather.) But the biologists also assure us that there are many possible species that haven't yet existed, and probably never will—short-legged, fat horses good only for eating, say, or blotchless giraffes. Only a small portion of the possible variations ever appear.

In probability theory, we take it that a coin toss has two possible outcomes: heads or tails.

> When witnessing the toss of a coin, X will normally envisage as possibly true the hypothesis that the coin will land heads up and that it will land tails up. He may also envisage other possibilities—e.g., its landing on its edge. However, if he takes for granted even the crudest folklore of modern physics, he will rule out as impossible the coin's moving upward to outer space in the direction of Alpha Centauri. (Levi 1980, p. 3)

Everywhere one looks, one finds reliance on claims about what things can be in what states, what outcomes are possible, and what is impossible but not *logically* impossible (self-contradictory).

If this elusive sense of "can" has nothing particular to do with *agency*, it nevertheless makes it appearance vividly in that area. In "Ifs and Cans," Austin (1961) offers a famous series of criticisms of the attempt to define "could have done otherwise" as "would have done otherwise if . . ." for various different fillings of the blank. Austin's objections to this strategy have been ably criticized by several philosophers (see especially Chisholm, 1964a). But more important than those objections and criticisms, which have received a great deal of attention from philosophers, is Austin's abrupt, unargued, and all too influential dismissal (in one footnote and one aside) of the most promising approach to the residual, froggy problem.

Austin notes in passing that "There is some plausibility, for example, in the suggestion that 'I can do X' means 'I shall succeed in doing X, if I try,' and 'I could have done X' means 'I should have succeeded in doing X, if I had tried.'" But a famous long footnote dismisses the suggestion:

> Plausibility, but no more. Consider the case where I miss a very short putt and kick myself because I could have holed it. It is not that I should have holed it if I had tried: I did try, and missed. It is not that I should have holed it if conditions had been different: that might of course be so, but I am talking about conditions as they precisely were, and asserting that I could have holed it. There is the rub. Nor does 'I can hole it this time' mean that I shall hole it this time if I try or if anything else: for I may try and miss, and yet not be convinced that I could not have done it; indeed, further experiments

may confirm my belief that I could have done it that time, although I did not.

But if I tried my hardest, say, and missed, surely there *must* have been *something* that caused me to fail, that made me unable to succeed? So that I *could not* have holed it. Well, a modern belief in science, in there being an explanation of everything, may make us assent to this argument. But such a belief is not in line with the traditional beliefs enshrined in the word *can:* according to *them,* a human ability or power or capacity is inherently liable not to produce success, on occasion, and that for no reason (or are bad luck and bad form sometimes reasons?). (p. 166)

But then what should give way, according to Austin—"a modern belief in science" or the "traditional beliefs enshrined in the word *can*"? Austin does not say, and leaves the impasse unresolved. The impasse is an illusion; modern science needs the same "can" that traditional beliefs about human agency need. And what must give is Austin's insistence that he was "talking about conditions as they precisely were." As we have seen, there is never any purchase to be gained by talking about microprecise conditions; when we talk about what someone—or something—*can do* we are always interested in something general.

This point is made well by Honoré (1964), in a seldom-cited critical commentary on Austin's paper. Honoré proposes that we distinguish between two senses of "can": "can" (particular) and "can" (general)—and notes that the particular sense is almost degenerate: it "is almost equivalent to 'will' and has predictive force." (p. 464) In the past tense, particular "can" is only appropriate for describing success: "Thus 'I could see you in the undergrowth' is properly said only when I have succeeded in seeing you."

> Success or failure, on the assumption that an effort has been or will be made, is the factor which governs the use of the notion: if the agent tried and failed, he could not do the action: if he tried and succeeded, he was able to do it. (Honoré 1964, p. 464)

The more useful notion is "can" (general), which in the case of an agent imputes skill or ability, and in the case of an inanimate thing, imputes the sort of potentiality discussed in chapter five (for example, the different states that something can be in). But as we saw then, that sense of "can" is a manifestly *epistemic* notion; that is, it is generated by any self-controlling planner's need to partition the world into those things and their "states" that are all possible-*for-all-it-knows.*

Philosophical tradition distinguishes several varieties of possibility. Among them:

(a) *logical* or "alethic" possibility: the complement of logical impossibility; something is logically possible if it is consistently describable; it is logically possible that there is a unicorn in the garden, but (if the biologists are right) it is not biologically or physically possible.

(b) *physical* or "nomic" possibility: something is physically possible if it does not violate the laws of physics or the laws of nature (*nomos* = law, in Greek). It is physically impossible to travel faster than the speed of light, even though one can describe such a feat without contradicting oneself.

(c) *epistemic* possibility: something is epistemically possible *for Jones* if it is consistent with everything Jones already *knows*. So epistemic possibility is generally viewed as subjective and relative, unlike logical and physical possibility, which are deemed entirely objective.[11]

It is customary in philosophical discussions of free will to distinguish epistemic possibility from its kin, and then dismiss it as of no further interest in that context.[12] Austin's dismissal is one of the briefest. After considering two other senses of "could have," he mentions a third sense,

> in which sense 'I could have done something different' means 'I might, for all anyone could know for certain beforehand, have done something different.' This third kind of 'could have' might, I think, be held to be a vulgarism, 'could' being used incorrectly for 'might': but in any case we shall not be concerned with it here. (Austin 1961, p. 207)

It is a shame that philosophers have not been concerned with it, for it is the key to the resolution of the riddle about "can." The useful notion of "can," the notion that is relied upon not only in personal planning and deliberation, but also in science, is a concept of possibility—and with it, of course, interdefined concepts of impossibility and necessity—that are, contrary to first appearances, fundamentally "epistemic."

As Slote points out in his pioneering article, "Selective Necessity and Free Will" (Slote 1982), the sorts of concepts of necessity and possibility relied upon in these contexts obey different modal principles from the concept of "classical" alethic necessity. In particular, such necessity is not "agglomerative," by which Slote means closed with respect to con-

---

11. See Hacking 1975 for important complications and qualifications.

12. See, for example, van Inwagen's brief paragraph (van Inwagen 1983, pp. 9–10), and Ayers' much more cautious approach, which begins: "Discussions of power and potentiality, especially as they occur in the freewill controversy, are fairly haunted by the notion of epistemic possibility, and the related notions of certainty and uncertainty, predictability and unpredictability. This is not mere confusion . . ." (Ayers 1968, pp. 13ff.)

junction introduction.[13] Slote illustrates the concept with an example of an "accidental" meeting: Jules happens to meet his friend Jim at the bank; he thinks it is a happy accident, as indeed it is. But Jules' being at the bank is not an accident, since he always goes there on Wednesday morning as part of his job; and Jim's being there is also no accident, since he has been sent by his superior. That Jules is at L at time t is no accident; that Jim is at L at time t is no accident. But that Jules is at L at time t *and* Jim is at L at time t—*that* is an accident. (Slote 1982, esp. pp. 15–17)

This is apparently accidentality or coincidentality from-a-limited-point-of-view. We imagine that if we knew much, much more than Jules and Jim together know, we would have been able to predict their convergence at the bank; *to us,* their meeting would have been "no accident." But this is nevertheless just the concept of accidentality we need to describe the "independence" of a thing's powers or abilities from the initial conditions or background conditions in which those powers are exercised. For instance, it is no accident that this particular insect has just the evasive flight pattern it does have (for it was designed by evolution to have that pattern). And it is no accident that the predatory bird that catches that insect has the genes it does (for it too was designed to have those genes). But it is an accident—happy for the bird and its progeny, unhappy for the insect—that a bird with just those genes caught just that evasive insect. And out of thousands of such happy accidents better birds—and better insects—come to be designed. Out of a conspiracy of accidents, by the millions, comes the space of "possibility" within which selection can occur.

The eminent biologist, Jacques Monod, describes the importance for evolution of chance, or what he calls "absolute coincidence" (Monod 1972, p. 112ff.), and illustrates absolute coincidence with an example strikingly like Slote's:

> Suppose that Dr. Brown sets out on an emergency call to a new patient. In the meantime Jones the contractor's man has started making emergency repairs on the roof of a nearby building. As Dr. Brown walks past the building, Jones inadvertently lets go of his hammer, whose (deterministic) trajectory happens to intercept that of the physician, who dies of a fractured skull. We say he was a victim of chance. (p. 114)

---

13. Slote overlooks the possibility that the form of "selective necessity" he describes is in fact disguisedly epistemic. But he offers a variety of observations which lead in that direction. Schotch and Jennings (1980) offer several philosophical reasons for doubting the universal appeal of full aggregation or agglomeration principles in modal logic, but miss the most compelling cases, which Slote presents.

But when Monod comes to define the conditions under which such coincidences can occur, he apparently falls into the actualist trap. Accidents must happen if evolution is to take place, Monod says, and accidents can happen—"Unless of course we go back to Laplace's world, from which chance is excluded by definition and where Dr. Brown has been fated to die under Jones' hammer ever since the beginning of time." (p. 115)

If "Laplace's world" means just a deterministic world, then Monod is wrong. Natural selection does not need "absolute" coincidence. It does not need "essential" randomness or perfect independence; it needs *practical* independence—of the sort exhibited by Brown and Jones, and Jules and Jim, each on his own trajectory but "just happening" to intersect, like the cards being deterministically shuffled in a deck and just happening to fall into sequence. Would evolution occur in a deterministic world, a Laplacean world where mutation was caused by a nonrandom process? Yes, for what evolution requires is an <u>unpatterned</u> generator of raw material, not an <u>uncaused</u> generator of raw material. Quantum-level effects may indeed play a role in the generation of mutations, but such a role is not required by theory.[14]

It is not clear that "genuine" or "objective" randomness of either the quantum-mechanical sort or of the mathematical, informationally incompressible sort is ever required by a process, or detectable by a process. (Chaitin (1976) presents a Gödelian proof that there is no decision procedure for determining whether a series is mathematically random.) Even in mathematics, where the concept of objective randomness can find critical application within proofs, there are cases of what might be called practical indistinguishability.

In number theory, the Fermat-Lagrange Theorem states that every natural number is the sum of four perfect squares:

$$n = x^2 + y^2 + z^2 + w^2$$

The theorem is easy enough to prove, I gather, but finding the values for x, y, z, and w for a given n is a tedious business. There is a straightforward, "brute force" algorithm that will always find the values by simple exhaustive trial and error, but it has the alarming property of requiring, on the average, 2^n steps to terminate. Thus, for a natural number as small as, say, 203, the algorithm could not be expected to find the answer before the heat death of the universe. It is not what the jargon calls a

---

14. Monod's very interesting discussion (see esp. pp. 77–80 and 111–117) is equivocal and conflicted on this point. See also the valuable discussion of this question in Wimsatt 1980, esp. section 3, "Periodic, Almost-Periodic, and Chaotic Behavior in Simple Models of Population Growth and Regulation."

feasible algorithm, even though *in principle* (as a philosopher would note) it always yields the correct answer.

But all is not lost. Rabin and others have developed so-called random algorithms, which rely in extremely counterintuitive ways on randomization. One such algorithm has been discovered by Rabin for finding values for the Fermat-Lagrange theorem. It is not logically guaranteed to find the right answer any faster than the brute force algorithm, but its *expected* termination time (with the right answer) is only $(\log n)^3$ steps, a manageably small number even for large values of n. The probability of a much longer or much shorter termination time drops off so steeply as to be entirely negligible. The formal proof that this is its expected termination time makes essential mention of the invocation of random sequences in the algorithm.

Question: in the actual world of hardware computers, does it make any difference whether the computer uses a genuinely random sequence or a pseudo-random sequence? That is, if one wrote Rabin's program to run on a computer that didn't have a radium randomizer but relied instead on a pseudo-random number generating algorithm, would this cheap shortcut work? Or would attempts to find the values for a particular n run longer than the expected number of steps in virtue of the hidden, humanly undetectable nonrandomness of the sequence? Would the number system, in its hauteur, punish the mathematician for trying to plumb its secrets with mere pseudo-random exploration? As it turns out, experience to date has been that one can indeed get away with pseudo-random sequences. In the actual runs that have been attempted, it has made no difference.[15]

But surely mere practical indistinguishability, even in the limit, is not the Real Thing—real, objective possibility. That is the intuition we must now examine. It is at the heart of the brusque rejection, by philosophers, of epistemic possibility as a building stone in the foundation of free will. So-called "classical" or Newtonian physics is deterministic, but as several physicists have recently noted, many of the most mundane macroscopic phenomena in a Newtonian world would be, *by Newtonian principles,* unpredictable by any being that fell short of being an *infinite* Laplacean demon, for they would require infinite precision of initial observation. That is, errors in observation, however minuscule, would propagate and grow exponentially (Berry 1983 and Ford 1983).

In Newtonian physics, there are stable systems (precious few of them) and unstable or chaotic systems. "For nonchaotic systems, error

---

15. Rabin, personal communication, New York Academy of Sciences meeting, April 1983. See also Rabin 1980 and Jauch 1973 (discussed in Hofstadter 1979, pp. 408–409).

propagates less rapidly and . . . even a coarse-grained past suffices to determine precisely a coarse-grained future." Eclipses, for instance, may be predicted centuries in advance. But "a chaotic orbit is random and incalculable; its information content is both infinite and incompressible." (Ford 1983, p. 7) The trajectory of a pinball (the example is Berry's) after bumping, say, twenty posts (in a few seconds) is unpredictable *in the limit,* far outstripping the limits of accuracy of any imaginable observation devices. Now this result is surely "just epistemic." What could it have to do with free will?

Just this, I think: such chaotic systems are the source of the "practical" (but one might say infinitely practical) independence of things that shuffles the world and makes it a place of continual opportunity. The opportunities provided are not just *our* opportunities, but also those of Mother Nature—and of oxygen atoms which can join forces on occasion with hydrogen atoms. It is not any parochial fact about *our* epistemic limitations that distinguishes the world into stable, predictable systems and unstable, chaotic systems; it is a fact about the world itself—because it is a fact about the world's predictability by any predicting system at all, however powerful. There is no higher perspective (unless we count the perspective of an infinite being) from which the "accidental" collisions of locally predictable trajectories are themselves predictable and hence "no accident" after all.

It is this contrast between the stable and the chaotic that grounds our division of the world into the enduring and salient features of the world, and those features that we *must* treat statistically or probabilistically (in effect, either averaging over them and turning them into a blur, or treating them as equi-possible members of some ensemble of alternatives). And this division of the world is not just our division; it is, for instance, Mother Nature's division as well. Since for all Mother Nature knows (or could know) it is possible that these insects will cross paths (sometime, somewhere) with these insectivorous birds, they had better be designed with some avoidance machinery. This endows them with a certain power (a bit of "can do," as slang has it) that will serve well (in general).

(These all too sketchy remarks about "can" are at best a pointing gesture toward the final, finished surface of this part of my sculpted portrayal of the free agent. This is another area where much more work needs to be done, and some of the work, certainly, is quite beyond me. But if I am even approximately right in this first, rough pass over the region, the work still to be done will at least move the investigation off of stale, overworked surfaces into new spaces.)

Why Do We Want Free Will?

> It was in *this* sphere then, the
> sphere of legal obligations, that the
> moral conceptual world of "guilt,"
> "conscience," "duty," "sacredness
> of duty" had its origin; its
> beginnings were, like the
> beginnings of everything great on
> earth, soaked in blood thoroughly
> and for a long time.
> —Nietzsche, *On The Genealogy of
> Morals*

1. Nihilism Neglected

The varieties of free will we deem worth wanting are those—if there are any—that will secure for us our dignity and responsibility. If, inspired by some philosophical analysis, we develop a yearning for "contra-causal freedom" or the capacity to exhibit "agent causation," for instance, it is because we have been convinced by that analysis rightly or wrongly that just such a metaphysical blessing is a necessary condition for the sort of free will that any responsible, dignified, moral agent must have. If it turns out that there is no such sort of free will, the very idea of responsibility will lose its foundation.

It is interesting that when people hit upon this suggestion, they do not as a rule view it as the prospect of a welcome holiday, a chance to do whatever they like without running the risk of feeling—or being— guilty. One might think that the supposition that responsibility was a baseless concept would be liberating, exhilarating, a breath of fresh air blowing away the gloomy old dogmas of guilt and sin. But strangely enough, it seems that we want to be held responsible. Why?

Perhaps because our dignity is threatened by the prospect that we ourselves might not be responsible agents. But could we be wrong to feel this way? What is this *dignity* that is so special? And why should we care about it? Are we perhaps enchanted by an outmoded world view, a Morality that is no longer defensible in this clear-eyed age of Science? (Skinner 1971)

Are there even darker reasons for our allegiance? How should we interpret the fact that we want to hold *others* responsible? We don't want to let Hitler, or Nixon, or the kid who steals our hubcaps, off the hook. Perhaps we think that if the price we must pay for holding others responsible is holding ourselves responsible, this is a bargain well worth striking. But why do we want so much to hold others responsible? Could it be a streak of sheer vindictiveness or vengefulness in us, rationalized and made presentable in civilized company by a gloss of moral doctrine?

No doubt there are some atavistic and bloodthirsty elements in our current vision of responsibility, dignity, and guilt. In Nietzsche's brilliant Just So Story in *On the Genealogy of Morals,* we are told that the moral concepts of guilt and punishment grew out of prior *legal* concepts of debt and credit, according to which "the creditor could inflict every kind of indignity and torture upon the body of the debtor." (Nietzsche 1887, p. 64) Among the debts our forerunners recognized were the debts of gratitude owed to their own ancestors. And as the sense of indebtedness to these ancestors grew (and of course could not be repaid), these ancestor-creditors became transformed into a creditor God, and the debt to him became an intolerable burden. This sets the stage for Nietzsche's bold speculation: he describes the (no doubt free-floating) rationale behind the unconscious invention of the guilty conscience by the priests of *ressentiment:*

> —suddenly we stand before the paradoxical and horrifying expedient that afforded temporary relief for tormented humanity, that stroke of genius on the part of Christianity: God himself sacrifices himself for the guilt of mankind, God himself makes payment to himself, God as the only being who can redeem man from what has become unredeemable for man himself—the creditor sacrifices himself for his debtor, out of *love* (can one credit that?), out of love for his debtor! (p. 92)

The story is too compelling to be all wrong. But even if Nietzsche's tale—or another one with similar themes—were entirely true, this would not show that there could not also be a vindication of our conceptual scheme—or important parts of it. True conclusions can be born of fallacious reasoning, and many a good idea has arisen out of unconscionable activities.[1]

---

1. Nietzsche himself draws attention to this now familiar point of evolutionary theory: the *raison d'être* of an organ, behavior, or practice can shift under the pressure of circumstances. "The cause of the origin of a thing and its eventual

I think there is an entirely presentable defense of our desire to preserve our "moral conceptual world." The distinction between responsible moral agents and beings with diminished or no responsibility is coherent, real, and important. It is coherent, even if in many instances it is hard to apply; it draws an empirically real line, in that we don't all fall on one side; and, most important, the distinction matters: the use we make of it plays a crucial role in the quality and meaning of our lives.

The argument I will give for this view is, of necessity, an argument to the effect that *it is rational* for us to esteem free will and covet responsibility. No other sort of argument could be a *defense* of those concepts; nevertheless, such an argument must inevitably appear to be question-begging in its appeal to the rational judgment of an audience of fellow agents. Am I not assuming that we—the readers and the author—are just the sorts of free, responsible agents my argument is supposed to support? Moreover, my argument will assume that *something matters*—that some things are for better and some are for worse. (Without that assumption, our assumed rationality would have nothing on which to get a purchase.) Isn't this anti-nihilistic assumption even more obviously question-begging?

Throughout this book I have taken for granted my own rationality as well as yours, and have not put in question the meaningfulness of the enterprise we have been engaged in. The very decision to write a book—a traditional book like this, composed of sentences and not, say, a bound collection of pages smeared with various jams and jellies—may seem to beg the question in favor of free will. If so, then those who have written books and articles denying the reality of free will are in an even more embarrassing position: they are left advising (pretending to advise? seeming to advise?) the reader that advising is pointless.[2] But there are other alternatives, such as silence or suicide, and the suspicion may still be strong in some quarters that we have been averting our eyes from the deepest, most terrifying visions.

Let us examine that suspicion. I have been assuming the meaningfulness of my enterprise. I might, of course, be wrong about that, since my particular enterprise might be so defective as to be meaningless. But the view that *no* enterprise could be meaningful is *nihilism:* according to it, *nothing* matters. Some suspect that if determinism is true, so is nihilism. Anyone harboring that suspicion must find my project precarious at

---

utility, its actual employment and place in a system of purposes, lie worlds apart." (Nietzsche 1887, p. 77)

2. Skinner's attempts (1971) to convince his readers that they were not free, dignified agents have often been claimed to be systematically self-stultifying. For another discussion, see Wolf 1981, esp. p. 399.

best, for I have not yet made any attempt to take nihilism seriously. Beyond acknowledging this neglect, what can I say about nihilism?

I cannot say that it would be a great pity, a crying shame, an instance of "cosmic unfairness" if nihilism turned out to be true. For if nihilism were true, *all* value judgments would be illusory; the brute fact of anyone's sorrow or pain wouldn't mean a thing, and bemoaning our predicament would be as misguided as regretting that the square root of two isn't one and a half. Nihilism might, I suppose, be true; it *might* even follow from determinism, as some suspect (though I see no reason to believe this). Nevertheless, we may assume that nihilism is false. How can I make that complacent (or cavalier) claim? Shouldn't we even stop to consider carefully the prospect that it might be true? Well, if it were true that we ought to take the possibility of nihilism that seriously, then nihilism would be false, for if we *ought* to do *anything* nihilism is false. But then we may as well assume that it is false, since either it is false or, if it isn't, nothing matters and we may do whatever we want. Nihilism is, quite literally, a *negligible* position.

Since there could be nothing better to do, we might just as well affirm our confidence in our starting point. We may assume that something matters, and that we are rational enough so that there can be a point to our attempts to understand the world. I do not see how those assumptions could be coherently criticized—which is not to say that they must be true. But that still leaves slightly less radical possibilities well worth considering. It is one thing to assume that there is better and worse, good and bad, room for hope and regret; it is another thing to assume that our traditional moral concepts are in good order. It could be, for instance, that the concept of personal responsibility enshrined in traditional (Western) morality is subtly incoherent, and that we ought to revise or even jettison that concept and the family of ideas surrounding it: guilt, desert, moral praise, and punishment, to mention the most important. We might, for instance, have to demote ourselves somewhat from our traditionally elevated status as moral agents in order to secure a defensible morality.

2. Diminished Responsibility and the Specter of Creeping Exculpation

We already saw in chapter two that if, in order to be a genuine moral agent, one had to have a perfect Kantian Will, infinitely sensitive to the sweet voice of Reason, there could be no moral agents in our universe. And in chapter four we saw that a completely self-made self, one hundred per cent responsible for its own character, was an impossibility. But the prospect was seen to be good that we finite and imperfect beings are worthy approximations of these imaginary absolutes. We should look for a similar resting place for our concept of moral responsibility.

We want to hold ourselves and others responsible, but we recognize that our intuitions often support the judgment that a particular individual has "diminished responsibility" because of his or her infirmities, or because of particularly dire circumstances during upbringing or at the time of action. We also find it plausible to judge that nonhuman animals, infants, and those who are severely handicapped mentally are not responsible at all. But since we are all more or less imperfect, will there be anyone left to be responsible after we have excused all those with good excuses?

At our best, we behave "responsibly"—that is to say, morally. But how should we treat those cases in which people fall short of the sort of rational well-designedness they exhibit at their best? Are we equally responsible for the good things and the bad things we do? For Kant, there seems to have been an asymmetry: we are only *really* responsible for the right things we do. (For a contemporary version of a similar asymmetry, see Wolf 1980.) This theme first surfaced in Socrates' "paradoxical" claim that no one ever knowingly desires to do evil. It has been a perennial topic of philosophical discussion ever since, but the issue has nevertheless been addressed only obliquely and skittishly. What are we afraid of? Certainly one thing we fear is that no one ever really deserves the punishment society metes out—since all miscreants are *ipso facto* deluded, deranged, or radically ignorant in one way or another.

A task that faces us, then, is drawing and defending a line between exculpating pathology (the sort that is claimed in the notorious "insanity defense") and varieties of falling-short that still leave agents genuinely culpable. We are looking, then, for some elbow room for us sinners in between the saints and the monsters.[3] This is not merely a problem in the law. Our strongest moral opinions hinge on just such issues, and there can be little doubt that our everyday intuitions are deeply conflicted. We heap scorn on Nixon, for instance, and in the same breath marvel at how transparently and grotesquely self-deceived he was. But then is he more properly the victim (poor fellow) of that deception or doubly guilty because he is the perpetrator of (self-)deception in addition to his other crimes? Self-deception (whether or not it is a well-named affliction) is ubiquitous. If it exculpates, does it exculpate us all? Always?

---

3. Slote has drawn to my attention the medieval doctrine that the most saintly and blessed are those unable to sin (*"non posse peccare"*). See, for instance, St. Augustine, *De libero arbitrio* ("On Free Will"); St. Anselm, *De libero arbitrio,* cap. I. col. 489–491; St. Thomas, *De veritate,* q. 23, a. 4.

We may feel the temptation to hold out for some version of Cosmic Responsibility as a metaphysical bulwark against Creeping Exculpation, but once again philosophical absolutism of that sort is almost always forlorn. If we are to be found responsible at all, it will have to be a modest, naturalized, slightly diminished responsibility, for we are no angels. As Williams notes, commenting on the failure of Kant's absolutism, "No human characteristic which is relevant to degrees of moral esteem can escape being an empirical characteristic, subject to empirical conditions, psychological history and individual variation." (Williams 1973, p. 228)

When are people responsible for the bad things they do? To answer this question, we must pause to consider the point of *holding* people responsible. The judgment of responsibility, whether in a court of law, or by a private individual with regard to another, sets the stage for a decision about sanctions: What shall we do? What response should be made to this responsible agent?

> Moral assessment of persons is important because of the bearing it has on how to behave *vis-a-vis* the persons assessed. It is offenders, not conduct, we must incarcerate or treat or blame, and our behavior is rational only insofar as it fits with what we can discover about offenders from their conduct. (Cummins 1980, p. 212)

We may decide to forgive, or we may decide to reproach, or denounce, or scold, or even punish the culprit. Each of these alternatives has a distinct place and rationale in our interpersonal economy, and contributes to the depth of our institution of holding people responsible. But for simplicity I will concentrate on the most explicit (public, codified, instituted) response: punishment. There is an idea—one might call it a strategic idea—embedded in the rationale of punishment, which I take to be the key to understanding our status as responsible moral agents. I will bring this idea into focus by presenting a simplified "rational reconstruction" of what I take to be the traditional justification (one might say it was the somewhat free-floating rationale) of the institution of criminal law, with its elaborate system of enforcement and punishment. Since my main goal is to expose an idea, not to present an impregnable defense of the institution of criminal law, I will ignore the subtleties.[4]

Why do we want to punish people who "commit crimes"? One may

---

4. The classic examination of these issues is Hart 1968. See especially his essays "Prolegomenon to the Principles of Punishment," pp. 1–27, "Negligence, *Mens Rea*, and Criminal Responsibility," and "Punishment and the Elimination of Responsibility," pp. 136–186. See also Gross 1979.

speculate with Nietzsche about dark undercurrents of violence in our psyches, but whatever the merits of such hypotheses, there are also some good reasons for this peculiarly human institution. We can readily identify sorts of harms we would like to see minimized in our society, and we have reason to believe that if we prohibit the causing of these harms, and give force to the prohibition by threatening sanctions, we will thereby diminish the frequency of those harms. We believe this institution is at least somewhat effective, and we believe this for good reasons. First, it follows from our conception of rationality that if the members of society are even approximately rational, they will see that it is not at all in their interests to be caught having committed the prohibited deeds, and will hence in general be deterred. And we have plenty of empirical evidence that the citizenry, taken as a whole, is appropriately sensitive to such institutions.[5] Laws (backed by sanctions) do make a difference, and in the desired direction. But we recognize that these desirable effects fall short of the ideal.

In an ideal world, it seems, everyone would see the right thing to do and do it, just for that reason, so we would have no need of laws and a system of threatened punishments. Everyone would behave like angels. Heaven on Earth, in short. It might seem that in a somewhat less ideal world ("one step down") we would need the system of laws, since people (if they were like us) would be selfish and aggressive. But this system of laws would deter perfectly, because (unlike us) everyone would be so rational. People—all people—would see as plain as the noses on their faces that crime didn't pay, and hence would all abstain from it. Judges and policemen and jailers would be appointed and trained, and would sit around, like the Swiss Army, waiting to be called into action, but rather doubting that it would ever happen in their lifetimes.

Why isn't that the situation we find ourselves in? If we're really *homo sapiens,* the "rational animal," why are our prisons overcrowded and our judges overworked? One reason seems to be that we skimp on our institutions of enforcement, and hence people, being rational indeed, see that under certain conditions crime *does* pay, or at any rate is likely enough to pay to be worth the risk. The deterrent power of laws is (ideally) a function of people's perception of the likelihood of their being apprehended and the severity of the penalty that might be inflicted. Increasing either factor increases deterrence. The incidence of running red lights could be dramatically reduced by either installing a squad car at every intersection 24 hours a day (making apprehension very likely) or

---

5. The difficulty of establishing (in the court of science) particular hypotheses about the deterrent effects of particular laws should not be underestimated. See Gibbs 1975.

by making the penalty life imprisonment. But again, being rational, the citizenry determines that either option—or indeed any combination of these options watered down—would probably not be worth the cost to society. Better a few red lights should be run than we should have to devote so much of our wealth to enforcement, or to inflict such brutal (and brutalizing) punishments on miscreants. So our skimping is itself rational it seems.[6]

Since rapidly diminishing returns would be the result of any further investment in strengthening our enforcement, the optimal institution will be one in which a certain amount of lawbreaking, apprehension, and conviction is "tolerated." That is not to say our present system needs no serious reform, but—runs this argument—it would be irrational to hold out any hope of devising a system of *perfect* deterrence. So lawbreakers will always be among us; the jailer will never have—should never have—an entirely ceremonial position.

But recognizing the value in minimizing the amount of lawbreaking (while also trying to minimize the costs of enforcement and punishment), we see that there are improvements (fine tuning) of the laws that are called for. Deterrence depends on several factors, and one is "publicity": deterrence has a chance to succeed only with people who *know* the law and *understand* the conditions and sanctions. There may be individuals, we recognize, who fail to meet these conditions, and hence may commit the prohibited deed because the deterrent effect of the law never reaches to them. That is why a part of the cost of the institution of laws is public education; secret laws are useless as deterrents. The cost-effective way of achieving a suitably high level of knowledge is to combine a sufficiently energetic public information program with a somewhat peremptory (and hence bracing) legal wrinkle: ignorance of the law is no excuse.

This latter condition provides a motivation to all to maintain a state of mild inquisitiveness about the law and any new changes in it, and would be outrageous, rationally unacceptable, in the absence of a "sufficiently" energetic public information program. That is why the two elements must operate together; provided that the state does its part in making the information available, it is not asking too much to hold the citizenry responsible for knowing it. It is important to note that the principle that ignorance of the law is no excuse has a measure of arbi-

6. But wait—if we made the penalties severe enough, and credible enough to deter everyone, would it be so costly after all? Yes. For one thing, while the prisons would be almost empty, the police force would still have to be huge, for with penalties so severe, the attractiveness of evasion and simply resisting arrest would rise. And of course there are other good objections to such a proposal, though it is a perennially suggested reform.

trariness about it. It does not suppose that there *couldn't be* intuitively valid grounds for pleading ignorance as an excuse; it simply declares that such pleas *will not (normally) even be entertained.* Life is too short; the law must be efficient, and we have to draw the line somewhere.[7] (This is the strategic idea, illustrated simply in this instance, that we will find as the basis of our sense of personal moral responsibility.)

When all this is in place, we still recognize that there are those whom the laws will fail to move in the desired way. There is a tacit requirement that laws be made as straightforward and comprehensible as possible, so that it is not asking too much to suppose people under their jurisdiction can comprehend them, but for some people this *is* asking too much. These are, paradigmatically, the mentally incompetent and insane. We excuse them from criminal liability because they manifestly do not meet the minimal conditions for deterrability, and the attempt to educate them, to bring them up to the knowledge and comprehension threshold, would be fruitless—or at least too costly. To punish them as if they were responsible citizens would be to undermine the very institution of pun- ishment (which depends on its credibility) by undermining its rationale. It would be as outrageous—as offensive to the rationality of the citizenry at large—for the law to refuse to distinguish these people as nonrespon- sible, as it would be for the law to maintain its "ignorance is no excuse" rule while passing and enforcing secret laws. So in order to preserve the credibility and defensibility of the system, we add explicit provisions excluding various types of people from legal responsibility.

This has the effect of diminishing the pool of eligible punishees, the genuinely responsible and guilty-as-charged. But we recognize that per- haps the principles used to demarcate this class are crude, and the ques- tion arises whether the law's credibility and acceptability (its justice, in short) could be further improved by making finer-grained distinctions. But then the subversive proposal is suggested: why not excuse *all* who commit crimes, on the grounds that since (obviously) the law didn't deter them on the occasion, they were—at least on that occasion— undeterrable. (Compare: "How dare you advertise this shirt as machine-washable! I just washed it, and look at it!")

But if we were to take this step, our whole system of deterrence would crash. The bracing effect of the laws and their sanctions on the deliberations of (somewhat) rational citizens would be dissipated, and

---

7. Having drawn the line, we do expect judges to exercise some discretion. The point is that by drawing the line the burden is shifted: a judge *may* consider that the accused's ignorance is due to extenuating circumstances—"justifiable igno- rance of the law" (Gross 1979, p. 155)—but he is not obliged in general to consider the question.

the undesirable harms of the state of nature would return. So we must get arbitrary again, and draw the line—exactly where is no more important in this case than it is in the case of setting a legal age for drinking or driving. We must set up some efficiently determinable threshold for legal competence, never for a moment supposing that there couldn't be intuitively persuasive "counterexamples" to whatever line we draw, but declaring in advance that such pleas will not be entertained. We mustn't look too closely at the particular micro-details of the accused's circumstances, but just try to establish (crudely and swiftly) that *in general* this agent is deterrable, even though he was not deterred on this occasion. (This is the home, in the law and morality, of the elbow room we sought in chapter six in order to stave off actualism.)[8]

Our refusal, beyond some arbitrary point, to delve further into causes and circumstances may strike a chord of suspicion in some. Can this policy be fair? Indeed it can. Remember that the breaks average out; we could not improve basketball by disallowing the fluke shots and unlucky breaks. (My claim here is in effect that *holding people responsible* is the best game in town.) Recall that a certain tolerance for risk-taking lawbreakers was built into the rationale for skimping on law enforcement. It is not even a *prima facie* sign of irrationality if our miscreant has simply calculated the odds, decided that on this occasion law breaking is worth a shot, and lost. We cannot conclude from the fact that a wager was lost that it was irrationally made. So long as the risk was taken in full knowledge of the consequences of the loss, the agent can hardly complain that the sanctions now imposed are unfairly applied to him.

The effect of such an institution, with such a rationale, is to create—to *constitute*—a class of legally culpable agents whose subsequent liability to punishment maintains the credibility of the sanctions of the laws. The institution, if it is to maintain itself, must provide for the fine tuning of its arbitrary thresholds as new information (or misinformation) emerges that might undercut its credibility. One can speculate that there is an optimal setting of the competence threshold (for any particular combination of social circumstances, degree of public sophistication, and so on)

---

8. Fingarette (1972, p. 203) defines insanity as "failure to respond relevantly to what is essentially relevant . . . by virtue of a grave defect in *capacity* to do so inherent at least for the time in the person's mental makeup." This person must be understood, in Honoré's terms (see chapter six), as someone who no longer "can" (general) respond relevantly; if instead we interpreted this "can" as "can" (particular), every well-attested instance of particular folly (for example, punching the arresting officer) would be *conclusive* evidence of (temporary?) insanity. No doubt much of the suspicion and disfavor in which the very idea of temporary insanity is held is owing to a dim recognition that this might be the thin edge of a most subversive wedge.

that maximizes the bracing effect of the law. A higher than optimal threshold would encourage a sort of malingering on the part of defendants, which, if recognized by the populace, would diminish their respect for the law and hence diminish its deterrent effect. And a lower than optimal threshold would yield a diminishing return of deterrence and lead to the punishment of individuals who, in the eyes of society, "really couldn't help it." The public perception of the fairness of the law is a critical factor in its effectiveness.

I take the foregoing sketch to be a version of the standard, presumptive defense of our institution of law, trial, and punishment as an institution of deterrence. (There are other defenses I choose to pass over here.) It exhibits, in the daylight of familiar surroundings, the sort of rationale I suppose to exist for our more fundamental (but probably historically later) "institution": the "moral conceptual world" of personal responsibility.

Why do we hold ourselves and others *morally* responsible? At first it may appear that this inquiry is parasitic on a metaphysical question about the conditions under which someone truly *is* responsible. (In criticizing a particular setting of the thresholds for *legal* responsibility, we might argue that the law treated as responsible some people who were not really morally responsible for their conduct or vice versa.) Surely, it seems, we can make a distinction between the question of why we *hold* people responsible, or *take* responsibility ourselves for various things, and the question of why or whether we actually *are* responsible. We know that sometimes mistakes are made; people are held responsible who were not responsible—either for the deed in question or for their actions in general. And sometimes someone who (jolly well) is responsible refuses to take responsibility.

But whatever responsibility is, considered as a metaphysical state, unless we can tie it to some recognizable social desideratum, it will have no rational claim on our esteem. Why would anyone care whether or not he had the property of responsibility (for some particular deed, or in general)? Of course people can want just about anything, and a yearning for responsibility might arise when one was in the mood for satisfying a purely metaphysical hankering. (Imagine someone who managed to work himself into the state of contracting a desire to eat a piece of bread composed of molecules all of which had once been part of a piece of bread eaten by Alexander the Great. Now imagine someone who managed to affect a yearning for metaphysical responsibility—whatever that is.)

Why then do we want to hold people—ourselves included—responsible? "By holding someone responsible and acting accordingly, we may cause him to shed an undesirable trait, and this is useful regardless of whether the trait is of his making." (Gomberg 1978, p. 208) Once again, the utility of a certain measure of arbitrariness is made visible. Instead of investigating, endlessly, in an attempt to *discover* whether or not a particular trait is of someone's making—instead of trying to assay exactly to what degree a particular self is self-made—we simply *hold* people responsible for their conduct (within limits we take care not to examine too closely). And we are rewarded for adopting this strategy by the higher proportion of "responsible" behavior we thereby inculcate.

Consider the implications of this vision for the question we so often address to ourselves about our own personal guilt or innocence. When we *accept* responsibility for misdeeds are we deceiving ourselves? If one supposed there were some sort of cosmic, absolute responsibility one either had or was excluded from, then the prospect of mistakenly accepting or mistakenly disclaiming responsibility would be a knotty and apparently insoluble problem. How would one ever know? Worse still, following Kant, we would seem to be bound to agree that only perfectly moral behavior could be responsible behavior; real culpability would be as impossible as a round square. Wolf provides a recent formulation:

> Like the compatibilists, then, I am claiming that whether an agent is morally responsible depends not on whether but on how that agent is determined. . . . However, since on my view the satisfactory kind of determination is determination by reasons that an agent ought to have, it will follow that an agent can be both determined and responsible only insofar as he performs actions that he ought to perform. If an agent performs a morally bad action, on the other hand, then his action can't be determined in the appropriate way. (Wolf 1980, p. 163)

It seems on this account that there must inevitably be something wrong, something criticizable, in the design or implementation of the causal train of reasoning leading to a morally bad action.

But we have seen that this need not be so. At every level of organization, from the presumably "hard-wired" level of memory organization to the level of the design of social institutions, the *best possible* designs, given the constraints of finitude and time pressure, would have to include some measure of arbitrariness and wise risk taking. The (entirely unconscious) organization of memory guarantees that only some approximately appropriate subset of relevant points will occur to one in the time available (Cherniak 1983). Any individual's personally developed style of self-control must buy some efficiencies at the expense of gambles on what is apt to be encountered. Particular instances of conscious problem solving or decision making must include a somewhat arbitrary decision (conscious or not) to terminate deliberation about the main decision while knowing full well that there still are uncanvassed relevant considerations. And at the level of social institutions, there is not only the arbitrariness (in strategic locations) of the criminal law, but other arbitrariness as well, such as the use of lotteries to speed up otherwise intractable decision problems (such as who should be drafted into the armed forces) in a fair and timely manner.

Any finite control system (such as a human brain) will always be prone to making mistakes or arriving at decisions that a more leisurely analysis would condemn; it is an inevitable feature of human character, even perfected to its limit. Original Sin, naturalized. It is wise, however, to adopt policies that minimize the bad effects of these inevitable defects of character. And the corrective feedback forces needed to accomplish this are analogous to those we just sketched in our rationale of punishment in the law. By somewhat arbitrarily holding people responsible for their actions, and making sure they realize that they will be held responsible, we constrain the risk-taking in the design (and redesign) of their characters within tolerable bounds. When in spite of these best measures people get caught in wrong deeds, their gambles (wise or foolish) have simply lost and they ought not to object to paying the assigned penalty.

In fact, I submit, we do commonly take just this attitude to our own transgressions (at least the minor ones) when we are confronted with them. I recently *simply forgot* to obtain the proper, obtainable permission to park my car in a restricted zone, making myself liable for a considerable fine. Did I plead a pitiable flaw in my memory, or the well-known absentmindedness that accompanies my trade, or the mitigation of "temporary distraction beyond my control"? Of course not. Some such account of my inappropriate behavior on the occasion must have been true, but a clearer case of a straightforwardly culpable—if venial—sin of omission would be hard to find.

When the stakes are higher, when graver crimes are the issue, this ready acquiescence in culpability is not as uniform. But it certainly is widespread. Many a murderer has no doubt of his own culpability, and if this may well sometimes be socially fostered self-deception, it need not be. Skepticism about the very possibility of culpability arises from a misplaced reverence for an absolutist ideal: the concept of total, before-the-eyes-of-God Guilt. The fact that *that* condition is never to be met in this world should not mislead us into skepticism about the integrity of our institution of moral responsibility.

3. The Dread Secret Denied

It is hard to be so optimistic in the cold hours of the morning when one reflects back on one's own appalling weakness and stupidity, at the width of the chasm between one's public self-presentation and the unpresent-able private thinking that apparently determined one's action. But what is the correct or even coherent response to this realization of such la-mentable defects of character? Self-reproach?

> How do we reproach ourselves? We say to ourselves, "How negli-gent of me!" "How thoughtless!" "How selfish!" "How hasty and unrestrained!" "That I should have been capable even for a moment of taking such a petty, irritated view!" etc. In other words, we are attributing to ourselves at the time of the act, in some respect and measure, a bad character, and regretting it. And that is the entire point of our self-reproach. We are turning upon ourselves with disapproval and it may be with disgust; we wish we could undo what we did in the past, and, helpless to do that, feel a peculiar thwarted poignant anger and shame at ourselves that we *had it in us* to perpe-trate the thing we now condemn. (Hobart 1934, p. 4)

But is our regret, remorse, and self-condemnation any less incohe-rent than the thwarted wish to undo the deed? Now that we see the social utility of the myth of free will, we may well wonder if we are obliged by any further reasons to go along with the institution and, in the private arena of our own hearts, hold ourselves responsible. What at-titude might we then take as an alternative? The attitude that goes with an embarrassed shrug? Or perhaps the impassivity of a disengaged spec-tator? Or rage at the unfairness of having been determined to be such a nasty and contemptible member of the human race?

How should one respond to the idea that one is guilty? If the con-cept of guilt one is contemplating applying to oneself is the traditional, absolute concept of guilty-before-the-eyes-of-God, then one has as much reason to dismiss it as one does to dismiss the other dubious absolutist notions that are its kin: the perfect Kantian will, the Sartrian self-created self, the ideal Socratic agent who can never knowingly do wrong, the Chisholmian agent as unmoved mover. No one, not monsters like Hitler or Eichmann, not ordinary sane criminals like Agnew or Vesco, and not you when you last broke a law, or broke a promise, is or could be guilty in that sense. For that sense of guilt has been screwed so tight by philo-sophical and theological tradition that the condition it purports to name defies description.

For that very reason, of course, there is small solace in the recogni-tion that one is not guilty in that sense. One can still be guilty-as-charged—either in the strictly legal sense, or in the related sense that arises from our practice of holding individuals personally, morally re-sponsible. Is there a place in either of those notions for regret or re-morse? This is a large question that deserves careful treatment on its own (see Strawson 1962 and Bennett 1980), but I will venture a few fairly obvious points. The conscience that manifests itself only retrospectively in agonies of remorse, and never prospectively in overcoming some base urge, is a singularly unattractive trait of character, and one that any moral world could well do without. The sort of remorse that (on the other hand) is a manifestation of some significant, projectible, nonmomentary shift in priorities for decision is precisely the sort of attitude the institution of holding people responsible exists to achieve. So that sort of remorse has an entirely appropriate place in our naturalized institution of guilt.

But suppose that what you see when you contemplate your own biography is that whatever else may be true, you have been, are, and no doubt will continue to be one of the villains. For the rest of your life you will be in trouble—vilified, condemned, punished, shunned. There are such people. They make the grade as responsible agents, but are so thoroughly mean-spirited, so untouched by human warmth that, in a word, we despise them. Isn't it unfair that we should treat them so? The retort suggests itself: who more deserves to be despised than someone utterly despicable? Can they help being despicable? They *may* not be able to help it *now,* for they may be too far gone (like the drunk who is responsible for having made himself drunk), but in chapter four we saw that one can be as responsible for one's character as for any other artifact arising from one's past efforts. If the person has managed to turn himself into a monster, there may be no one left to hold responsible, but that is the extreme case.

What advice or consolation could one give to someone who confessed that he was a despicable villain? The answer is obvious: if one was interested in "saving his soul" one could urge, in whatever manner seemed most likely to be effective, that he reform his ways and strive to overcome his deservedly evil reputation. If, on the other hand, one was interested in compounding his misery (at whatever cost to society), one could urge on him a vision of his own utter degradation and helplessness, and foster in him an attitude of apathy and fatalism, thereby achieving (perhaps) an almost complete dissociation of his reflection from his deeds and projects and encouraging in him a cynical tolerance of his own worst side.

We all know the feeling at times: the terrible existential funk in which we recognize that we have slid self-defeatingly into the passive spectator attitude, fecklessly wondering what we are going to do, or think, next. Instead of thinking ahead, planning and hoping and trying to anticipate the world, we spiral down into a regress of self-preoccupation that squanders our time, virtually guaranteeing that our self-image of futility and indecision will come true. Fortunately for most of us, these depressions soon pass, and we return to some constructive engagement or other with the world. We break out of our slump, like the golfer who finally sees the wisdom in the curious advice of the pro: keep your head down and follow through (see p. 16).

Since we all know this feeling, we can all appreciate the ominousness of anything that purported to be the discovery or proof that free will is impossible for us. Having good reasons for wanting free will is not, of course, having good reasons for believing one has free will. It seems to be, however, that having good reasons for wanting free will *is* having good reasons for trying to get oneself to believe one has it. For it is very likely, as we have seen, that believing that one has free will is itself one of the necessary conditions for having free will: an agent who enjoyed the other necessary conditions for free will—rationality, and the capacity for higher order self-control and self-reflection—but who had been hoodwinked into believing he lacked free will would be almost as incapacitated for free, responsible choice by that belief as by the lack of any of the other necessary conditions.

This sets up a delicate position for the agnostic who is still uncertain whether all the other conditions for free will (have we identified them all?) are met. If he can overcome or ignore his doubts and achieve the state of mind of a frank believer in free will, he will thereby achieve one of two states: (a) genuine free will (if free will is otherwise possible for him), or (b) at least the illusion of free will.

The former state is manifestly desirable, but the latter, if it were the best we could hope for, *might* be worth wanting. It seems that it would be a member of the familiar class of life-enabling or life-enhancing illusions: the illusion that one is still loved by one's loved ones; the illusion that one has several more years to live when one hasn't; the illusion that in spite of one's physical ugliness, one's inner beauty is readily manifest to others.

If the agnostic instead sinks into doubt, or worse, into the conviction that he lacks free will, he is certain to be right: his attitude toward his own opportunities for choice and action will be such that he is essentially disabled as a chooser. He ceases to act under the idea of freedom. We seem constitutionally unable to maintain that conviction for more than a few bad moments; hunger or boredom or curiosity soon sets in and lures us back into action—a bit of sphexishness for which we can be grateful, perhaps. Still the experience, however brief, is grim. And its implications if we take it seriously are almost too grim to contemplate. Small wonder then that we should be highly motivated to look on the bright side and find the case for free will compelling if we possibly can. The circumstances are ripe for self-deception, and any defense of free will against the skeptics invites the suspicion of wishful thinking at best, hypocrisy at worst.

Still, what one hopes very much to be true may be true. And there is nothing better to do, given our irrepressible curiosity and skepticism, and our aspirations to rationality, than to conduct a patient examination of the issues to see if our hoped-for conclusion can be sustained. This I have attempted to do, and my conclusion is optimistic: free will is not an illusion, not even an irrepressible and life-enhancing illusion. When we look closely at the sources of our suspicion and dread, we find again and again that they are not indisputable axioms or overwhelmingly well-supported, empirical discoveries, but unfocused images, hastily glanced at—like the shadows on the bedroom wall that take on an apparent robustness and menace precisely because we do not look at them closely.

What we want when we want free will is the power to decide our courses of action, and to decide them wisely, in the light of our expectations and desires. We want to be in control of ourselves, and not under the control of others. We want to be agents, capable of initiating, and taking responsibility for, projects and deeds. All this is ours, I have tried to show, as a natural product of our biological endowment, extended and enhanced by our initiation into society.

We want, moreover, to have enough elbow room in the world so that when we exercise these powers, it is not always a matter of settling for the only desperate course of action that has a chance of fulfilling our desires. We can have this elbow room as well, and it is well worth striving for, but not guaranteed. There are real threats to human freedom, but they are not metaphysical. There is political bondage, coercion, the manipulation inducible by the dissemination of misinformation, and the "forced move" desperation of hunger and poverty. No doubt we could do a lot more to combat these impositions on our freedom, were it not for another sort of straitjacket we often find ourselves wearing: the curious sort of self-imposed bondage that we create by the very exercise of our freedom, and in the very acknowledgment of our responsibility: the chains, ropes, strings, and threads of commitment (explicit and tacit) that tie us to our family and friends, that tie us into our life projects, and that make us increasingly immovable by appeals for radical action.

Our experiences with these real and variable threats to our freedom generate the anxieties and provide the metaphors that motivate and (often covertly) guide the arguments and analyses that have been at the center of philosophers' attention. My strategy has been to pause to examine the metaphors, and to disclose their role in the thought experiments—the intuition pumps—that have dominated our imaginations.

We are afraid that science has shown, or will soon show, or threatens to show, that we can't be what we want to be. The threat is not determinism—if it were, we could all relax, since physicists now seem to agree that our world is fundamentally indeterministic—but science itself, or the "naturalism" that is its enabling world view.

This fear, like most, survives on ignorance. It is fostered by oversimplified visions of what science has to tell us about ourselves and the rest of the universe, about causation, about time, about possibility. So long as we refuse to look closely at the details of what the scientific image of humanity might be—for fear of what we might find—the suspicion will always persist that abstract philosophical arguments purporting to prove the compatibility of freedom and science are just so much whistling in the dark. The threats, after all, take so many different forms.

I have attempted to exorcise each bugbear in turn—some of them keep returning in new guises—showing how the very compelling arguments that give birth to them are enabled, in virtually every case, by misuse of intuition pumps, in particular, by focusing on simple models in which it is the simplicity of the model, and nothing else, that generates the illusory intuitions.

An ineliminable part of philosophical method, and indeed of scientific method, is the tactic of judging what is possible and impossible by reflecting on what one can and cannot imagine or conceive. One says, "It is inconceivable to me that p," and then shortens it to "It is inconceivable that p"—or in other words, "As anyone can see: p is impossible." You say you cannot imagine that p, and therefore declare that p is impossible? Mightn't that be hubris? One of my tactics has been to respond to traditional philosophical claims about what is unimaginable by urging: try harder.

My own intuition pumps are designed to help. Yes, if we try hard, we can imagine a being that listens to the voice of reason and yet is not exempted from the causal milieu. Yes, we can imagine a being whose every decision is caused by the interaction of features of its current state and features of its environment over which it has no control—and yet which is itself *in control,* and not being controlled by that omnipresent and omnicausal environment. Yes, we can imagine a process of self-creation that starts with a non-responsible agent and builds, gradually, to an agent responsible for its own character. Yes, we can imagine a rational *and deterministic* being who is not deluded when it views its future as open and "up to" it. Yes, we can imagine a responsible, free agent of whom it is true that whenever it has acted in the past, it could not have acted otherwise.

It is not just that we can imagine those things we suspected we could not imagine, thus undercutting the impossibility arguments; the project of imagining them in some detail pays dividends. We get a clearer vision of the very ideas we felt were threatened—the ideas of rationality, self-

control, self-authorship, opportunity, avoidance and prevention, moral
responsibility, and self-improvement, for instance. When we see how
robust a naturalized vision of ourselves can be, we are less apt to be
attracted to absolutist and perfectionist doctrines that defy assimilation
into science, or its offspring, common sense. We see that a more realistic
view of human rationality—one that takes our finitary predicament seriously—is actually more versatile and powerful than the preposterously
idealized "theories" that generate all the traditional paradoxes.

I know that the naturalistic attitude I have espoused, the attitude
that encourages us to think of ourselves, imaginatively, as organic robots,
as designed portions of the material universe, is odious to many human-
ists. I have tried to show them that in shunning it, they turn their back on
a fruitful source of *philosophical* ideas. This theme is implicit, of course,
in my citations and footnotes to works in a variety of fields that philosophers—especially philosophers writing about free will—have tended to
ignore. My own conviction is that a sympathetic consideration of the
fruits of these other disciplines gives one a perspective that is simply
*un*obtainable by someone who studies only the traditional philosophical
literature. And I have found my own philosophical curiosity frustrated
time and again by my inability to drive myself as deeply into these alien
and often forbiddingly technical disciplines as I have thought was
needed. There is much more to be mined from them by philosophers
with the right training and talents.

There is, of course, much more to be said about free will in any case.
I have run out of quarries, at least for the time being, but certainly there
are ideas that I have not taken seriously that others deem to be crucial.
Some, for instance, must be appalled by my abrupt parenthetical dismissal in chapter six of the "problem" of reconciling free will with the
hypothesis of an infinite, all-knowing Being. This central and traditional
version of the free will problem was the primary focus of the issue for
centuries, but its interest depends on a very literal and anthropomorphic
vision of God as Knower. That is not the way to take the idea of God
seriously today, I think. In the end I decided I simply could not take this
version of the problem seriously enough to think it warranted a careful
discussion. It is in my opinion a mere historical puzzle, or an intellectual
amusement, and I did not want to convey the impression that (what with
all the fun I've been having) I've been playing games.

Other challenges to our conviction that we have free will can be
expected, of course, and welcomed, since we want to know the truth in
the end. It is virtually certain that the incompatibilists and "hard determinists" and other skeptics will devise ingenious new arguments to demonstrate that no one in fact has free will, or would have free will if

determinism or mechanism or some other "ism" were true. I close with some advice on how to respond to these challenges.

First, inquire closely about just what variety of free will is supposedly jeopardized by the argument. Is it, in fact, a variety worth caring about? Ask yourself whether you have any clearly statable reason to hope you have that variety, any reason to fear that you might not. Would lacking this freedom really be like being in prison, or like being a puppet? For perhaps the conclusion of the new argument is only that no one could have some metaphysical property that is of academic interest at best. Or worse, the yearned-for freedom in question may turn out on inspection to be an incoherently conceived blessing. Ask yourself: can I even conceive of beings whose wills are freer than our own? What regrettable feature of our lot as physical organisms is not a feature of their lot? If the ideal of freedom we hold out for is simply self-contradictory, we should hardly feel bereft when we learn we cannot have it. There's no sense wringing our hands because we can't undo the past, and can't prevent an event that actually happens, and can't create ourselves *ex nihilo,* and can't choose both alternatives at a decision point, and can't be perfect. If the proposed argument passes all these tests, so that a dire conclusion does seem to be in the offing, then and only then must we take it very seriously and see exactly what the argument is.

Bibliography

Anscombe, G. E. M. (1957). *Intention*. Oxford: Blackwell.

Austin, J. L. (1961). "Ifs and Cans," in Austin, *Philosophical Papers,* edited by J. O. Urmson and G. Warnock. Oxford: Clarendon Press, pp.153–180.

Ayer, A. J. (1954). "Freedom and Necessity," in *Philosophical Essays*. New York: Macmillan, pp.271–284.

Ayer, A. J. (1980). "Free-will and Rationality," in van Straaten 1980.

Ayers, M. (1968). *The Refutation of Determinism: an Essay in Philosophical Logic*. London: Methuen.

Bennett, J. (1976). *Linguistic Behaviour*. Cambridge: Cambridge University Press.

Bennett, J. (1980). "Accountability," in van Straaten 1980.

Berlin, I. (1954). *Historical Inevitability*. Oxford: Oxford University Press.

Berofsky, B., ed. (1966). *Free Will and Determinism*. New York: Harper & Row.

Berry, M. (1983). "Breaking the Paradigms of Classical Physics From Within," in J. Petitot, ed., *Proceedings of the Cerisy Symposium ("Logos et Theorie des Catastrophes")*.

Boër S., and W. Lycan (1980). "Who, Me," *The Philosophical Review*, 89, pp.427–466.

Brewer, W. F. (1974). "There is No Convincing Evidence for Operant or Classical Conditioning in Adult Humans," in W. B. Weimer, ed., *Cognition and the Symbolic Processes*. Hillsdale, New Jersey: Erlbaum.

Brown, N. (1959). *Life Against Death*. New York: Random House.

Campbell, D. (1975). "On the Conflicts Between Biological and Social Evolution and Between Psychology and Moral Tradition," *American Psychologist*, 30, pp.1103–1126.

Cartwright, H. (1970). "Quantities," *The Philosophical Review*, 79, pp.25–42.

Chaitin, G. (1976). "Randomness and Mathematical Proof," *Scientific American*, 232, pp.47–52.

Chappell, V. (1962). *The Philosophy of Mind*. Englewood Cliffs, NJ: Prentice-Hall.

Cherniak, C. (1983). "Rationality and the Structure of Human Memory," *Synthese*, 57, pp.163–186.

Chisholm, R. (1961). "Responsibility and Avoidability," in Hook 1961.

Chisholm, R. (1964a). "J. L. Austin's Philosophical Papers," *Mind*, 73, pp.1–26. (Parts of this article are reprinted in Berofsky 1966.)

Chisholm, R. (1964b). "Human Freedom and the Self," the Lindley Lecture, 1964, University of Kansas. (Reprinted in Watson 1982.)

Chisholm, R. (1976). *Person and Object: a Metaphysical Study*, the Paul Carus Lectures. Lasalle, Ill: Open Court.

Cohen, L. J. (1981). "Can Human Irrationality be Experimentally Demonstrated?" *Behavioral and Brain Sciences*, 4, pp.317–331.

Cummins, R. (1980). "Culpability and Mental Disorder," *Canadian Journal of Philosophy*, X, pp.207–232.

Danto, A. (1965). "Basic Actions," *American Philosophical Quarterly*, 2, pp.141–148.

Davidson, D. (1970). "How is Weakness of the Will Possible?" in Joel Feinberg, ed., *Moral Concepts*. Oxford: Oxford University Press, pp.93–113.

Davidson, D. (1973). "On the Very Idea of a Conceptual Scheme," *Proceedings and Addresses of the American Philosophical Association*, 1973–1974, 67, pp.5–20.

Dawkins, R. (1976). *The Selfish Gene*. Oxford: Oxford University Press.

Dawkins, R. (1980). "Good Strategy or Evolutionarily Stable Strategy?" in G. W. Barlow and J. Silverberg, eds., *Sociobiology: Beyond Nature/Nurture?*, AAAS Selected Symposium. Boulder, Colorado: Westview Press.

Dawkins, R. (1982). *The Extended Phenotype*. New York: W. H. Freeman.

Dennett, D. (1969). *Content and Consciousness*. London: Routledge & Kegan Paul, and New York: Humanities Press.

Dennett, D. (1971). "Intentional Systems," *J. Phil.*, 68, pp.87–106.

Dennett, D. (1972). Review of J. R. Lucas, *The Freedom of the Will*, in *J. Phil.*, 67, pp.91–97.

Dennett, D. (1973). "Mechanism and Responsibility," in Honderich 1973. (Reprinted in Dennett 1978a.)

Dennett, D. (1975). "Why the Law of Effect Will not Go Away," *Journal of the Theory of Social Behaviour*, 5, pp.169–187. (Reprinted in Dennett 1978a.)

Dennett, D. (1976). "Conditions of Personhood," in A. Rorty 1976. (Reprinted in Dennett 1978a.)

Dennett, D. (1978a). *Brainstorms: Philosophical Essays on Mind and Psychology.* Montgomery, Vt: Bradford Books, and Hassocks, Sussex: Harvester.

Dennett, D. (1978b). "Current Issues in the Philosophy of Mind," *American Philosophical Quarterly*, 15, pp.249–261.

Dennett, D. (1980). "The Milk of Human Intentionality," (commentary on Searle 1980), *Behavioral and Brain Sciences,* 3, pp.428–430.

Dennett, D. (1981a). "Three Kinds of Intentional Psychology," in R. Healey, ed., *Reduction, Time and Reality.* Cambridge: Cambridge University Press, pp.37–61.

Dennett, D. (1981b). "True Believers: the Intentional Strategy and Why it Works," in A. F. Heath, ed., *Scientific Explanation.* Oxford: Oxford University Press.

Dennett, D. (1982a). "Beyond Belief," in A. Woodfield, ed., *Thought and Object.* Oxford: Oxford University Press.

Dennett, D. (1982b). "Notes on Prosthetic Imagination," *New Boston Review*, June, pp.3–7. (Reprinted, with revision, as "The Imagination Extenders," in *Psychology Today*, December 1982, pp.32–39).

Dennett, D. (1982c). "Why do we think what we do about why we think what we do?" (a commentary on Goodman 1982), *Cognition*, 12, pp.219–237.

Dennett, D. (1982d). "How to Study Consciousness Empirically: or Nothing Comes to Mind," *Synthese*, 53, pp.159–180.

Dennett, D. (1982e). "Comments on Rorty," *Synthese*, 53, pp.349–356.

Dennett, D. (1983a). "Styles of Mental Representation," *Proc. Aristotelian Soc.,* New Series 83 1982–1983, pp.213–226.

Dennett, D. (1983b). "Intentional Systems in Cognitive Ethology: the 'Panglossian Paradigm' Defended," in *Behavioral and Brain Sciences*, Vol. 6, pp.343–390.

Dennett, D. (forthcoming-a). "Cognitive Wheels: the Frame Problem of Artificial Intelligence," in C. Hookway, ed., *Minds, Machines and Evolution.* Cambridge: Cambridge University Press.

Dennett, D. (forthcoming-b). "The Self as a Center of Narrative Gravity," in P.M. Cole, D. L. Johnson, and F. S. Kessel, eds., *Self and Consciousness*, New York: Praeger.

Descartes, R. *Oeuvres de Descartes*, edited by C. Adam and P. Tannery. Paris: Leopold Cerf, 1897–1913.

de Sousa, R. (1970). "Self-Deception," *Inquiry*, 13, pp.308–321.

Dewey, J. (1922). *Human Nature and Conduct.* New York: Henry Holt.

Doan, B., and J. Macnamara. *Free Will and Scientific Insight,* in preparation.

Dretske, F. (1981). *Knowledge and the Flow of Information*. Cambridge, Mass.: Bradford/MIT Press.

Dyson, F. (1979). *Disturbing the Universe*. New York: Harper.

Eccles, J. C. (1953). *The Neurophysiological Basis of Mind*. Oxford: Oxford University Press.

Edwards, P. (1961). "Hard and Soft Determinism," in Hook 1961.

Eells, E. (1982). *Rational Decision and Causality*. Cambridge: Cambridge University Press.

Everett, H. (1973). In *The Many-Worlds Interpretation of Quantum Mechanics*, edited by B. S. Dewitt and N. Graham. Princeton, N.J.: Princeton University Press.

Farrell, B. A. (1950). "Experience," *Mind*, 1950. (Reprinted in Chappell 1962.)

Fingarette, H. (1972). *The Meaning of Criminal Insanity*. Berkeley: University of California Press.

Fischer, J. (1982). "Responsibility and Control," *J. Phil.*, Jan. 1982, pp.24–40.

Fishman, G. S. (1973). *Concepts and Methods in Discrete Event Simulation*. New York: Wiley.

Flew, A. (1955). "Divine Omniscience and Human Freedom," in A. Flew and A. MacIntyre, eds., *New Essays in Philosophical Theology*. London: SCM Press, pp.141–169.

Fodor, J. (1980). "Methodological Solipsism Considered as a Research Strategy in Cognitive Psychology," *Behavioral and Brain Sciences*, 1980, Vol 3. (Reprinted in Haugeland 1981 and in Fodor, J. (1981). *RePresentations*. Cambridge, Mass.: Bradford/MIT Press.

Fodor, J. (1983). *The Modularity of Mind*. Cambridge, Mass.: Bradford/MIT Press.

Foot, P. (1973). "Nietzsche: the Revaluation of Values," in R. Solomon, ed., *Nietzsche: a Collection of Critical Essays*. New York: Doubleday, pp.156–168.

Ford, J. (1983). "How Random is a Coin Toss?" *Physics Today*, April 1983, pp.1–8.

Frankfurt, H. (1969). "Alternate Possibilities and Moral Responsibility," *J. Phil.*, 65, pp.829–833.

Frankfurt, H. (1971). "Freedom of the Will and the Concept of a Person," *J. Phil.*, 68, pp.5–20. (Reprinted in Watson 1982.)

Frankfurt, H. (1973). "Coercion and Moral Responsibility," in Honderich 1973.

Frankfurt, H. (1976). "Identification and Externality," in A. Rorty 1976.

Gale, G. (1981). "The Anthropic Principle," *Scientific American*, 254, December, pp.154–171.

Gallup, G. (1977). "Self-recognition in Primates: A Comparative Approach to

Bidirection Properties of Consciousness," *American Psychologist*, 32, pp.329–338.

Gallwey, T. (1979). *The Inner Game of Tennis*. New York: Bantam.

Gazzaniga, M., and J. Ledoux, (1978). *The Integrated Mind*. New York: Plenum.

Gibbs, J. P. (1975). *Crime, Punishment, and Deterrence*. New York/Oxford/Amsterdam: Elsevier.

Gibson, J. J. (1966). *The Senses Considered as Perceptual Systems*. Boston: Houghton Mifflin.

Gibson, J. J. (1979). *The Ecological Approach to Visual Perception*. Boston: Houghton Mifflin.

Gomberg, P. (1978). "Free Will as Ultimate Responsibility," *American Philosophical Quarterly*, 15, p.208.

Goodman, N. (1965). *Fact, Fiction and Forecast*. New York: Bobbs-Merrill.

Goodman, N. (1982). "Thoughts Without Words," *Cognition*, 12, pp.205–218.

Greenspan, P. (1976). "Wiggins on Historical Inevitability and Incompatibilism," *Philosophical Studies*, 29, pp.235–247.

Greenspan, P. (1978). "Behavior Control and Freedom of Action," *Phil. Review*, 87, pp.25–40.

Gross, H. (1979). *A Theory of Criminal Justice*. New York: Oxford University Press.

Hacking, I. (1975). "All Kinds of Possibility," *The Philosophical Review*, 84, pp.321–337.

Hampshire, S. (1959). *Thought and Action*. London: Chatto and Windus.

Hart, H. L. A. (1968). *Punishment and Responsibility*. Oxford: Oxford University Press.

Haugeland, J. (1981). "Semantic Engines: an Introduction to Mind Design," in Haugeland, ed., *Mind Design*. Cambridge, Mass.: Bradford/MIT Press.

Hintikka, K. J. J. (1973). *Logic, Language-Games and Information*. Oxford: Clarendon.

Hintikka, K. J. J. (1976). *The Semantics of Questions and the Questions of Semantics* (Acta Philosophica Fennica), Vol. 28, # 4. Amsterdam: North-Holland.

Hobart, R. E. (1934). "Free Will as Involving Determinism and as Inconceivable Without It," *Mind*, 43, pp.1–27.

Hobbes, T. (1841). *The Questions Concerning Liberty, Necessity, and Chance*, in *The English Works of Thomas Hobbes*, Vol. V, edited by Sir W. Molesworth. London: John Bohn. (Excerpted in Morgenbesser and Walsh 1962.)

Hofstadter, D. R. (1979). *Gödel, Escher, Bach: an Eternal Golden Braid*. New York: Basic Books.

Hofstadter, D. R. (1981). "Reflections" (on Searle), in Hofstadter and Dennett 1981, pp.373–382.

Hofstadter, D. R. (1982a). "Undercut, Flaunt, Hruska, behavioral evolution and other games of strategy," *Scientific American,* 247, August 1982, pp.16–24.

Hofstadter, D. R. (1982b). "Can Creativity be Mechanized?" *Scientific American,* 247, September 1982, pp.18–34.

Hofstadter, D. R. (1982c). "Variations on a Theme as the Essence of Imagination," *Scientific American,* 247, October 1982, pp.20–29.

Hofstadter, D. R. (1983). "The Calculus of Cooperation is Tested Through a Lottery," *Scientific American,* 248, June 1983, pp.14–28. (See also M. Gardner, "The Topology of Knots and the Results of Douglas Hofstadter's Luring Lottery," *Scientific American,* p.249, September 1983, pp.25–28.)

Hofstadter, D. R., and D. Dennett (1981). *The Mind's I: Fantasies and Reflections on Mind and Soul.* New York: Basic Books.

Honderich, T., ed. (1973). *Essays on Freedom of Action.* London: Routledge & Kegan Paul.

Honoré, A. M. (1964). "Can and Can't," *Mind,* 73, pp.463–479.

Holmstrom, N. (1977). "Firming up Soft Determinism," *The Personalist,* 58, pp.39–51.

Hook, S., ed. (1961a). *Determinism and Freedom in the Age of Modern Science.* New York: Collier.

Hook, S. (1961b). "Necessity, Indeterminism and Sentimentalism," in Hook 1961a.

Hospers, J. (1961). "What Means This Freedom?" in Hook 1961a.

Hume, D. (1739). *A Treatise of Human Nature,* edited by L. A. Selby-Bigge. Oxford: Clarendon, 1964.

Humphrey, N. (1982). "Consciousness: a Just So Story," *New Scientist,* 95, p.475.

Hutchings, E. (1983). "The Autonomous Viking," *Science,* 219, Feb. 18, 1983, pp.803–808.

Jacob, F. (1982). *The Possible and the Actual.* Seattle: University of Washington Press.

James, W. (1921). "The Dilemma of Determinism," in W. James, *The Will to Believe.* New York: Longmans, Green, pp.145–183.

Jauch, J. M. (1973). *Are Quanta Real?.* Bloomington, Indiana: Indiana University Press.

Jaynes, J. (1976). *The Origins of Consciousness in the Breakdown of the Bicameral Mind.* Boston: Houghton Mifflin.

Jennings, P. (1963). *The Jenguin Pennings.* Harmandsworth: Penguin.

Kahneman, D., P. Slovic, and A. Tversky, eds. (1982). *Judgment Under Uncertainty: Heuristics and Biases.* Cambridge: Cambridge University Press.

Kant, I. (1788). *Critique of Practical Reason* (T. K. Abbot translation). London: Longmans, 1873.

Krebs, J. R., A. Kacelnik, and P. Taylor (1978). "Test of Optimal Sampling by Foraging Great Tits, *Nature*, 275, pp.27–31.

Kyburg, H. (1983). "Rational Belief," *Behavioral and Brain Sciences*, 6, pp.231–274.

Laplace, P. (1820). *A Philosophical Essay on Probabilities*, translated by F. W. Truscott and F. L. Emory. New York: Dover, 1951.

Lem, S. (1974). "The Seventh Sally *or* How Trurl's Own Perfection Led to No Good," in *The Cyberiad*, translated by M. Kandel. New York: Seabury Press. (Reprinted in Hofstadter and Dennett 1981.)

Levi, I (1980). *The Enterprise of Knowledge*. Cambridge, Mass.: MIT Press.

Locke, J. (1690). *An Essay Concerning Human Understanding* (A. C. Fraser edition). New York: Dover, 1959.

Lucas, J. R. (1961). "Minds, Machines, and Gödel," *Philosophy*, 36, pp. 112–27. (Reprinted in A. R. Anderson, ed., *Minds and Machines*. Englewood Cliffs, N.J.: Prentice-Hall, 1964.)

Lucas, J. R. (1970). *The Freedom of the Will*. Oxford: Clarendon.

Lucretius, *The Nature of the Universe*, translated by R. E. Latham. Harmondsworth: Penguin, 1951.

MacIntyre, A. (1957). "Determinism," *Mind*, 66, pp.28–41.

MacKay, D. M. (1960). "On the Logical Indeterminacy of a Free Choice," *Mind*, 69, pp.31–40.

Mackie, J. L. (1974). *The Cement of the Universe*. Oxford: Oxford University Press.

McDermott, D. (1982). "A Temporal Logic for Reasoning about Processes and Plans," *Cognitive Science*, 6, pp.101–155.

Milgram, S. (1974). *Obedience to Authority: an Experimental View*. New York: Harper & Row.

Mill, J. S. (1867). *An Examination of Sir William Hamilton's Philosophy*. London: Longmans, Green, Reader and Dyer. (Chapter XXVI, "On the Freedom of the Will," is reprinted in Morgenbesser and Walsh 1962.)

Monod, J. (1972). *Chance and Necessity*. New York: Knopf.

Morgenbesser S., and J. Walsh, eds. (1962). *Free Will*. Englewood Cliffs, NJ: Prentice-Hall.

Nagel, T. (1974). "What is it Like to be a Bat?" *Philosophical Review*, 83, pp.435–450. (Reprinted in Nagel 1979, and, with commentary, in Hofstadter and Dennett 1981.)

Nagel, T. (1979). "Moral Luck," in Nagel, *Mortal Questions*. Cambridge: Cambridge University Press.

Nagel, T. (1981). "Freedom and Objectivity," unpublished manuscript dated July 6, 1981, quoted with permission.

Neisser, U. (1976). *Cognition and Reality*. San Francisco: Freeman.

Nietzsche, F. (1883). *Thus Spake Zarathustra*, translated by W. Kaufmann, in *The Portable Nietzsche*, ed. W. Kaufmann. New York: Viking.

Nietzsche, F. (1887). *On the Genealogy of Morals*, translated by W. Kaufmann and R. J. Hollingdale. New York: Vintage, 1967.

Nozick, R. (1979). "Coercion," in S. Morgenbesser, P. Suppes, and M. White, eds., *Philosophy, Science, and Method: Essays in Honor of Ernest Nagel*. New York: St. Martin's Press, pp.440–472.

Nozick, R. (1981). *Philosophical Explanations*. Cambridge, Mass.: Harvard University Press.

Pears, D. (1964). "Predicting and Deciding," *Proc. of the British Academy*, 50, 1964, pp.193–227. (Reprinted in P. F. Strawson, ed., *Studies in the Philosophy of Thought and Action*, Oxford University Press, 1968, pp.97–134.)

Popper, K. (1951). "Indeterminism in Quantum Physics and Classical Physics," *British Journal for the Philosophy of Science*, 1, pp.179–188.

Popper, K., and J. Eccles (1977). *The Self and its Brain*. New York: Springer.

Powers, L. (1978). "Knowledge by Deduction," *Phil. Review*, 87, pp.337–371.

Putnam, H. (1975). "The Meaning of 'Meaning'," in K. Gunderson, ed., *Language, Mind, and Knowledge*, Minnesota Studies in the Philosophy of Science, Vol. VII. Minneapolis: Univ. of Minnesota Press. (Reprinted in Putnam, *Mind, Language and Reality*. Cambridge: Cambridge University Press, 1975.)

Pynchon, T. (1973). *Gravity's Rainbow*. New York: Viking.

Quine, W. V. O. (1960). *Word and Object*. Cambridge, Mass.: MIT Press.

Raab, F. V. (1955). "Free Will and the Ambiguity of 'Could'," *Phil. Review*, 64, pp.60–77.

Rabin, M. (1980). "Probabilistic Algorithms in Finite Fields," *SIAM Journal of Computing*, 9, pp.273–280.

Rawls, J. (1971). *A Theory of Justice*. Cambridge, Mass.: Harvard University Press.

Rawls, J. (1980). "Representation of Freedom and Equality," Dewey Lectures, III, *J. Phil.*, Vol. 77, pp.535–559.

Reid, T. (1788). *Essays on the Active Power of the Human Mind*. Cambridge, Mass.: MIT Press edition, 1969.

Robbins, T. (1976). *Even Cowgirls Get the Blues*. New York: Bantam Books.

Rorty, A. (1972). "Belief and Self-Deception," *Inquiry*, 15, pp.387–410.

Rorty, A., ed. (1976). *The Identities of Persons*. Berkeley: University of California Press.

Rorty, R. (1979). *Philosophy and the Mirror of Nature*. Princeton: Princeton University Press.

Rorty, R. (1982). "Contemporary Philosophy of Mind," *Synthese*, 53, pp. 323–348.

Ryle, G. (1949). *The Concept of Mind*. London: Hutchinson.

Ryle, G. (1954). *Dilemmas*. Cambridge: Cambridge University Press.

Ryle, G. (1970). "Autobiographical," in O. P. Wood and G. Pitcher, eds., *Ryle: a Collection of Critical Essays*. Garden City, New York: Doubleday Anchor.

Ryle, G. (1979). *On Thinking*, edited by K. Kolenda. Oxford: Blackwell.

Saarinen, E., ed. (1979). *Game-Theoretical Semantics*. Dordrecht: Reidel.

Sanford, D. (1975). "Infinity and Vagueness," in *Phil. Review*, 84, pp. 520–535.

Sartre, J. P. (1946). *L'Existentialisme est un Humanisme: Dialogue avec P. Naville*. Paris: Nagel.

Sartre, J. P. (1956). *Being and Nothingness*, translated by H. Barnes. New York: Philosophical Library.

Schiffer, S. (1976). "A Paradox of Desire," *American Philosophical Quarterly*, 13, pp. 195–212.

Schneewind, J. (1981). Review of John Stuart Mill, in *Autobiography and Literary Essays*, edited by J. M. Robson and J. Stillinger (*Collected Works of John Stuart Mill*, Vol. I) in *M L N*, vol. 96, Dec. 1981, pp. 1231–1235.

Schotch, P. K., and R. E. Jennings (1980). "Modal Logic and the Theory of Modal Aggregation," *Philosophia*, 9, pp. 265–278.

Seidenfeld, T. (1981). "Levi on the Dogma of Randomization in Experiments," in R. J. Bogdan, ed., *Henry E. Kyburg, Jr. and Isaac Levi*. Dordrecht: Reidel, pp. 263–291.

Searle, J. (1980). "Minds, Brains and Programs," *Behavioral and Brain Sciences*, 3, pp. 417–457.

Sellars, W. (1963). *Science, Perception and Reality*. London: Routledge & Kegan Paul.

Sher, G. (1979). "Effort, Ability and Personal Desert," *Philosophy and Public Affairs*, 8, pp. 361–376.

Simon, H. (1957). *Models of Man*. New York: Wiley.

Simon, H. (1969). *The Sciences of the Artificial*. Cambridge, Mass.: MIT Press.

Skinner, B. F. (1953). *Science and Human Behavior*. New York: Macmillan.

Skinner, B. F. (1971). *Beyond Freedom and Dignity*. New York: Knopf.

Slote, M. (1982). "Selective Necessity and Free Will," *J. Phil.*, 74, pp. 5–24.

Sober, E. (1981). "The Evolution of Rationality," *Synthese*, 46, pp. 95–120.

Spinoza, B. (1677). *Ethics*, translated by R. H. M. Elwes. London: George Bell & Sons, 1891.

Straight, S. (1977). "Consciousness as a Workspace," *SISTM Quarterly*, 1, pp. 11–14.

Strawson, P. F. (1959). *Individuals*. London: Methuen.

Strawson, P. F. (1962). "Freedom and Resentment," *Proc. of the British Academy,* 1962. (Reprinted in Strawson 1968.)

Strawson, P. F., ed. (1968). *Studies in the Philosophy of Thought and Action.* Oxford: Oxford University Press.

Taylor, C. (1976). "Responsibility for Self," in A. Rorty 1976. (Reprinted in Watson 1982.)

Taylor, R. (1964). "Deliberation and Foreknowledge," *American Philosophical Quarterly,* 1, pp. 73–80. (Reprinted in Berofsky 1966.)

Thorp, J. (1980). *Free Will: a Defence Against Neurophysiological Determinism.* London and Boston: Routledge & Kegan Paul.

Ullman, S. (1979). *The Interpretation of Visual Motion.* Cambridge, Mass.: MIT Press.

van Inwagen, P. (1975). "The Incompatibility of Free Will and Determinism," *Phil. Studies,* 27, pp. 185–199. (Reprinted in Watson 1982.)

van Inwagen, P. (1978). "Ability and Responsibility," *Philosophical Review,* 87, pp. 201–224.

van Inwagen, P. (1983). *An Essay on Free Will.* Oxford: Clarendon.

van Straaten, Z., ed. (1980). *Philosophical Subjects: Essays presented to P. F. Strawson.* Oxford University Press.

von Neumann, J., and O. Morgenstern (1947). *Theory of Games and Economic Behavior.* (2nd edition.) Princeton: Princeton University Press.

von Wright, G. H. (1974). *Causality and Determinism.* New York: Columbia University Press.

Watson, G., ed. (1982). *Free Will.* Oxford: Oxford University Press.

Whitaker, H. (1976). "A Case of the Isolation of Language Function," in H. Whitaker and H. A. Whitaker, eds., *Studies in Neurolinguistics,* Vol II. New York: Academic Press.

Wiener, N. (1948). *Cybernetics: or Control and Communication in the Animal and the Machine.* Cambridge, Mass.: Technology Press, and New York: John Wiley & Sons.

Wiggins, D. (1973). "Towards a Reasonable Libertarianism," in Honderich 1973.

Williams, B. (1973). *Problems of the Self.* Cambridge: Cambridge University Press.

Williams, B. (1981). *Moral Luck.* Cambridge: Cambridge University Press.

Wimsatt, W. (1980). "Randomness and Perceived-Randomness in Evolutionary Biology," *Synthese,* 43, pp. 287–329.

Wittgenstein, L. (1953). *Philosophical Investigations,* translated by G. E. M. Anscombe. Oxford: Blackwell.

Wittgenstein, L. (1967). *Zettel,* edited by G. E. M. Anscombe and G. von Wright. Oxford: Blackwell.

Wolf, S. (1980). "Asymmetrical Freedom," *J. Phil.,* LXVII, pp. 151–165.

Wolf, S. (1981). "The Importance of Free Will," *Mind,* 190, pp. 386–378.

Wolff, R. P. (1973). *The Autonomy of Reason: a Commentary on Kant's Groundwork of the Metaphysic of Morals.* New York. Harper & Row, p. 216.

Wooldridge, D. (1963). *The Machinery of the Brain.* New York: McGraw Hill.

Wooldridge, D. (1968). *Mechanical Man: The Physical Basis of Intelligent Life.* New York: McGraw Hill.

Zaitchik, A. (1977). "On Deserving to Deserve," *Philosophy and Public Affairs,* 6, pp. 370–388.

Index

meta- (cont.)
level activity 36, 66, 114
level control 62–3, 85–7, 91
metaphor, 2, 7, 61–2, 83, 106, 121, 169
metaphysics, 5, 6, 16, 80n, 90, 120, 122, 128, 135–6, 138–9, 153, 158, 163, 169, 172
MI5, 24
microphysics and micro-level description, 91, 110, 112, 115, 119, 136–7, 139–42, 147, 162
midnight bull session, 5
Milgram, S., 13, 179
Mill, J. S., 54, 80n, 90, 179
Miller, D. S., 129n
mimicry, 54
mind, 28, 35, 40
philosphy of, 37
-reading, 10, 66–7
miracle, 125
modal logic, 123, 148, 149n
Monod, J., 21n, 59n, 149–50
monster, 157, 166–7
moral
agency, 154–7
conceptual world, 155–7, 167
decisions, 97
education, 96, 135
strength, 142
visions, 89
morality, 162–3
origin of, 44–5
Morgenstern, O., 63n, 182
Mother Nature, 24, 61, 72, 108, 126, 152
motivation
of citizens, 160
of philosophical projects, 4, 6–7, 10, 16
moved by reasons, 25–7
Mozart, W., 13, 75, 78
murder, premeditated, 103
murderer, 99, 132, 134, 165
mutation, 119, 150

Nagel, T.,17n, 32, 35n, 75, 92n, 97, 179
Napoleon, 8
narratization, 88n
NASA, 55, 57

naturalism, 49, 76, 80, 100, 158, 165, 170–1
nature, 48, 71, 129
does not play hide and seek, 118
laws of, 148
Mother Nature, 24, 61, 72, 108, 126, 152
state of, 17, 44–5, 162
nature's way, 44n
necessity, 145, 148
causal, 123, 128, 130
freedom as consciousness of, 65n
modal logic of, 123
selective, 148–9
"Need to Know" principle, 24, 38
Nefarious Neurosurgeon, 8, 64–5, 132
Neisser, U., 64n, 180
neuron, 74
Newton, I., 109n, 126, 151
New York Harbor, 82n
Niagara Falls, 127
Nietzsche, F., 9, 43, 46, 74, 81, 88, 153–4, 159, 180
nihilism, 153–6
Nixon, R., 154, 157, 166
noblesse oblige, 95
noise, 59n, 115
nomological impossibility, 140n, 148
normal, inertia of the, 126–7
noticing, 33, 39, 65, 99, 137
beneath notice, 109
now, zipping up the future, 102
Nozick, R., 9, 16n, 49–51, 56n, 58, 64–5, 70n, 91, 129, 138, 180
nuclear war, 14
number theory, 150–1

objectivity, scientific, 14
objet trouvé, 85
obliviousness, 23–4
obscurum per obscurius, 91
Oedipus, 104
ontological commitment, 127
open
to the agent, 63n, 113
fellowship, 117
future, 102, 112–3, 115, 139, 170
operant conditioning, 13
operations research, 141n

van Inwagen, P., 50n, 51n, 84n, 104n,
 105, 131, 132, 144, 148n, 182
Ventre, P. M., 62n
Venus, 95
Vesco, R., 166
Viking, the Autonomous, 55n, 72
virtue, 20
voice of reason. *See* reason
volcanic sculpture, 22
volition, 25n, 78n
voluntary, 77–9
von Neumann, J., 63n, 182
von Wright, 126n, 129, 182

wager, 10, 162
wasp, 10–13, 16, 50. *See also Sphex
 ichneumoneus*
Watson, G., 76, 182
wave packet, collapse of, 91
Wayneflete
 Lectures, 6n
 Professor, 7n
Western, free will as, 5
wheel of fortune, 2
Whitaker, H., 12, 182
Wiener, N., 33n, 67n, 108n, 109n,
 140n, 142, 144, 182
Wiggins, D., 51n, 58, 123, 182
will, 21
 power, 80
 rational, 26–7, 29, 49, 156, 166
 weakness of, 106, 165
Williams, B. A. O., 25n, 92n, 95,
 158, 182
Wimsatt, W., 67n, 95n, 109n, 110,
 142, 150n, 182
wisdom, common, 85, 96, 122
wishful thinking, 84, 107, 115, 168–
 70
Wittgenstein, L., 15, 18, 27, 182
Wolf, S., 25n, 155n, 157, 164, 182–3
Wolff, R. P., 28, 183
Woodfield, A., x
Wooldridge, D., 11, 183

Zaitchik, 85n, 183
zombie, 9, 134